The Campus History Series

KUTZTOWN UNIVERSITY

On the Front Cover: This is a c. 1940 image of Old Main. (Courtesy of KU Archives.)

On the Back Cover: This photograph shows a graduating class of Keystone State Normal School. (Courtesy of KU Archives.)

The Campus History Series

KUTZTOWN UNIVERSITY

EMMA E. BILLIG AND KAYLA L. FUSSELMAN

ARCADIA PUBLISHING

ISBN 978-1-4671-1705-0

Published by Arcadia Publishing
Charleston, South Carolina

Printed in the United States of America

Library of Congress Control Number: 2016940450

For all general information, please contact Arcadia Publishing:
Telephone 843-853-2070
Fax 843-853-0044
E-mail sales@arcadiapublishing.com
For customer service and orders:
Toll-Free 1-888-313-2665

Visit us on the Internet at www.arcadiapublishing.com

We dedicate this book to Dr. Robert Reynolds for going above and beyond with regard to his commitment and time put toward this project.

CONTENTS

FOREWORD

This book represents the fruition of the continued quest for excellence expected of our students at Kutztown University. Emma E. Billig and Kayla L. Fusselman developed this project in a history course taught by Prof. Robert W. Reynolds in the spring of 2015. Through two semesters of independent study and a big block of their winter break in the 2015–2016 academic year, both students have learned to write a book proposal, secure funding for publication, conduct in-depth archival research, network with key people who offered unique insight into Kutztown University's history, write strong descriptive prose, and make or exceed all the deadlines involved in the undertaking of publishing a book.

This book project required tremendous individual initiative that represents the ideals of Kutztown University's Honors Program. With this publication serving as their capstone honors project, Emma and Kayla have set a high standard of accomplishment.

How fitting that a student-driven sesquicentennial photographic history of Kutztown University, made possible by the caring and conscientious oversight of a faculty member, has resulted in a publication meant to share the pride and heritage that is Kutztown University. As we celebrate our sesquicentennial milestone, this book serves as a reminder of the purpose of this institution: to offer students the opportunity to exceed expectations in the pursuit of their academic dreams.

—Dr. Kenneth S. Hawkinson, President

ACKNOWLEDGMENTS

We never would have thought that taking an honors history class on local and community studies examining the history of Kutztown University would lead to this book. We would first like to thank Dr. Robert Reynolds for not only pushing to have the class but also for giving us the idea to write this book, as well as for guiding this project to completion. Thanks go to Jason Graver for providing an endless supply of photographs and information, along with fact-checking, editing, and historical research; and to Lauren Smith, who contributed to the early development of the project.

This book would not have been possible without the Kutztown University Foundation & Alumni Relations that funded the project. Specifically, we would like to thank Tracey Thompson, Alex Ogeka, and Ed Richmond; Mary Neuenschwander and Cheryl Swavely for their support in locating images; Matthew Santos and David Johnson of public relations for reading over our drafts and providing feedback, as well as tracking down photographs and information; and Camille DeMarco for providing us with information and pictures.

Thanks go to our families for keeping us sane during the three-month writing process and our friends for putting up with us; to Joshua Leiboff, Patrick Donmoyer, Phill Reed, and Gregory Bamberger for providing photographs and information; to Bill Donner for the image and information about Professor Horne; and to Bill Uhrich regarding information and images of Bruce Springsteen.

Additional recognition goes to Brendan Strasser and Craig Koller from the Kutztown Historical Society for photographs and information, and in memory of Bill Yurvati, who was a major contributor to the historical society's collection; and to John Paul Endress for photographing presidential portraits and other large framed pictures at his studio.

We especially need to thank Erin Vosgien and Jeff Ruetsche of Arcadia Publishing for their help throughout the writing process. We would also like to thank all university staff and faculty members who provided us with images and information.

Finally, thank-yous are extended to Sue Czerny and Miguel Nieves for providing us with access to the archives. Unless otherwise noted, all images are courtesy of the KU Archives; several others are courtesy of Kutztown University (KU), Kutztown University Relations (KUR), Kutztown Historical Society (KHS), or the Pennsylvania German Cultural Heritage Center (PGCHC).

Three works served as invaluable resources for this book: ***The Centennial History of Kutztown***, by William Wilburforce Deatrick (Kutztown Publishing Company, 1915); ***Beacon on the Hill: A Centennial History of Kutztown State College***, by Lee Graver Kutztown (Kutztown State College, 1966); and "History of State Teachers College, Kutztown, Pennsylvania," a master's thesis by Clara A. Myers (Temple University, 1934).

INTRODUCTION

A few months before the outbreak of the Civil War, the institution now named Kutztown University emerged from the vision of the Reverend J. Sassaman Herman, pastor of St. John's Reformed Church, Kutztown, who established a "select school" for the higher branches of education in his spacious home. At a synodical meeting, Reverend Herman communicated his vision for a school to the Reverend E.V. Gerhart, president of Franklin & Marshall College in Lancaster. Reverend Gerhart mentioned the name of Henry Rosenberger Nicks as a suitable person to organize such a school. On November 15, 1860, Nicks opened the proprietary Fairview Seminary in the three-story house owned by Reverend Herman with five pupils, including Nathan C. Schaeffer, the future third principal of Keystone State Normal School.

Nicks was forced to relocate his school to the second floor of the Kutztown Public School building when Herman sold his house in 1863. While in town, the school went by two names: the Kutztown Academy and the Kutztown Seminary. The new institution opened its doors at this temporary location on August 9, 1863, with nine pupils, including Nathan C. Schaeffer. With the enrollment of students continuing to rise, Allen S. Hottenstein was brought on as assistant teacher. Meanwhile, plans for a permanent school were put into place. By September 1864, the Maxatawny Seminary, a three-story brick building, had been completed on the site where Kutztown University's Old Main stands today, and Nicks's school moved into the new facility.

In the spring of 1865, Henry Nicks and Berks County Schools superintendent John S. Ermentrout held special classes for area teachers at the Maxatawny Seminary. The increase in teachers seeking instruction led to an interest in expanding the limited facilities of the seminary. The success of the school led to a local fundraising appeal to secure funds from the community to convert and expand Maxatawny Seminary into a state normal school for teacher training.

During the summer of 1865, a new joint stock company, with Lewis K. Hottenstein as president, David H. Hottenstein as secretary, and Henry Nicks as a member, set about the task of converting Maxatawny Seminary into a state normal school through construction and land acquisition. In 1865, five more acres were purchased next to the seminary, and a large structure, first called the Keystone Normal School, was constructed on the west side of the seminary building in accordance with the standards set by the Normal School Act of 1857. This law stated that a normal school must have at least 10 acres of land and buildings of sufficient size to accommodate 300 boarders, an auditorium to seat 1,000, and a library room. A three-story building of the same general size and appearance as the seminary was constructed on the west side of the center building.

On September 15, 1866, the commonwealth accepted the Keystone Normal School as the Keystone State Normal School (KSNS), the fourth Pennsylvania Normal School for the Third District, composed of Berks, Lehigh, and Schuylkill Counties. The first three normal schools in the state were Millersville in 1859, Edinboro in 1861, and Mansfield in 1862. September 15, 2016, marks the sesquicentennial of the establishment of the school that would eventually become Kutztown University, a state institution of higher education.

To recognize and honor the sesquicentennial celebration of Kutztown University, two of the school's undergraduate students who grew up in the local area developed this book as a capstone project for their honors program. The archival staff of the Rohrbach Library granted access and provided guidance to a vast array of research materials, including several hundred photographs, a century of yearbooks, and dozens of early-20th-century postcards. More images came from collections held by the Kutztown Historical Society, alumni, and faculty members. The Kutztown University Foundation graciously committed the funding needed to bring this project to fruition.

The 206 images in this book reflect the perspective and biases of two students and a KU history professor, each with his or her own viewpoint of what should be included in this volume. The images in the book were clustered into several categories: important staff and faculty, campus buildings, athletics, major events, and student life and traditions. Each of these themes has proven a vital part to the history of the university. The construction and renovation of buildings on campus have given a physical shape to the growth of the school. While academic and athletic achievements have played their parts in the institution's history, KU students were also affected by national historic events and local experiences. Readers will be able to see the growth and progress of the school, along with how the community affected the school and the students who attended.

This pictorial history of Kutztown University is divided into four chapters that mark the four names utilized in the growth of this institution as a state school. The first chapter, "Keystone State Normal School: 1866–1928," highlights the founding of the university and its growth from a modest seminary with five students to a successful state normal school with several hundred students. The second chapter, "Kutztown State Teachers College: 1928–1960," covers a period of challenges, including the Great Depression and World War II. The third chapter, "Kutztown State College: 1960–1983," covers an era of sustained growth highlighted by memorable concerts and changing traditions. The final chapter, "Kutztown University: 1983–Present," brings us to current times, with a strong focus on visiting dignitaries, as well as the creation of the Pennsylvania German Cultural Heritage Center.

Kutztown University is not an all-inclusive history, as limitations in size and format make that impossible. Not all of the important events that have occurred were captured with photographs, but much of what could be found is presented in this volume. These images capture the changing scene on campus over the generations. To learn more about Kutztown University's history, visit the archives website (http://library.kutztown.edu/digicoll), where the postcard collection and the centennial book *Beacon on the Hill* can be viewed.

Today, the university enrolls about 9,200 full- and part-time undergraduate and graduate students, with a ratio of 57 percent female and 43 percent male. Most students are Pennsylvania residents, but 41 states and 38 foreign countries are represented. Kutztown University offers more than 100 majors, minors, and concentrations for undergraduate degrees, as well as 23 graduate programs and two doctoral programs across its four colleges: business, education, liberal arts and sciences, and visual and performing arts. Yet, throughout 150 years of providing educational opportunities, Kutztown University has remained committed to the success of its students and the creation of alumni and friends, who through this publication will learn more about the school's rich history.

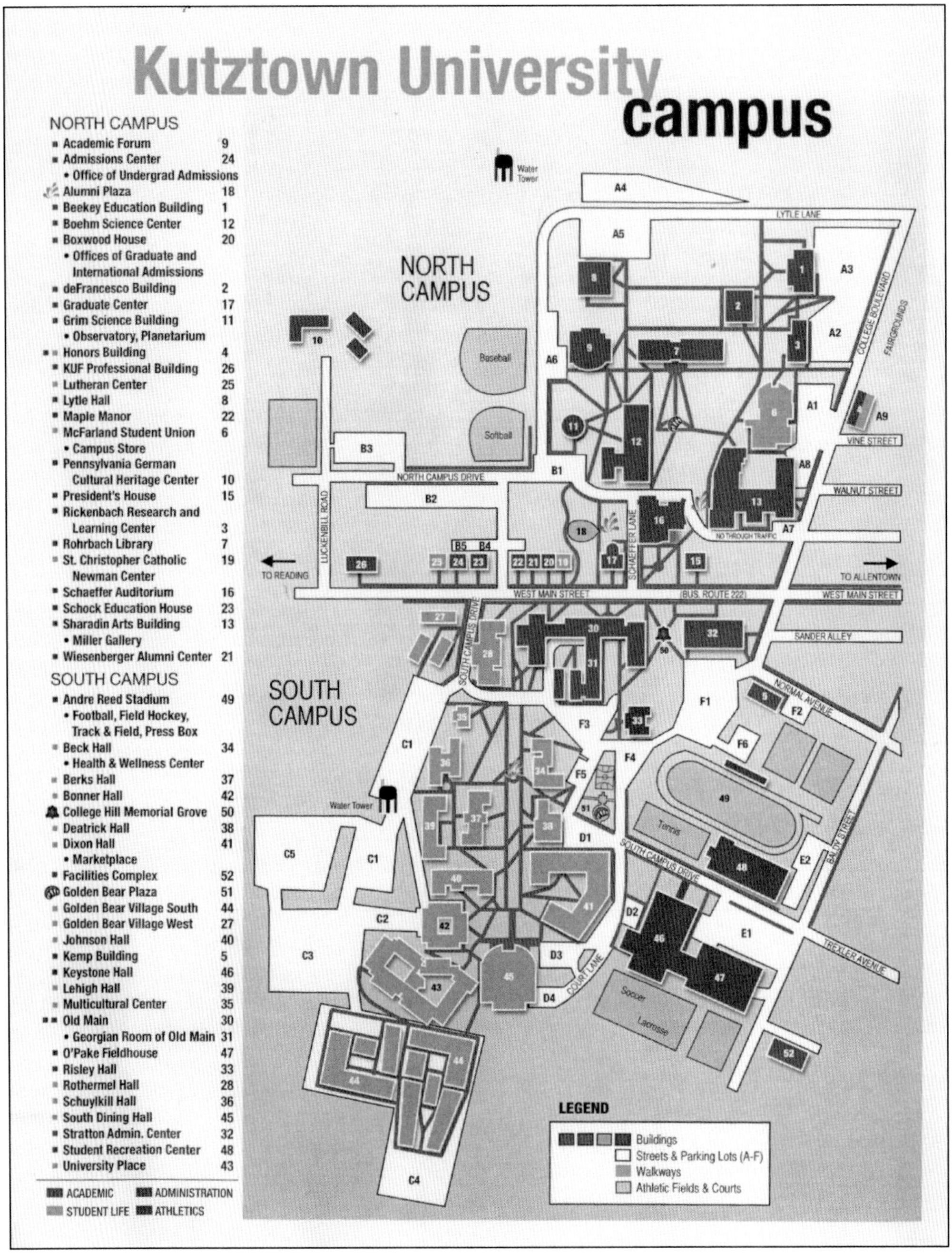

Kutztown University is located adjacent to the borough of Kutztown and in the heart of Pennsylvania Dutch Country. Shown here is a current map of all campus pathways, buildings, and facilities on the university's 289 acres. This map can be used as a reference for sites mentioned throughout the book.

One

Keystone State Normal School 1866–1928

In November 1860, Henry Nicks opened the Fairview Seminary in a three-story brick Kutztown home owned by the Reverend John S. Herman. Five students were present on the first day of school, including Reverend Herman's 12-year-old son Oscar C. Herman and Nathan C. Schaeffer, future principal of Keystone State Normal School and state superintendent of public instruction.

In August 1863, Nicks was forced to temporarily relocate his school to the second floor of the Kutztown Public School building when Herman made plans to sell his home. While there, the school went by two names: the Kutztown Academy and the Kutztown Seminary. During this time, plans for the construction of a permanent school were put into place. Through the efforts of Henry Nicks and other prominent residents of Kutztown, a three-story brick building had been completed by September 1864 on the site where Kutztown University's Old Main stands today, initially named the Maxatawny Seminary.

Due to the success of the Maxatawny Seminary, efforts were made to establish it as an official state normal school within a year. To meet state requirements, additions were made to the original building, and on September 15, 1866, the Keystone State Normal School (KSNS) was born. The university's sesquicentennial dates to the acceptance of the Maxatawny Seminary facility as a new normal school.

For his role in helping to establish the Keystone State Normal School, the Reverend John S. Ermentrout, Berks County Schools superintendent, was appointed as the school's first principal. Henry Nicks was named as steward for the school and later appointed as associate principal, but he resigned in the spring 1867. When Ermentrout resigned in 1871, the trustees of the school unanimously elected Henry Nicks as principal. When Nicks did not accept their offer, the Reverend Dr. Abraham Reeser Horne was appointed as the school's second principal.

As the school expanded in the 1880s, new sections were added to the original KSNS buildings. By 1893, all the buildings of the original Maxatawny Seminary and Keystone State Normal School had been completely replaced.

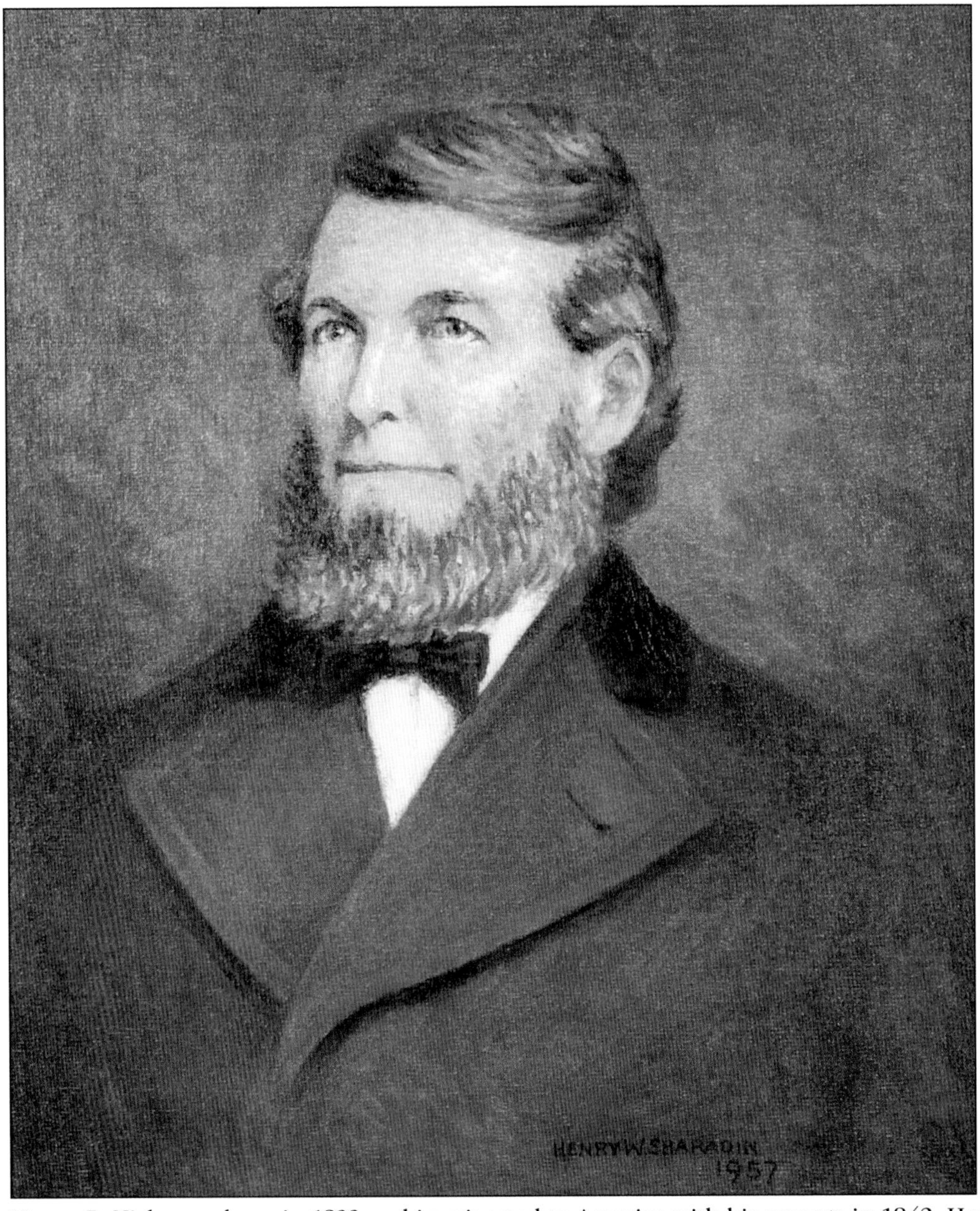

Henry R. Nicks was born in 1833 and immigrated to America with his parents in 1842. He studied at Cumberland Valley Institute, serving as associate principal to pay his way through before going to Franklin & Marshall College. There, he emerged as salutatorian of his class in 1858. In 1860, Nicks created and established the Fairview Seminary. Not only was he the first principal and teacher at the seminary, but his idea of higher education also led to the development of the Keystone State Normal School. Name changes to the seminary, after it was moved from Fairview Mansion, included Kutztown Seminary (Academy) and Maxatawny Seminary. During this time, the seminary relocated to what would become the east wing of the Keystone State Normal School. During Nicks's time at the normal school, he served as the associate principal before resigning in the spring of 1867. (Photograph by John Paul Endress, courtesy of KU.)

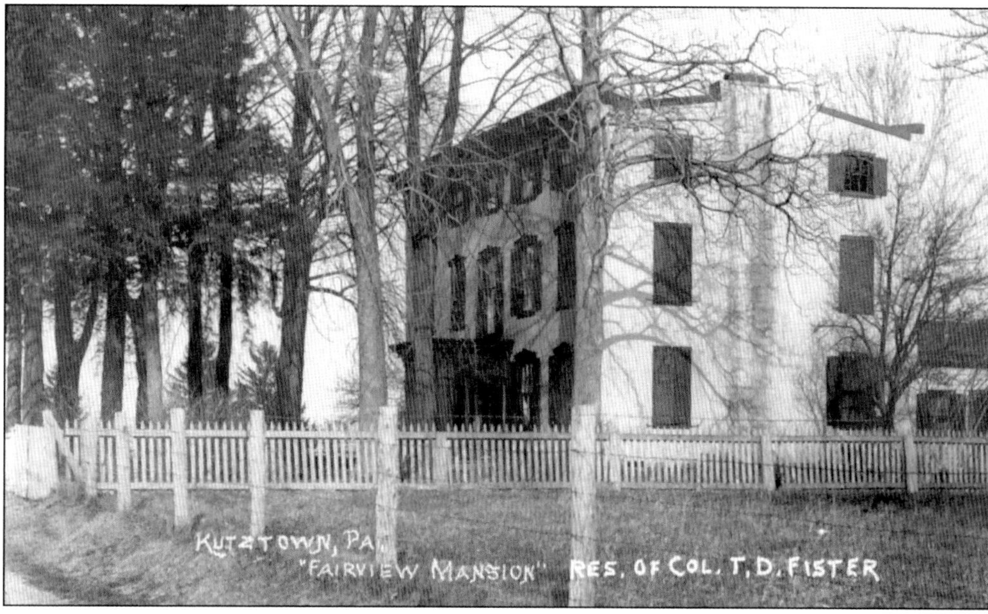

Fairview Mansion was the founding location of the seminary that later became the Keystone State Normal School. On November 15, 1860, Henry Nicks opened the Fairview Seminary, where he served as principal. In 1863, the seminary had to temporarily relocate to the Kutztown Public School building (below) before eventually ending up at the Maxatawny Seminary, where Kutztown University's Old Main is located today. In the summer of 1865, the task of converting Maxatawny Seminary into a state normal school began. Plans were drawn up for a four-story brick building to be attached to the three-story brick Maxatawny Seminary building. That four-story building would serve as the center, and next to it, on the west side, a three-story building with the same general size and appearance as the seminary would be constructed. (Above, photograph by W.W. Deatrick, courtesy of Jason Graver.)

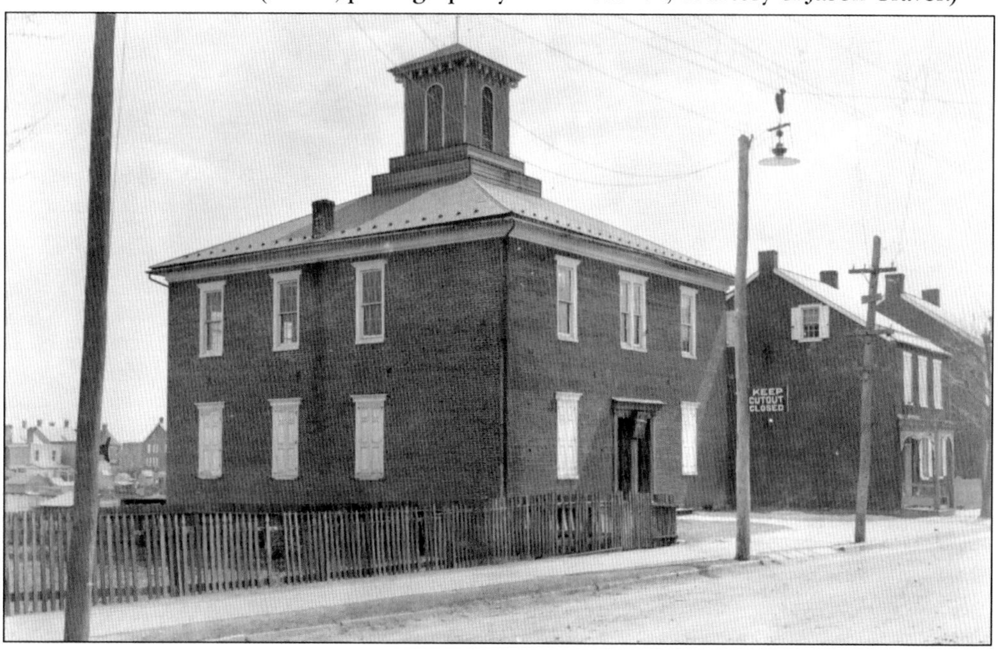

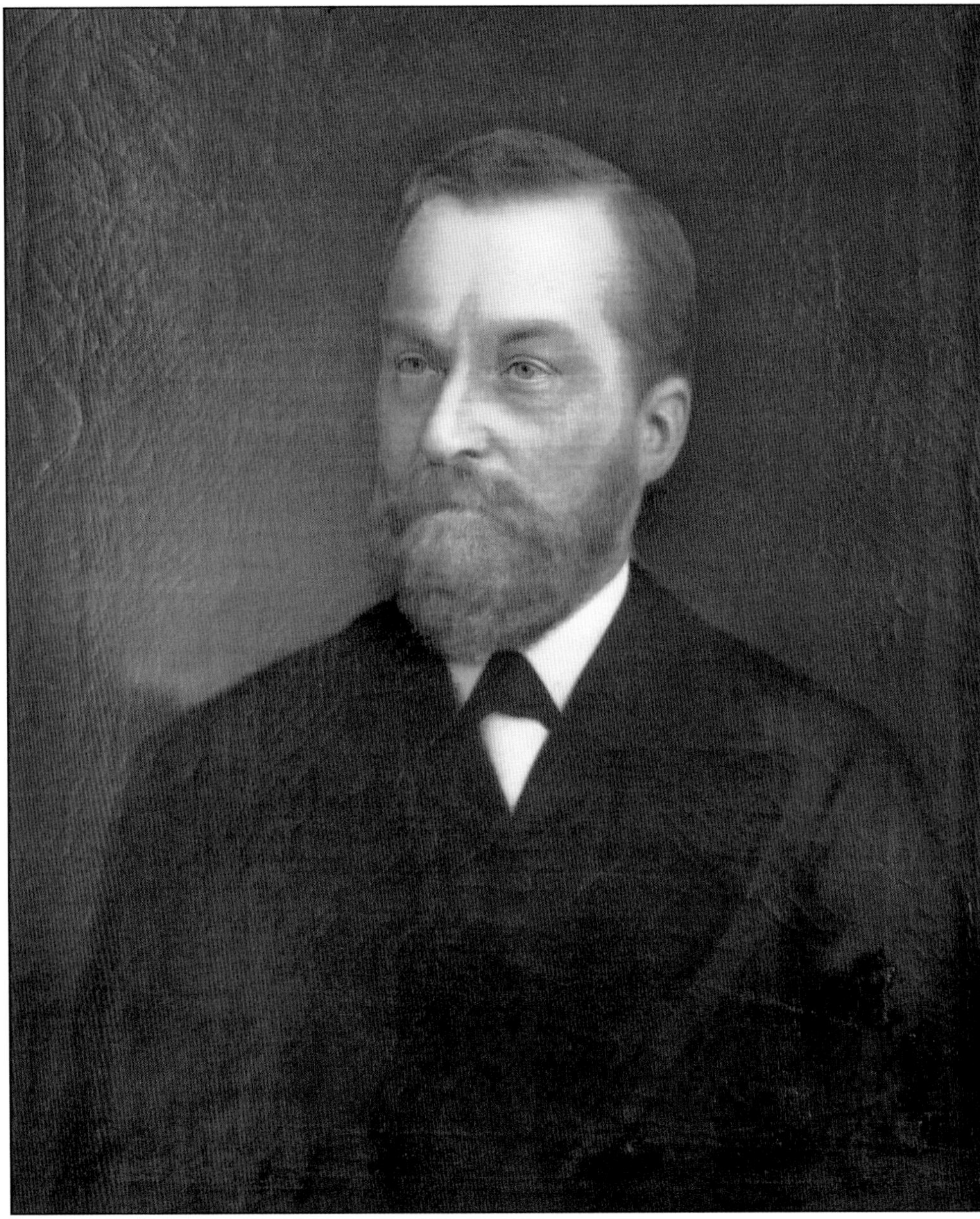

The Reverend John S. Ermentrout (1827–1881) earned his degree from Franklin & Marshall College in 1845, then studied for the ministry at the Reformed Theological Seminary, where he became an ordained clergyman. He was a pastor for a short time before being elected as Berks County superintendent. When the idea of establishing a normal school was raised, Ermentrout was elected to the board of trustees of Keystone Normal School on February 10, 1866. This name was utilized briefly until state affiliation was secured later that year, on September 15. Ermentrout served as the superintendent of Berks County Schools while acting as the full-time principal of Keystone State Normal School. He resigned as principal in 1871 and later was recalled by the board of trustees in 1873. He then became chair of mental and moral science and English literature until he passed away on July 21, 1881. (Photograph by John Paul Endress, courtesy of KU.)

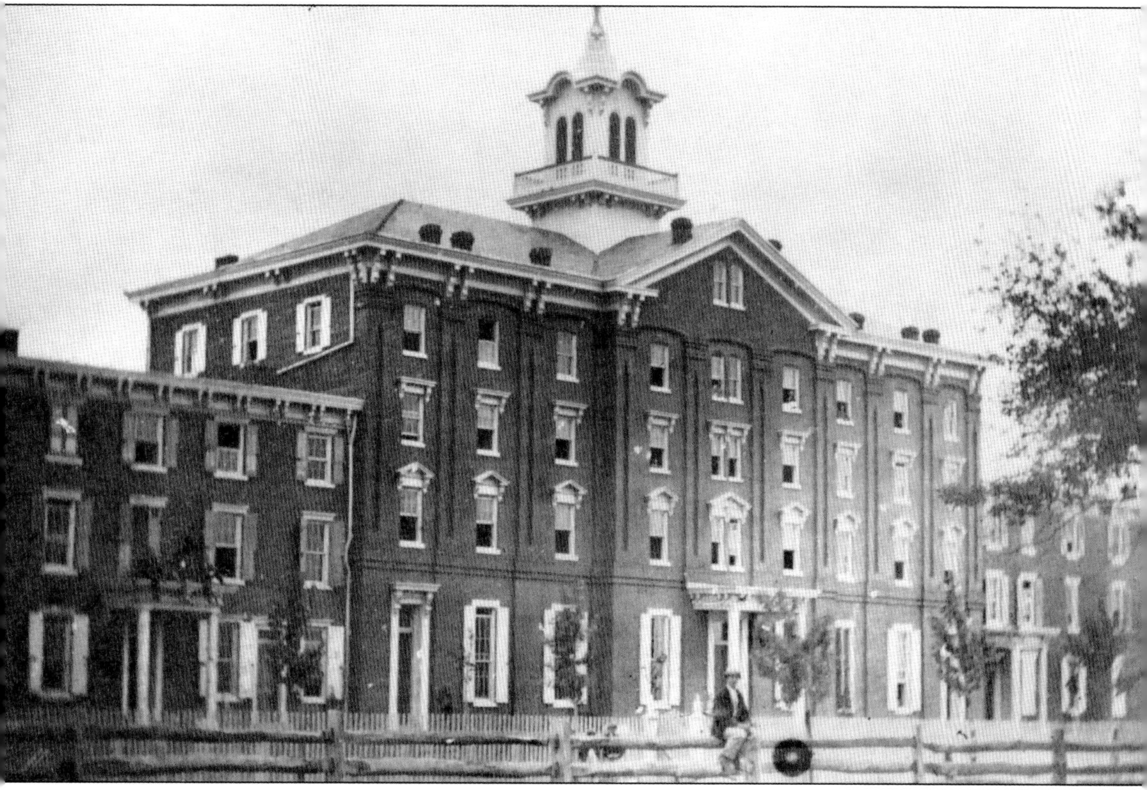

On September 17, 1865, Berks County Schools superintendent John S. Ermentrout laid the cornerstone to the Keystone Normal School building. Inside the stone, Ermentrout placed a Bible, a copy of the Apostles' Creed, and what Dr. Lee Graver refers to in his book *Beacon on the Hill* as "other significant items." During the first year of Keystone State Normal School, there were only 55 female students in attendance, with 263 male students. In 1867, about 56 percent of the teachers of the state were women. Students were permitted to enter the elementary course, from which they could graduate in two years with formal degrees in bachelor of the elements (BE) or bachelor of the sciences (BS). These degrees were special normal school degrees that were equivalent to at least one year of college. In 1880, the C wing of Old Main was built on the west side of the building for women's dormitories. The original Maxatawny Seminary building was razed in 1891 when the east wing of Old Main was built for the men's dormitories.

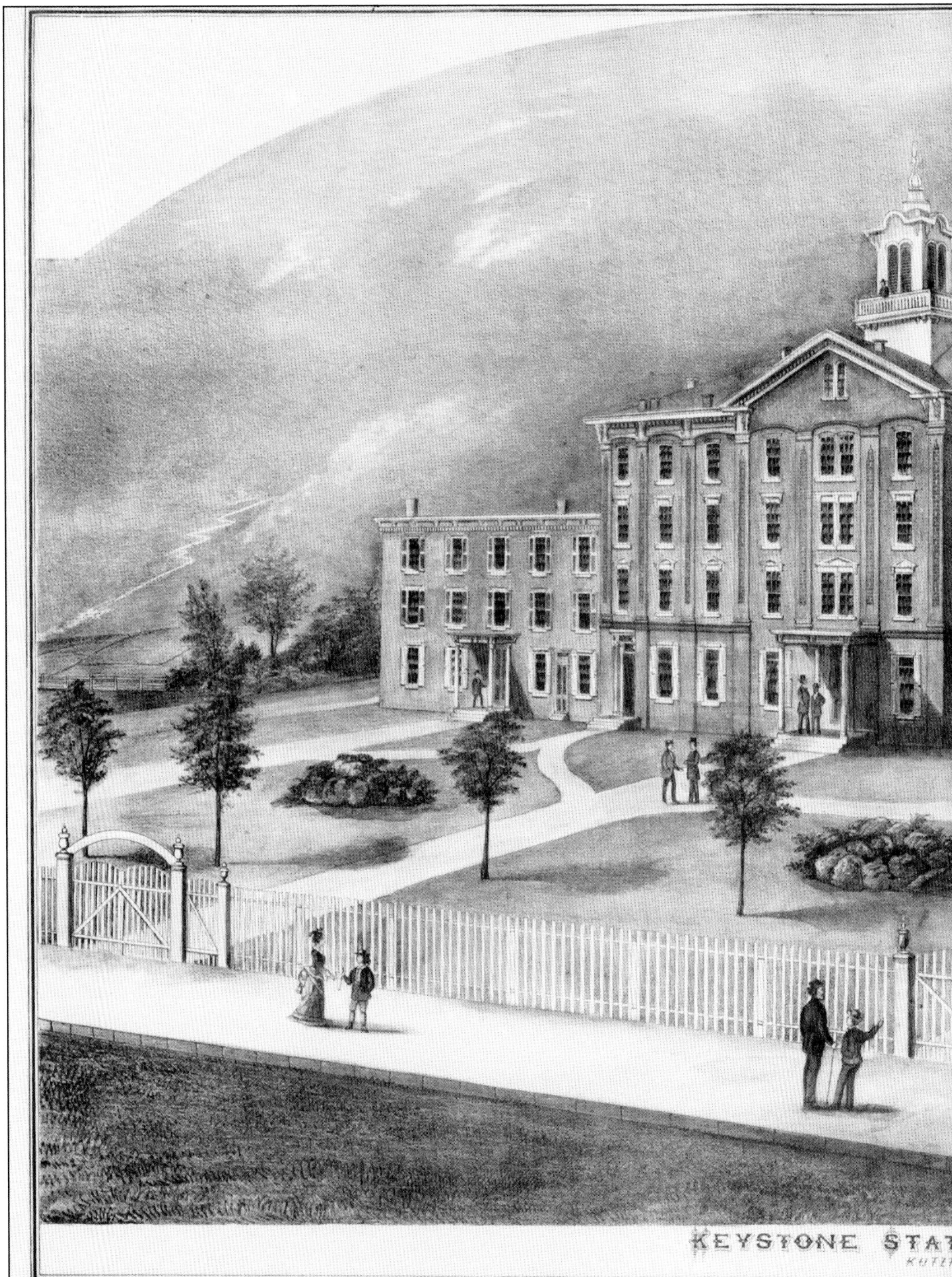

This lithograph first appears in the 1876 ***Historical Atlas of Berks County***. It shows the original Keystone State Normal School of 1866. The far left portion of the building housed the original Maxatawny Seminary from September 1864 to September 1866. As the years progressed, additions were made to the structure pictured here and older sections were

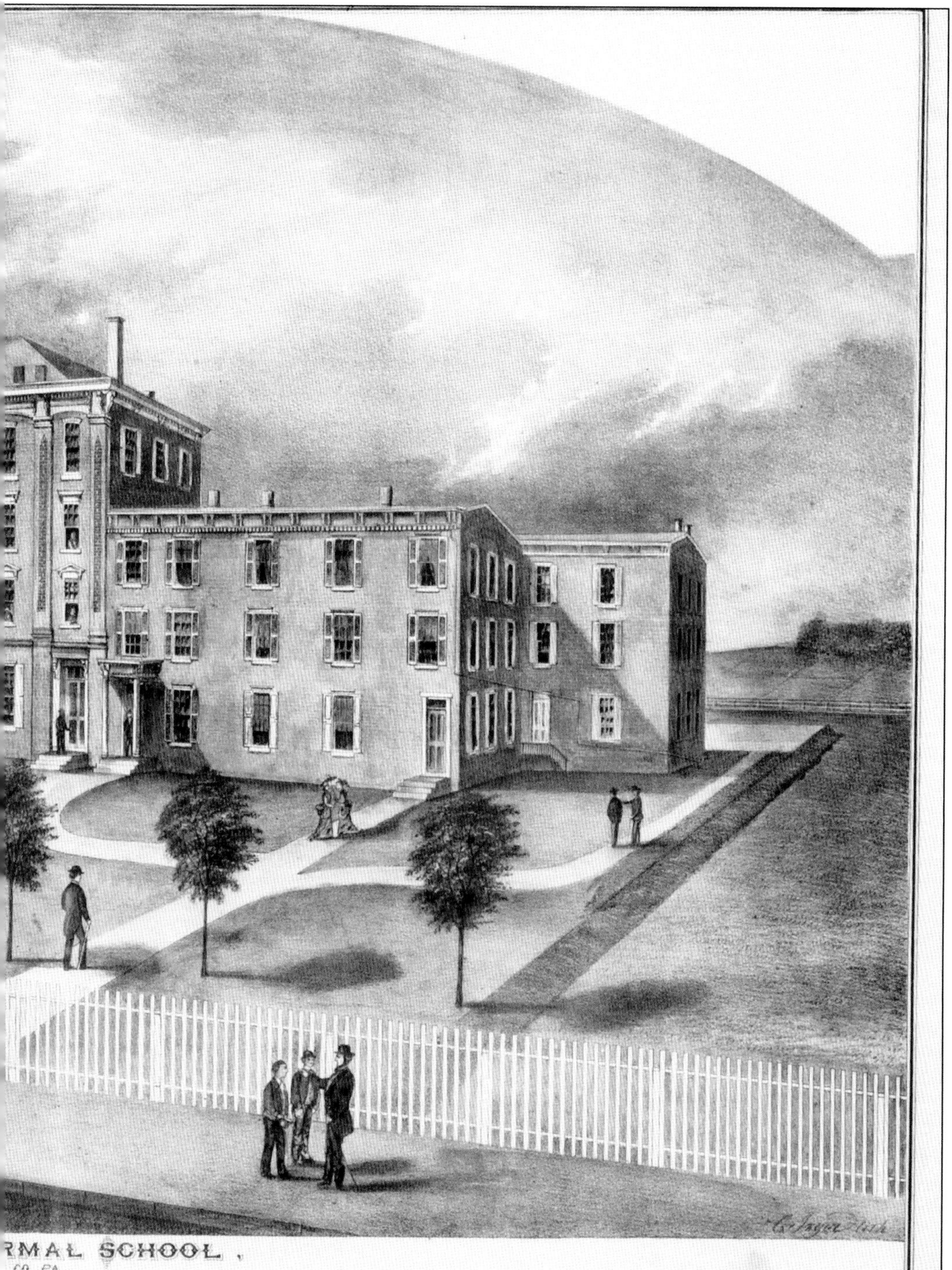

razed and replaced. The first addition was made to the west side of the structure in 1880 and housed the ladies' dormitories. Today, no parts of the building shown in this lithograph still stand. (Photograph by John Paul Endress, courtesy of KU.)

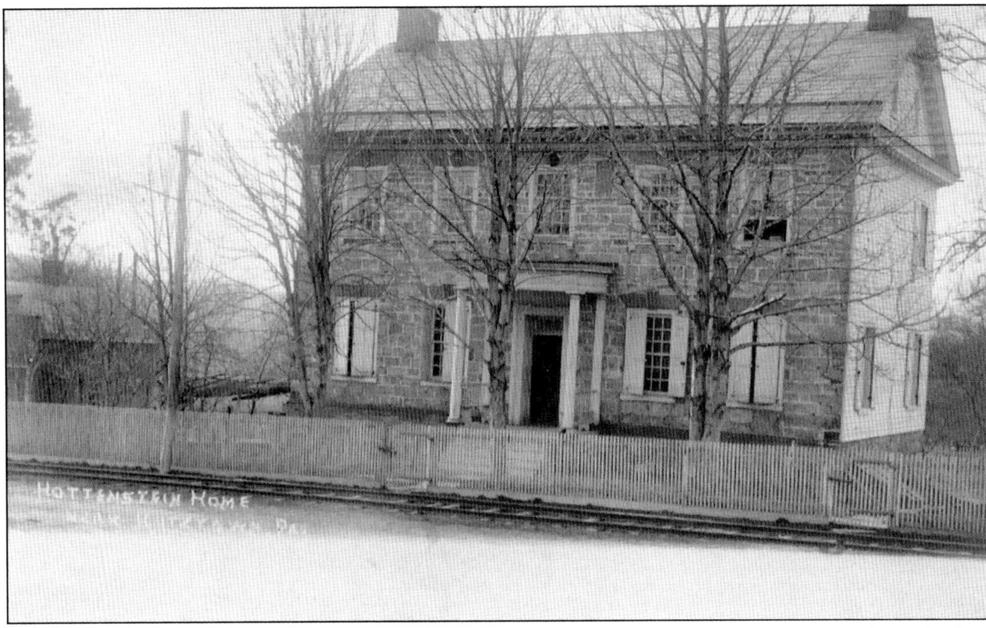

The Hottenstein family owned multiple adjoining farms along Kutztown Road, including the 1783 mansion where the meeting that launched public schools in Maxatawny Township occurred in 1852. Various Hottenstein family members contributed 20 percent of the cost to fund the seminary and 25 percent of the cost to build the normal school. Family members served on the board of trustees and worked in a variety of leadership positions for the school.

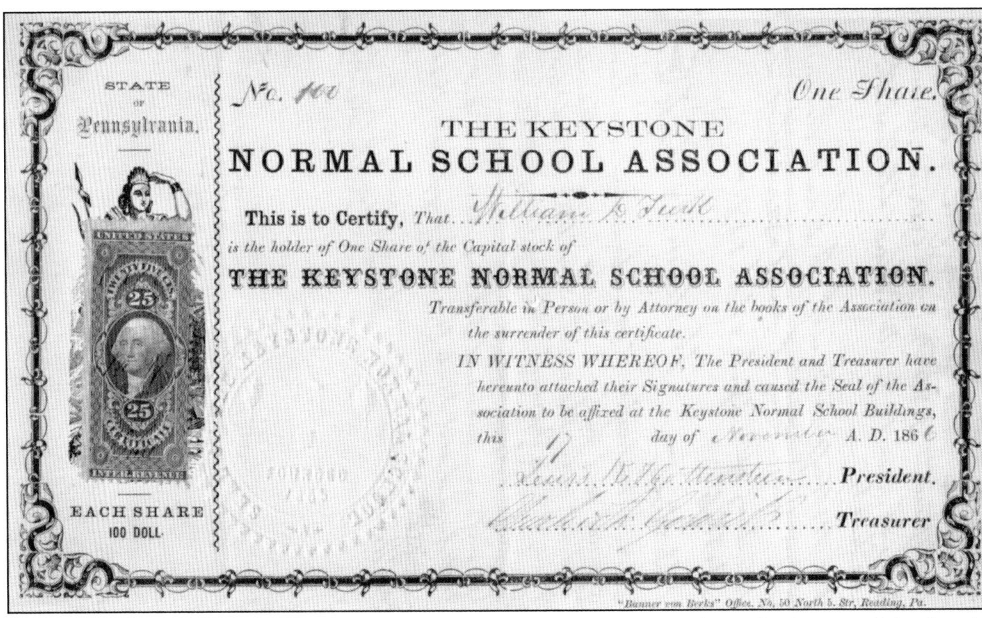
STATE OF Pennsylvania.

EACH SHARE 100 DOLL.

No.

One Share.

THE KEYSTONE

NORMAL SCHOOL ASSOCIATION.

This is to Certify, That William D. Seidel

is the holder of One Share of the Capital stock of

THE KEYSTONE NORMAL SCHOOL ASSOCIATION.

Transferable in Person or by Attorney on the books of the Association on the surrender of this certificate.

IN WITNESS WHEREOF, The President and Treasurer have hereunto attached their Signatures and caused the Seal of the Association to be affixed at the Keystone Normal School Buildings, this 17 day of November A. D. 186

..................President.

..................Treasurer

"Banner von Berks" Office, No. 50 North 5. Str, Reading, Pa.

John J. Hottenstein, a graduate of Keystone State Normal School, took charge of the books of the school, along with his duties as professor of bookkeeping and penmanship, for a salary of $400—one that was significantly lower than his associates. From 1877 to 1921, Hottenstein served as treasurer of Keystone. He was one of the longest-serving faculty members at the school.

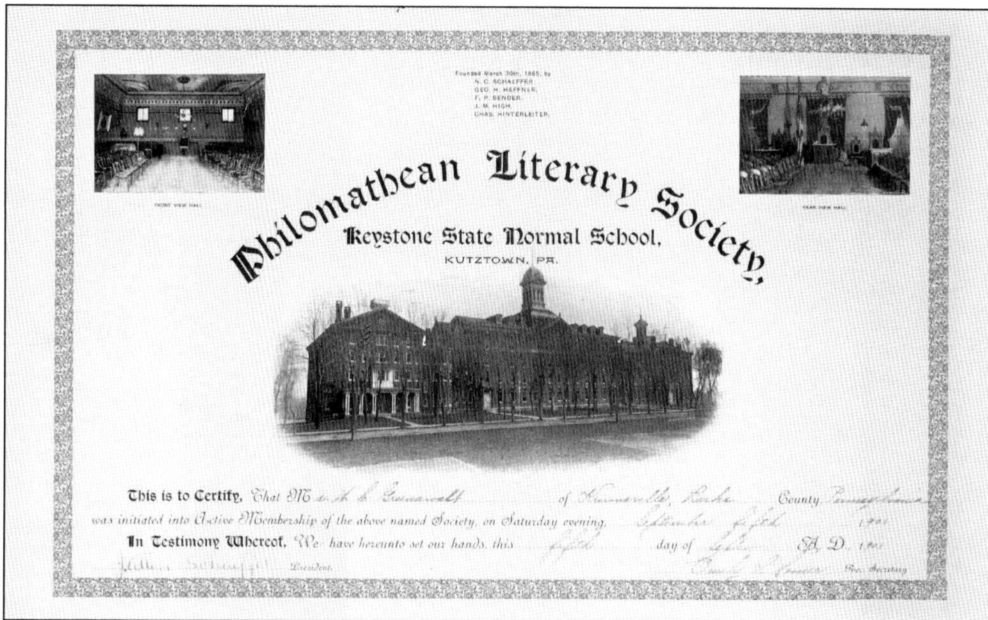

The Philomathean Literary Society dates back to the Maxatawny Seminary. Under the encouragement of Henry Nicks, the Philomathean Literary Society was organized on March 30, 1865. Nathan C. Schaeffer was a member of the first small group. The society provided an opportunity to all who desired to cultivate the art of expressing their thoughts in a clear and fluent manner and to become acquainted with the rules used in deliberative assemblies.

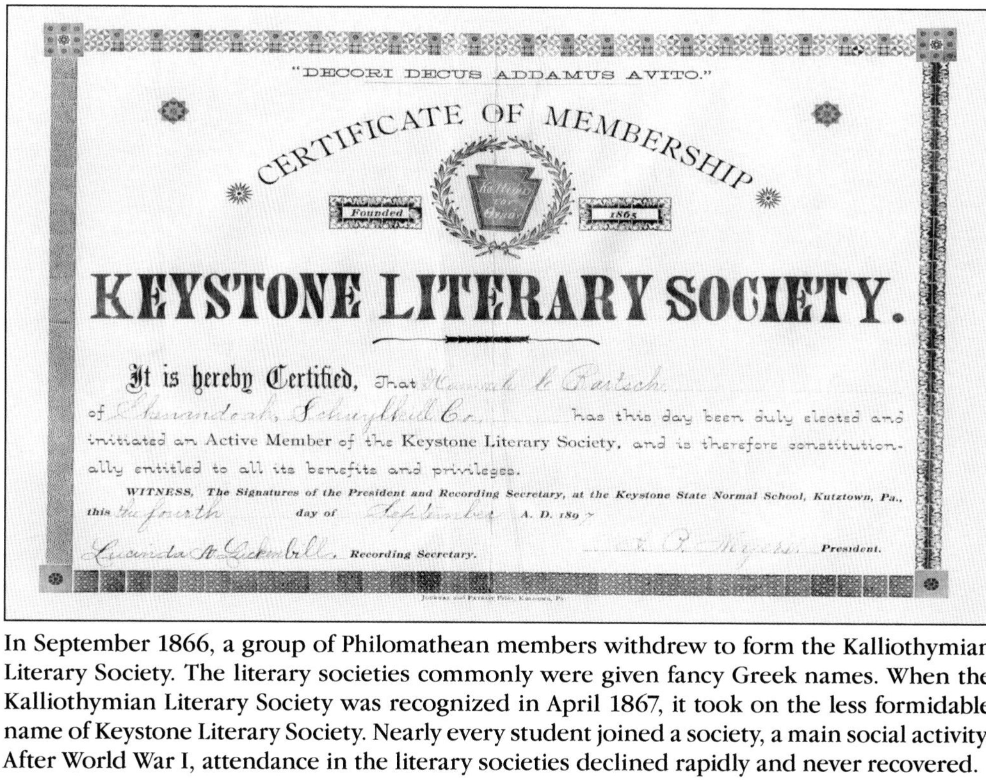

In September 1866, a group of Philomathean members withdrew to form the Kalliothymian Literary Society. The literary societies commonly were given fancy Greek names. When the Kalliothymian Literary Society was recognized in April 1867, it took on the less formidable name of Keystone Literary Society. Nearly every student joined a society, a main social activity. After World War I, attendance in the literary societies declined rapidly and never recovered.

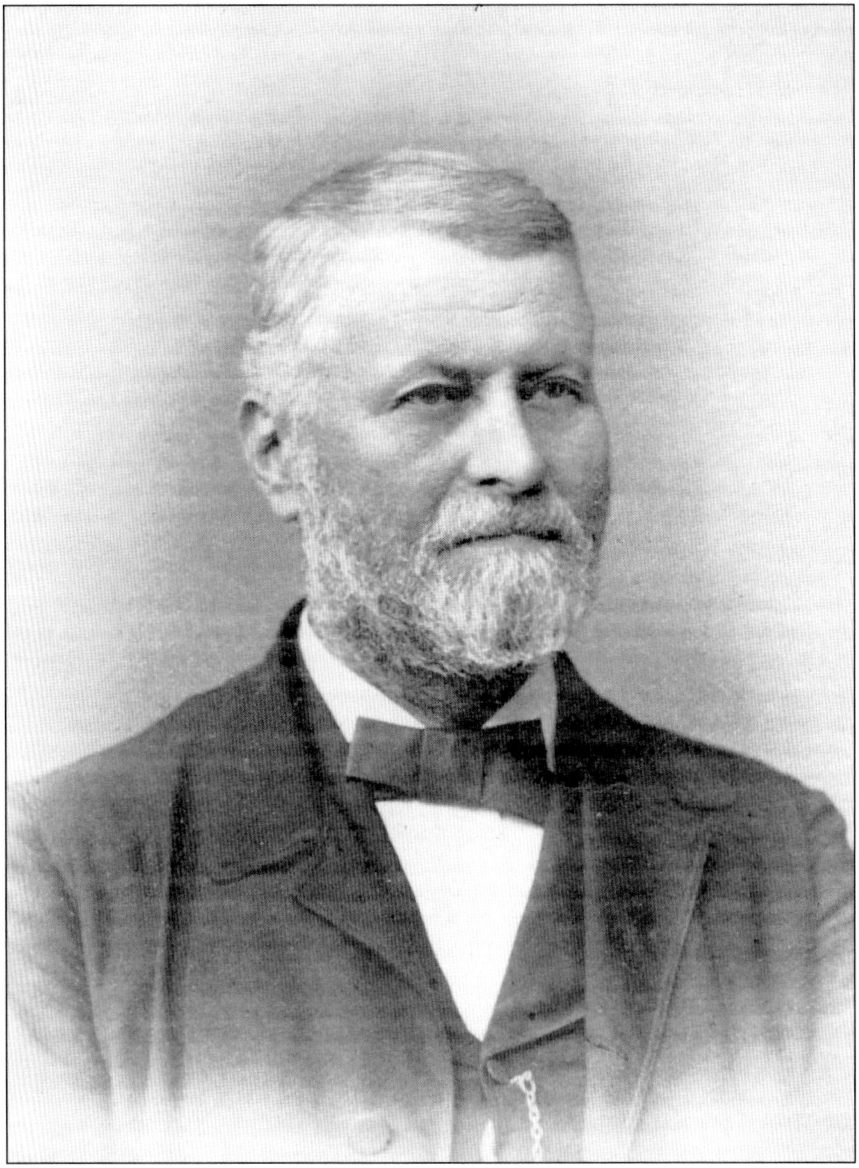

Abraham Reeser Horne (1834–1902) was principal of Keystone State Normal School from 1872 to 1877. Horne was a graduate of Pennsylvania College (now Gettysburg College) in 1858. As an ordained Lutheran pastor, he served several congregations, organized a normal school in Quakertown, served as superintendent of Williamsport School District, and after leaving Keystone, opened a preparatory and normal school at Muhlenberg College. He was editor of the *National Educator* journal from 1860 until 1902. While at Keystone, Horne also wrote one of the earliest books in the Pennsylvania German Deitsch language, *Horne's Pennsylvania German Manual*. The book is a very early example of a resource for reading and writing in an indigenous language and includes the earliest dictionary of the Pennsylvania German language. Far ahead of his time, Horne advocated for equal pay for female teachers and women's suffrage, and he proposed a form of bilingual education for Pennsylvania German children. By all accounts, Horne was a forward-thinking educator and a very inspiring teacher. (Courtesy of Dr. William Donner.)

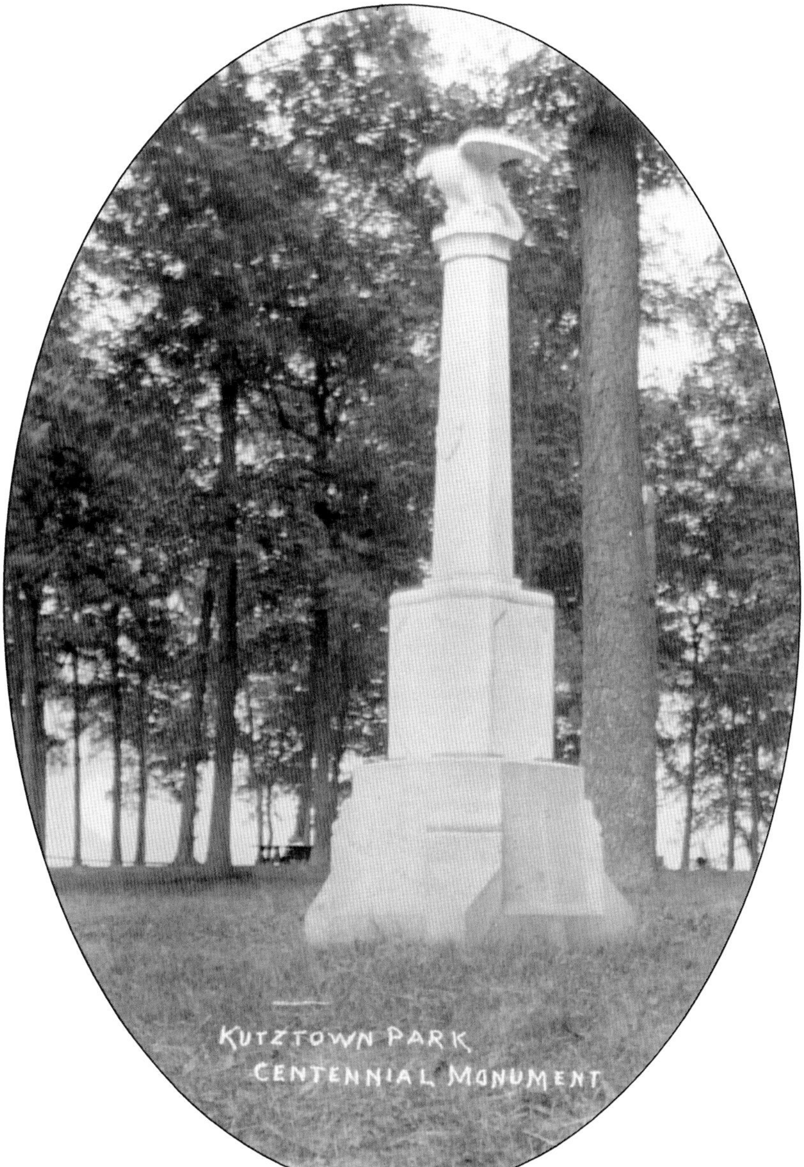

To celebrate the country's 100th birthday and the nearly 50 years of state-sponsored education since the passing of the 1834 Free School Act in Pennsylvania, the Historical Committee, chaired by John S. Ermentrout, former principal of Keystone State Normal School, decided to erect a local monument. On July 4, 1876, there was a centennial service held on the campus of Keystone State Normal School, and the monument was put in place in front of Old Main. On the four sides of the monument were the following inscriptions: "As God was with our fathers, so also is He with us," in German; "Nor is it necessary to know all," in Latin; "Virtue, Liberty & Independence," in English; and "Our free school system comes from the Pennsylvania Germans. Governor Wolf planned and started it, and Ritner and Shunk carried it out," in Pennsylvania German. The Latin inscription was later replaced with the following: "This monument was erected on the KSNS Campus, July, 4, 1876. Removed and rededicated in the Kutztown Park 1907."

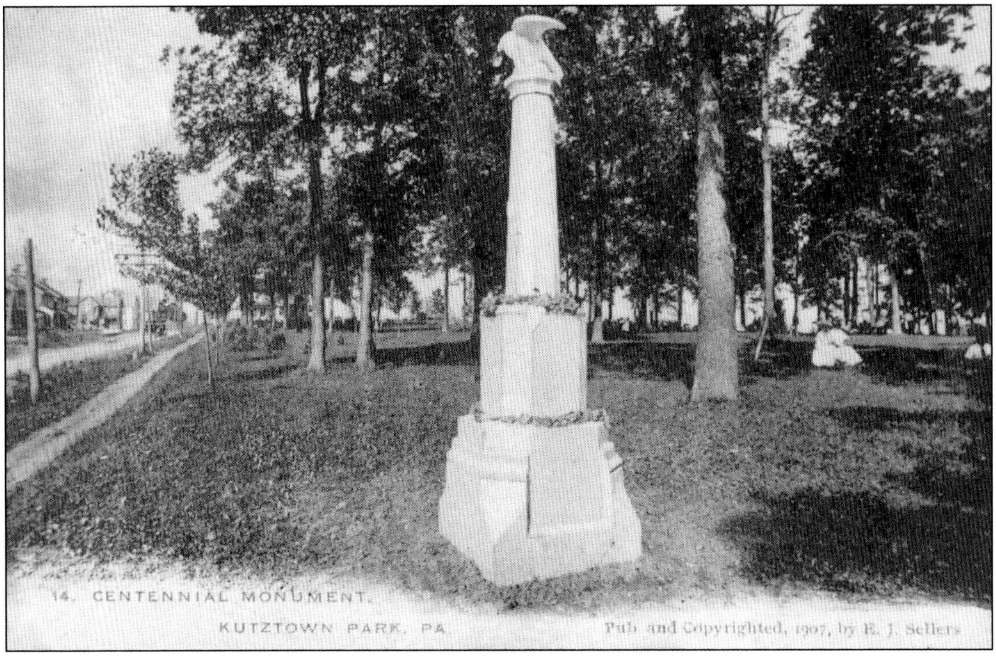

In August 1907, the centennial monument was moved from campus and rededicated near the entrance of Kutztown Park. In 1935, the monument was returned to campus east of what is now the administration building. In October 1983, the monument was placed under the protection of the Kutztown Historical Society. The remains of the centennial monument stand on the property of the society's headquarters, the 1892 Kutztown Public School building. (Courtesy of KHS.)

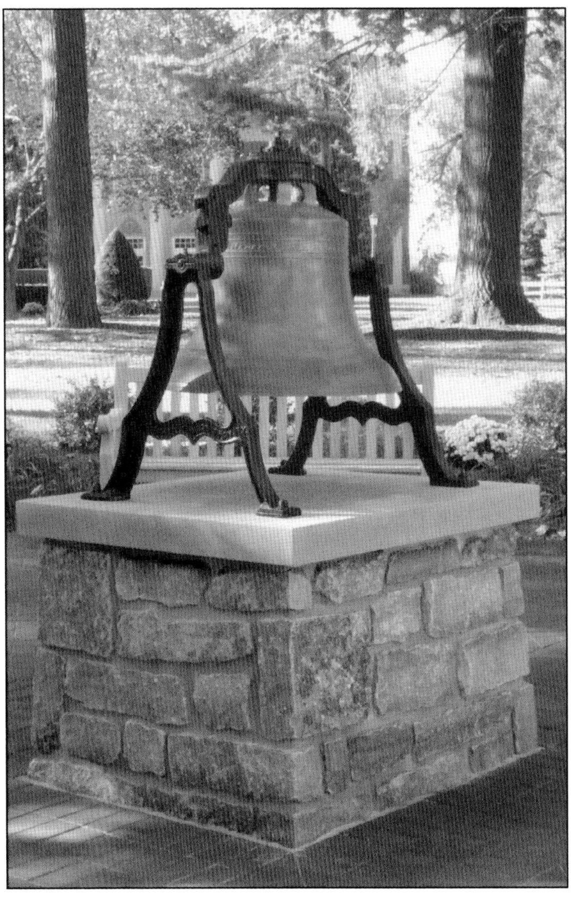

The original bell, housed within the Old Main tower since 1893 and concealed by the addition of a clock in 1910, was removed in 1995 to make room for new electronic controls to operate the clock. The functional bells that are rung are made by casting bell metal, a high-copper alloy of bronze. The bell now resides as a centerpiece in the College Hill Memorial Grove.

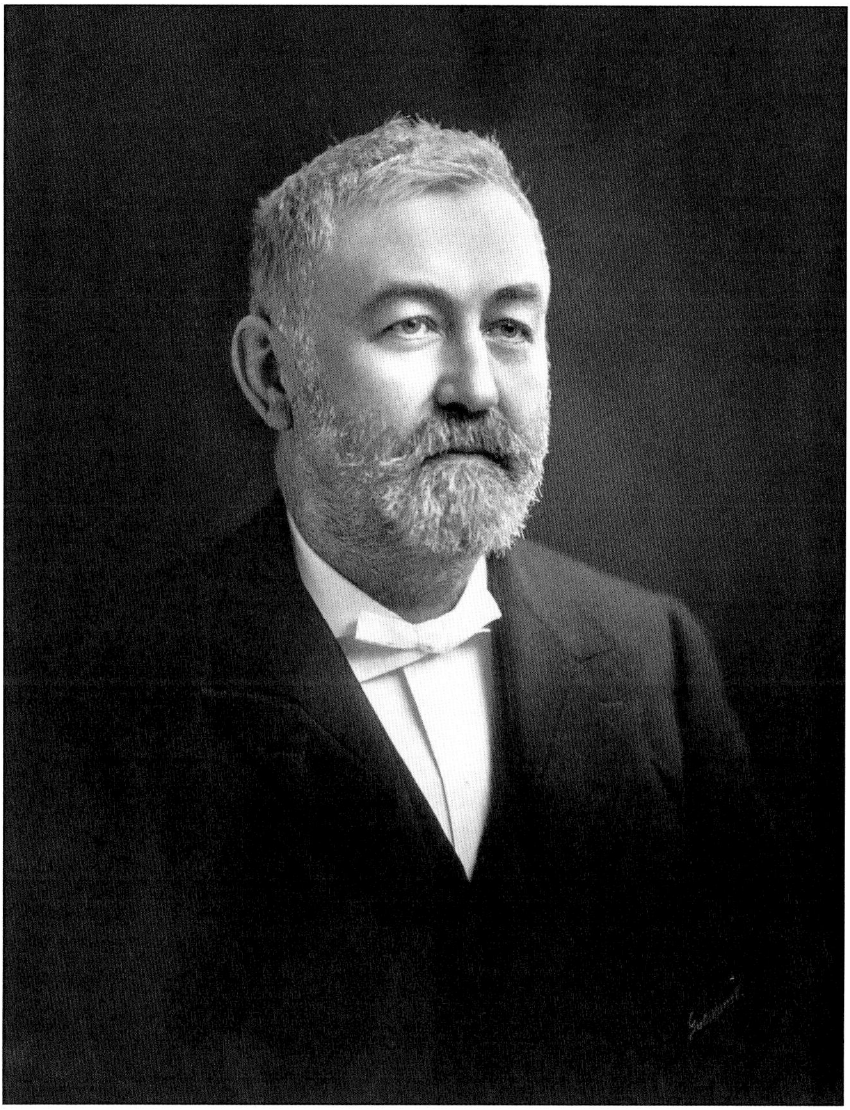

Nathan C. Schaeffer (1849–1919) was one of the original students of both Fairview Academy and Maxatawny Seminary. After he graduated from Maxatawny Seminary in 1865, Schaeffer spent the next several years continuing his education and, from time to time, returning to the Keystone State Normal School to teach mathematics, ancient languages, and history. At the age of 22, Schaeffer served the Keystone State Normal School as acting principal between 1871 and 1872. Eventually, in 1877, after continuing his education in Germany and teaching elsewhere, Schaeffer returned to the Keystone State Normal School as the third principal. During his 16 years as principal between 1877 and 1893, Dr. Schaeffer renovated and expanded the classrooms, dormitories, and curriculum of the school. His sense of humor, fairness, and patience earned him the respect of his colleagues and students. Dr. Schaeffer left the Keystone State Normal School in 1893 after being appointed Pennsylvania's superintendent of public instruction by Governor Pattison. Although the board of trustees always hoped its "illustrious son" would return to the Keystone State Normal School as principal, Dr. Schaeffer remained the state's superintendent until his death in 1919. (Photograph by John Paul Endress, courtesy of KU.)

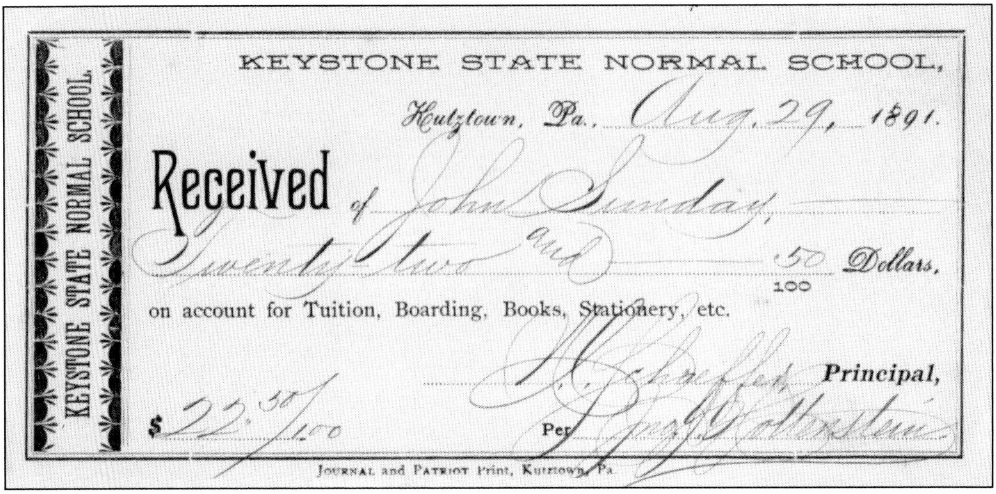

KEYSTONE STATE NORMAL SCHOOL.

KEYSTONE STATE NORMAL SCHOOL,

Kutztown, Pa., Aug. 29, 1891.

Received of John Sunday,

Twenty two and 50/100 Dollars,

on account for Tuition, Boarding, Books, Stationery, etc.

Principal,

$22.50/100 Per

Journal and Patriot Print, Kutztown, Pa.

This receipt for $22.50 was received from student John Sunday to pay for tuition during the fall term of 1891. The total cost for tuition, boarding, books, stationery, and so on for the fall term would have been $81. At the time, Nathan C. Schaeffer was principal, and John J. Hottenstein was secretary. Sunday graduated from the school in 1893.

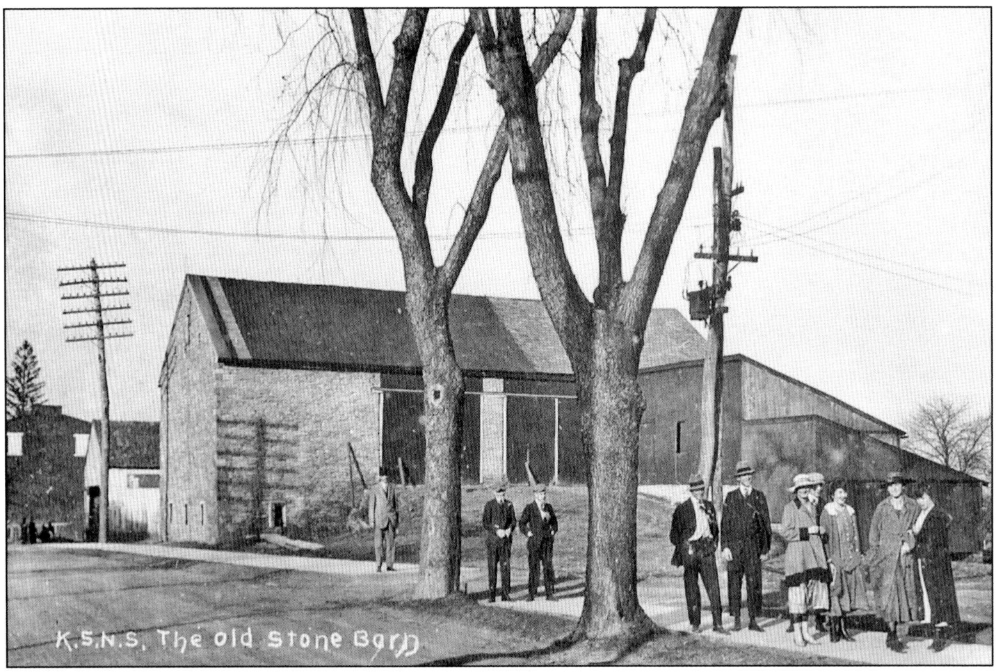

The old stone barn stood between Old Main and the edge of Kutztown. The brick building to the far left remains today as a pizza place at the intersection of Main Street and Normal Avenue. The barn served as a reminder that Keystone State Normal School was built on lands that had been farmed since the mid-18th century. It eventually came down in advance of the construction of the training school (today's south side of the Stratton Administration Building) in 1929.

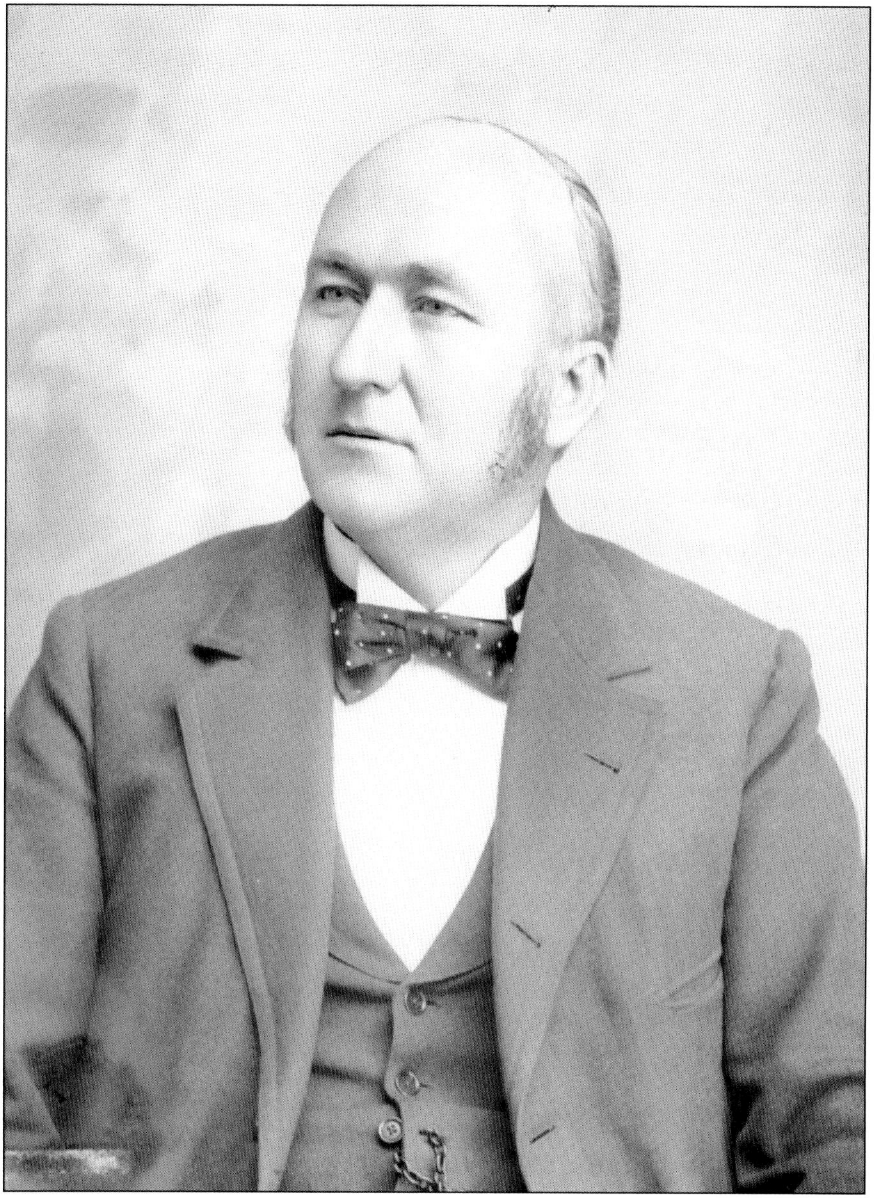

The Reverend Dr. George B. Hancher (1846–1915) spent his life as an educator and Lutheran minister. In 1882, Dr. Hancher started at the Keystone State Normal School as vice principal and professor of higher mathematics under the school's principal, Dr. Nathan C. Schaeffer. On June 16, 1893, two weeks after Dr. Schaeffer's resignation, Dr. Hancher was nominated to fill the principal position. The consideration to appoint Dr. Hancher as principal was pushed until June 23 by Franklin K. Flood (class of 1875) of the alumni committee. With only one dissenting vote, Dr. Hancher was elected principal and would serve from 1893 to 1899, with Amos C. Rothermel as his vice principal. During his term, Dr. Hancher was admired by his students and respected by the people of the area, who came to hear his lively sermons. Partly due to his temper and discipline issues, Dr. Hancher was not reelected in 1899. He accepted the decision without protest and retired to continue his work as a Lutheran pastor. (Courtesy of Jason Graver.)

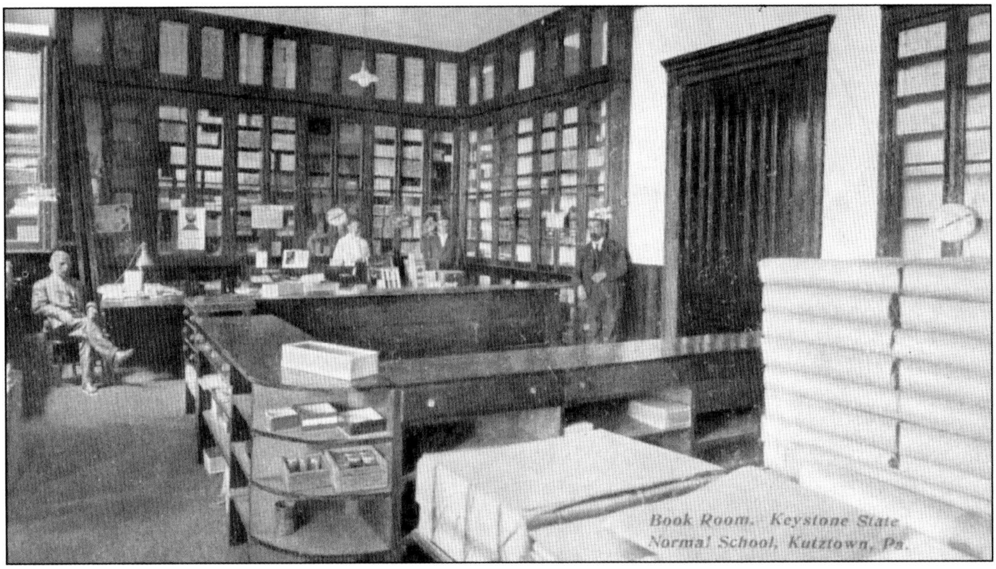

Early in the school's history, students had access to several libraries that were scattered throughout KSNS. The two literary societies of Keystone State Normal School, the Philomathean Literary Society and the Keystone Literary Society, had their own separate libraries. There was also a reference library, pictured here and described as "the Book Room," where professors helped students with their research. Eventually, a single faculty member was appointed to serve as the part-time librarian. (Photograph by David Keck.)

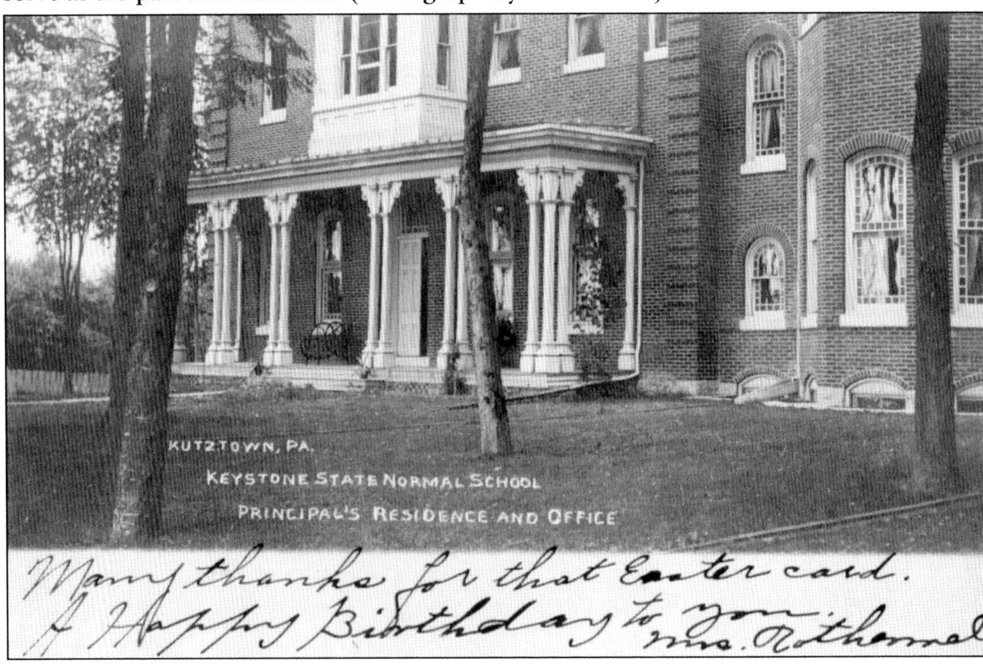

The school's principal was housed in the east wing of Old Main. His quarters included a living space and office, which was located in the same vicinity as the classrooms and dorm rooms that held the students of the normal school. Eventually, the porches and bay windows were torn down after the construction of the separate principal's residence across the street from Old Main in 1929. (Photography by W.W. Deatrick, courtesy of Jason Graver.)

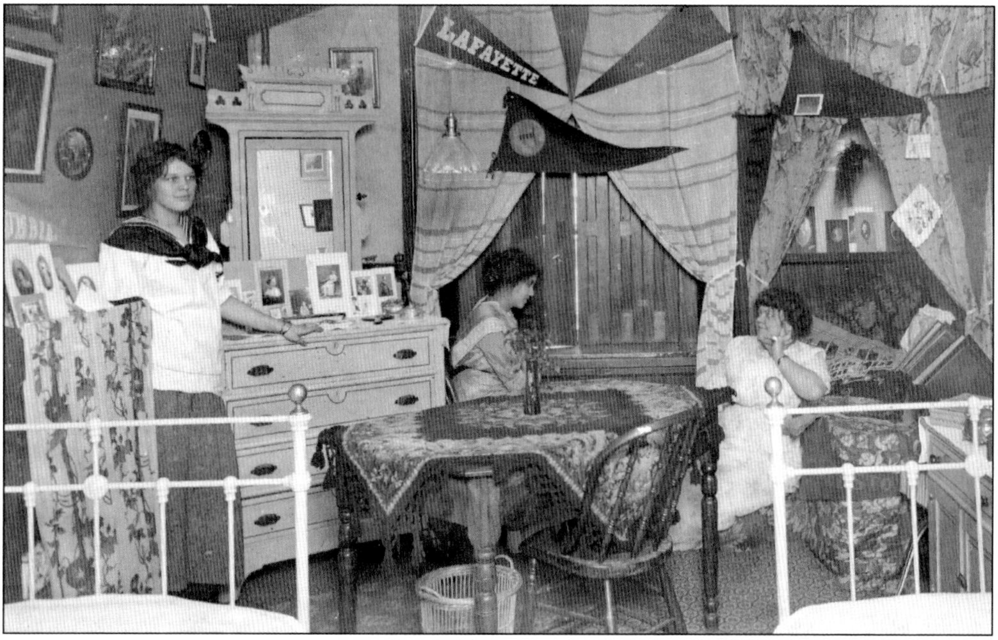

During the days of the Keystone State Normal School, all boarding students resided in Old Main. The rooms were small, and heat came from a central boiler. They were scantily furnished with iron bedsteads, thin mattresses, a table, chairs, a coal oil lamp, and two buckets, one of which was used for fire protection. Above is a women's dorm room where three KSNS students pose for a photograph. Men first had dorm rooms on the fourth floor of Old Main. A special staircase was installed so males would not trespass on female premises or mix in the stairwell. Later, in 1891, a separate male dormitory was built, with the first modern bathroom constructed in the basement of that dormitory in 1895. Below is a photograph of an 1897 men's dorm room. (Above, photograph by W.W. Deatrick; below, courtesy of KU.)

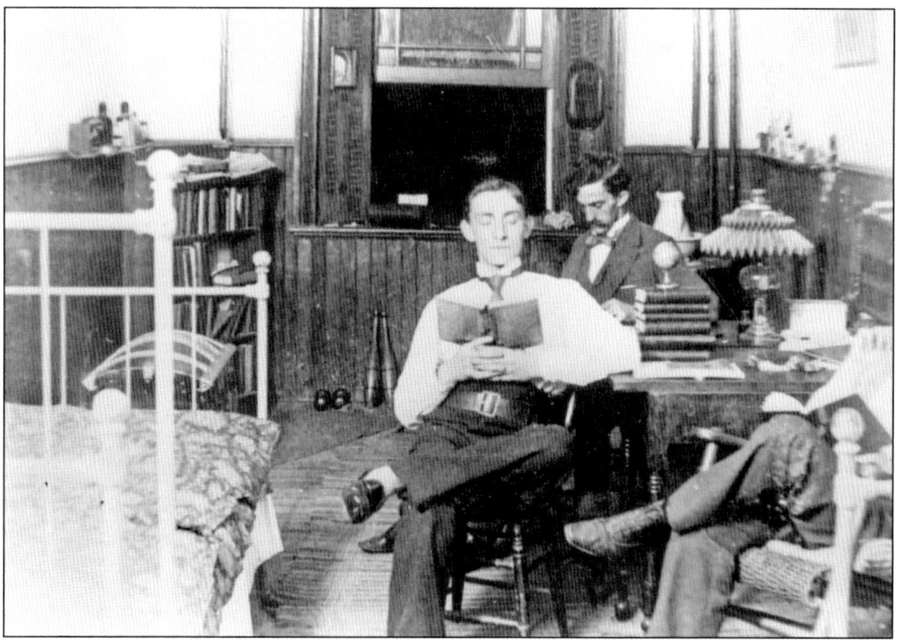

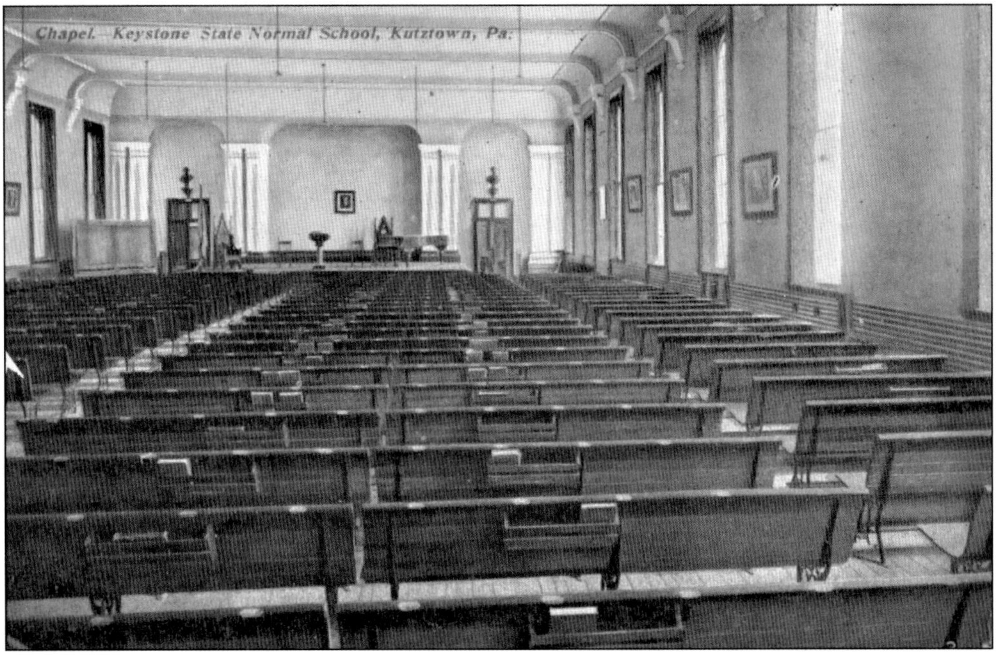

Construction of the chapel started in the fall of 1884 and was completed in April 1887. Daily morning devotional services were held here. Faculty were present during these services to set an example and enforce the rule that the sexes were not allowed to converse in the chapel. Today, this location is known as the Georgian Room. (Photograph by David Keck.)

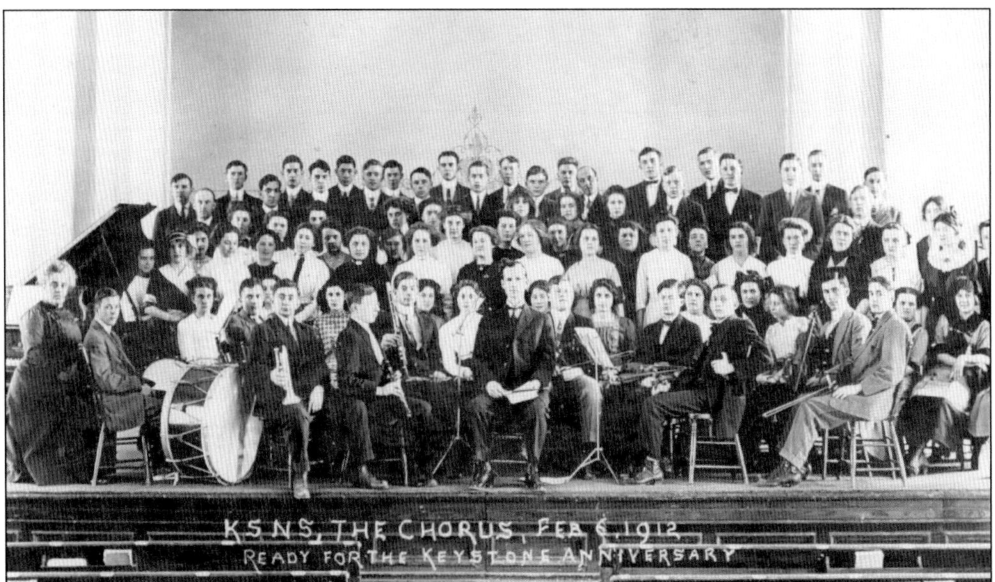

Each year, the literary societies held a public anniversary celebration. The anniversary showcased musical and literary highlights of the year. This photograph features the chorus and orchestra that performed at the Keystone Anniversary on February 6, 1912. The orchestra is seated in the front, with the chorus standing behind. Alumni and friends from far and wide gathered to attend. (Courtesy of KU.)

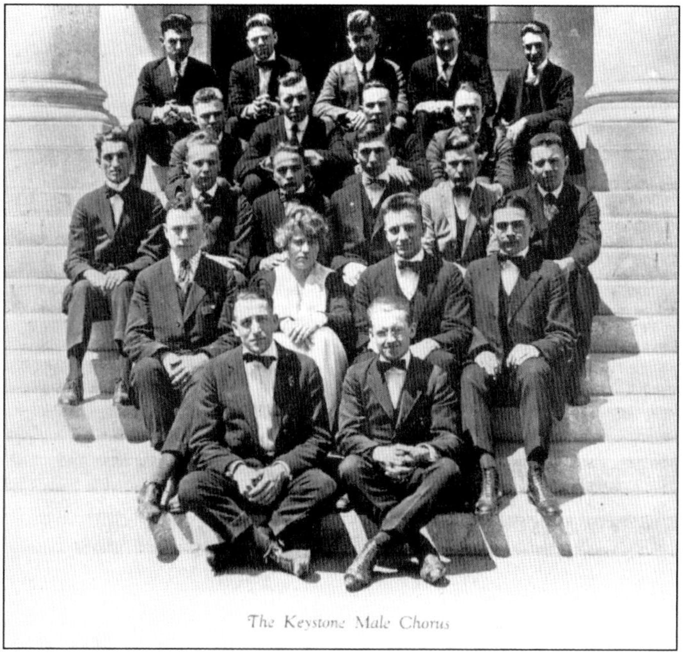

Ruth May Rothermel, adopted daughter of Dr. Amos C. and Ada Spate Rothermel and a 1914 graduate of Keystone State Normal School, created the Keystone Male Chorus in 1919 while serving as the school's music instructor. She directed the male chorus for many years. Here, Rothermel sits in the center of her mostly bow-tied chorus on the stairs of the library (today's Graduate Center).

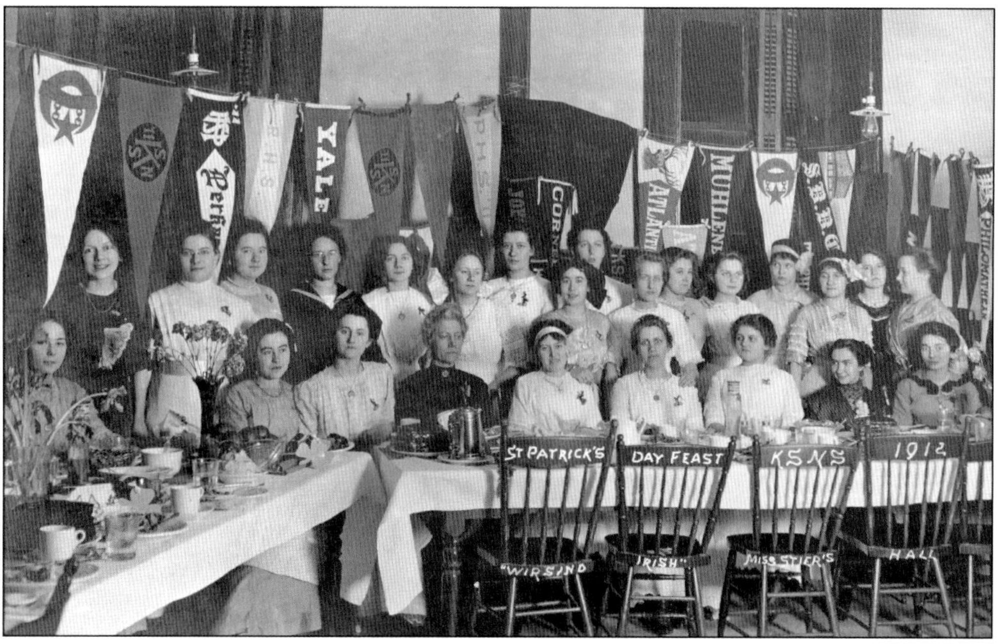

This image captures female students attending a St. Patrick's Day feast in Alma D. Stier's hall of Old Main. Stier was a professor of reading and elocution at the Keystone State Normal School. Professors were expected to live in Old Main and take responsibility for overseeing the hallways in which they lived. An inscription on the photograph reads, "Wirsind Irish," which is German for "We are Irish." (Photograph by W.W. Deatrick.)

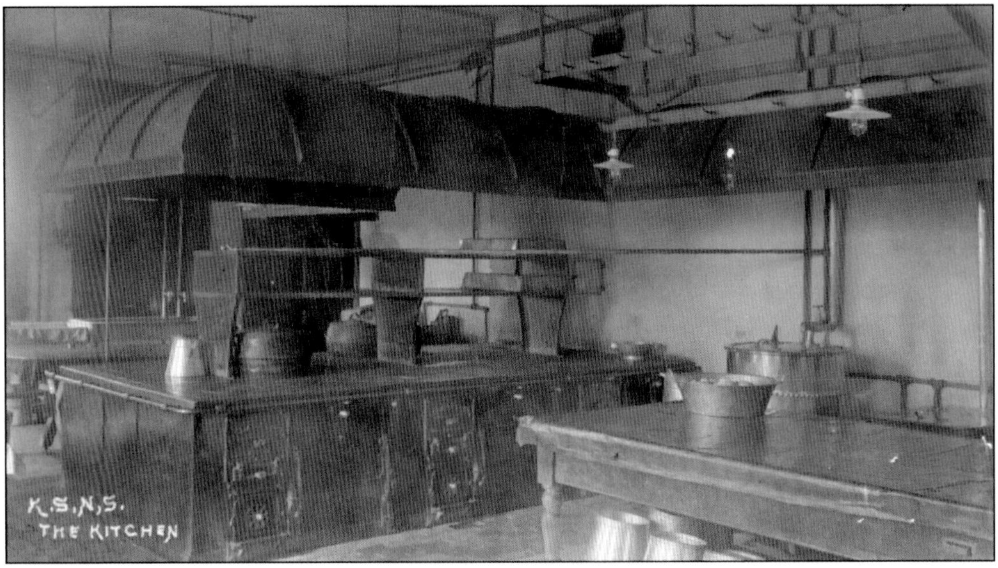

The kitchen, home to all meals for faculty and students, was originally located on the first floor of the chapel building. Also on the first floor was the dining room. Students were required to dress in their best and attend every meal. Professors would oversee the meals and ensure that all students behaved. (Courtesy of Jason Graver.)

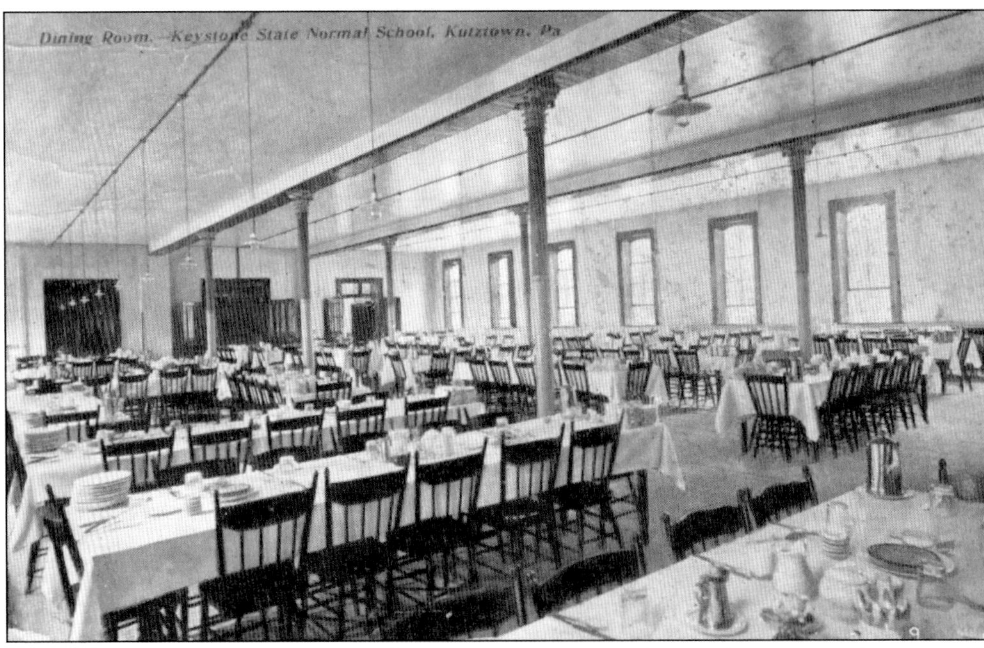

After the 5:30 a.m. rising bell, professors would ensure that students arrived punctually for a breakfast of cold meat, fried potatoes, oatmeal, bread, butter, molasses, and coffee. A gentleman could select a lady to sit opposite him. The ladies, instructed in table manners, were expected to help the gentlemen develop manners. The ban on talking between sexes in the dining room was not lifted until later. (Photograph by E.J. Moebius.)

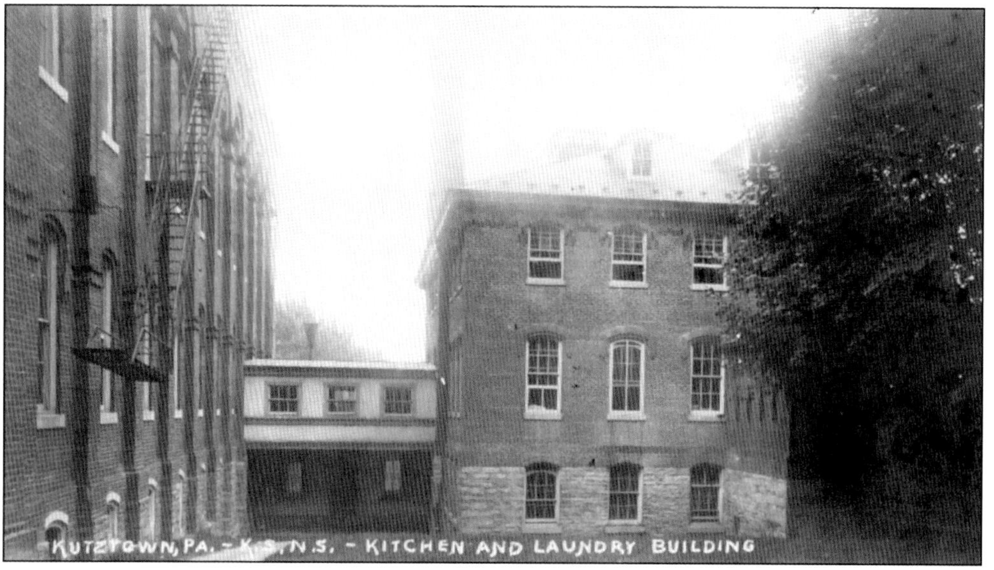

The kitchen and laundry building was completed in 1895. This facility was equipped to handle the production of 2,000 daily meals and all the laundry work of the school. In 1898, more improvements were made to the laundry facility at a cost of $824. The school laundry did custom work for the borough that earned it $800 per year. (Courtesy of Jason Graver.)

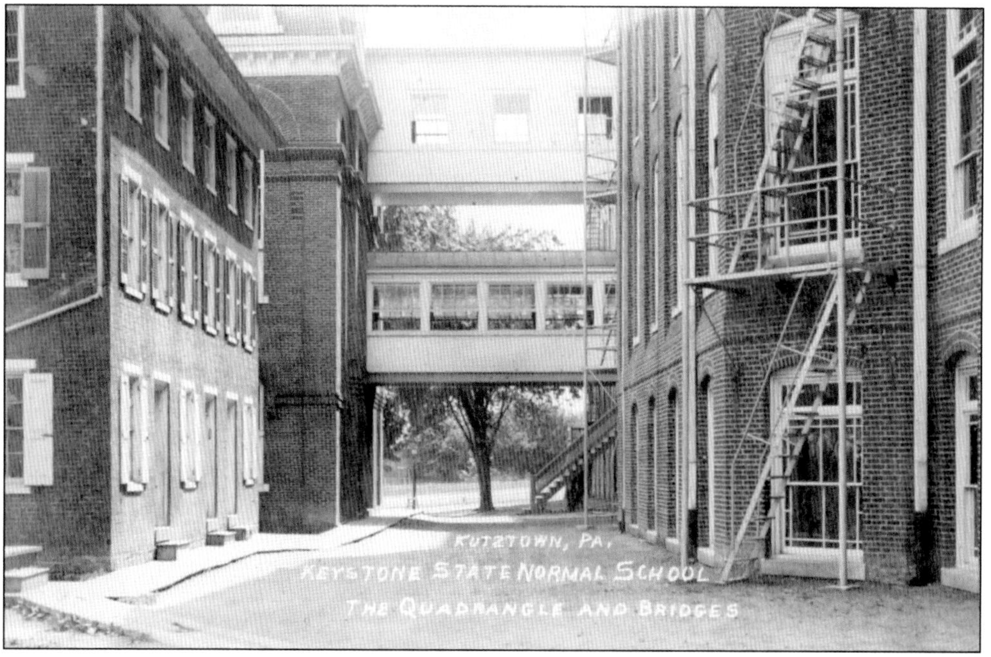

Two pedestrian bridges linked Old Main to newer buildings to the rear. The lower bridge connected to the chapel, and the top bridge led to a boys' dormitory above the chapel, which was eventually removed. This photograph was taken before the model school section of Old Main was built in 1900. The stewards' building, to the extreme left, was razed in the 1960s. (Courtesy of Jason Graver.)

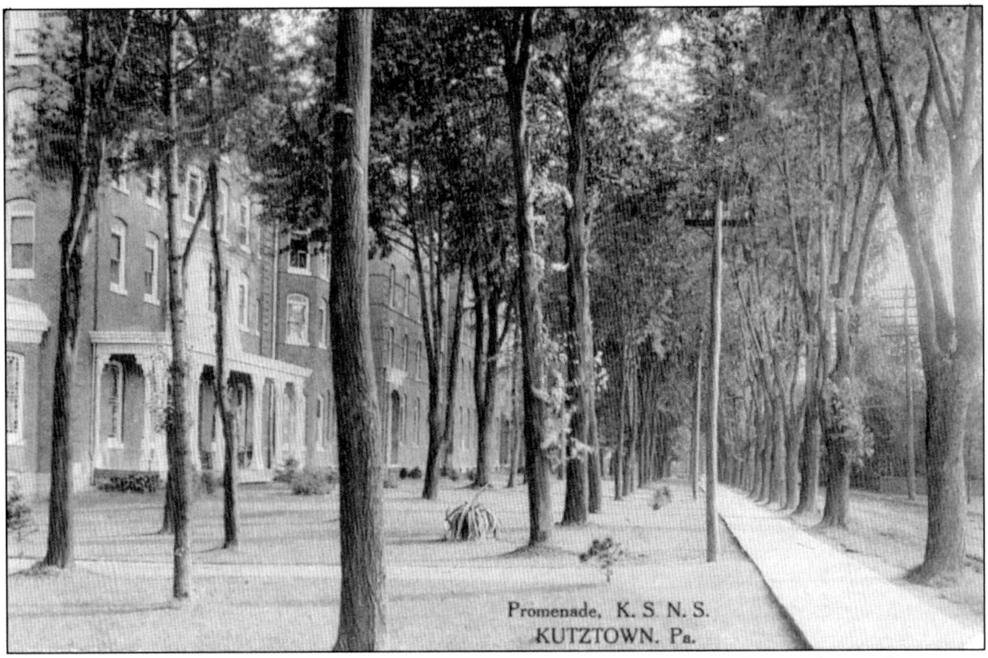

The promenade was located in front of Old Main. This photograph shows the view facing the east end of the school. The road beside the promenade was called Easton Road until the name was changed to Kutztown Road. Neither ladies nor gentlemen connected with the school were allowed to walk with a person of the opposite sex, except in cases of necessity and then only with permission. (Photograph by David Keck.)

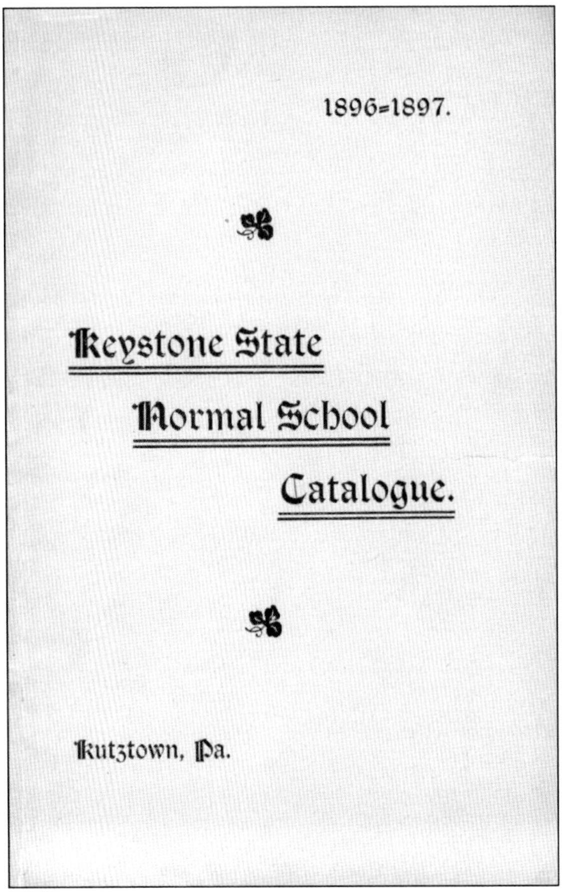

The *Keystone State Normal School Catalogue* of 1896–1897 was offered to students and alumni of the school. Among other things, it provides a directory of names and addresses, a summary of the total number of students for the year, and a list of the current courses offered.

Following a siege of typhoid fever in 1903, the board of trustees decided to drill a deep well and build a standpipe, even though the school continued to buy water from the local water company. The standpipe stood in the area of what is now the Rohrbach Library. (Photograph by Werner E. DeTurk, courtesy of Jason Graver.)

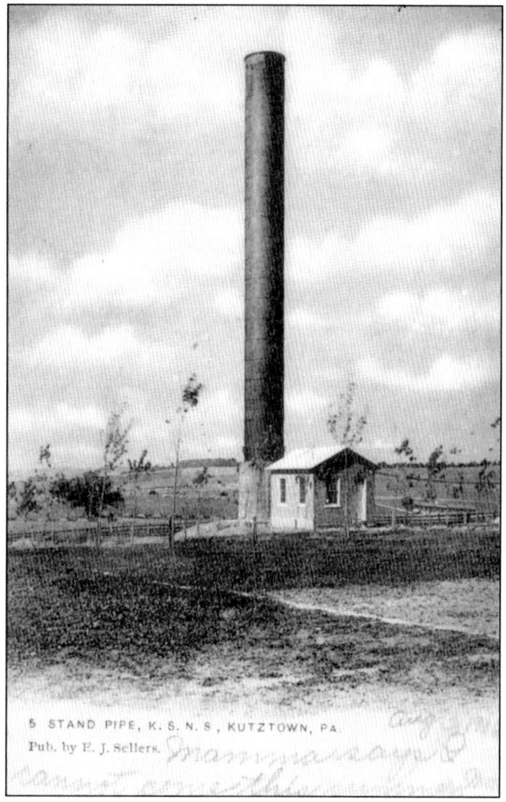

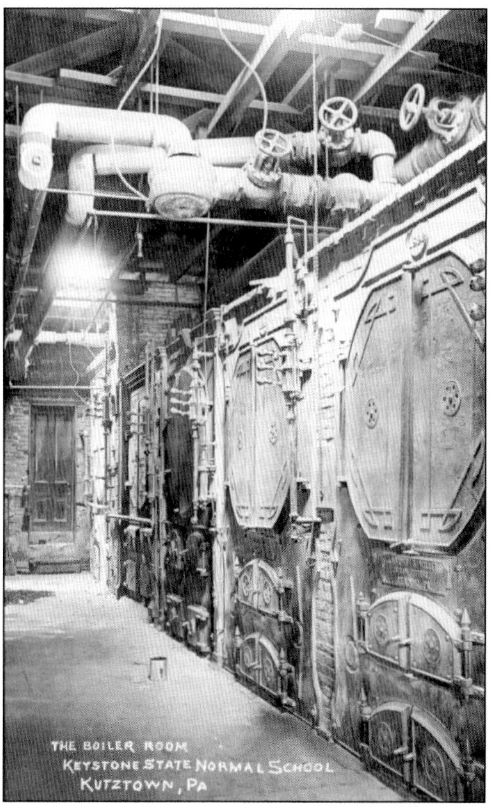

It took a mighty steam plant to provide central heating to a building as large as Old Main. Steam heat was likely original to Old Main (electricity came later), requiring students to light their rooms with coal oil lamps. Steam heat must have been a new amenity for many of the students at the Keystone State Normal School who had stoves fueled with wood or coal back home. (Photograph by W.W. Deatrick, courtesy of Jason Graver.)

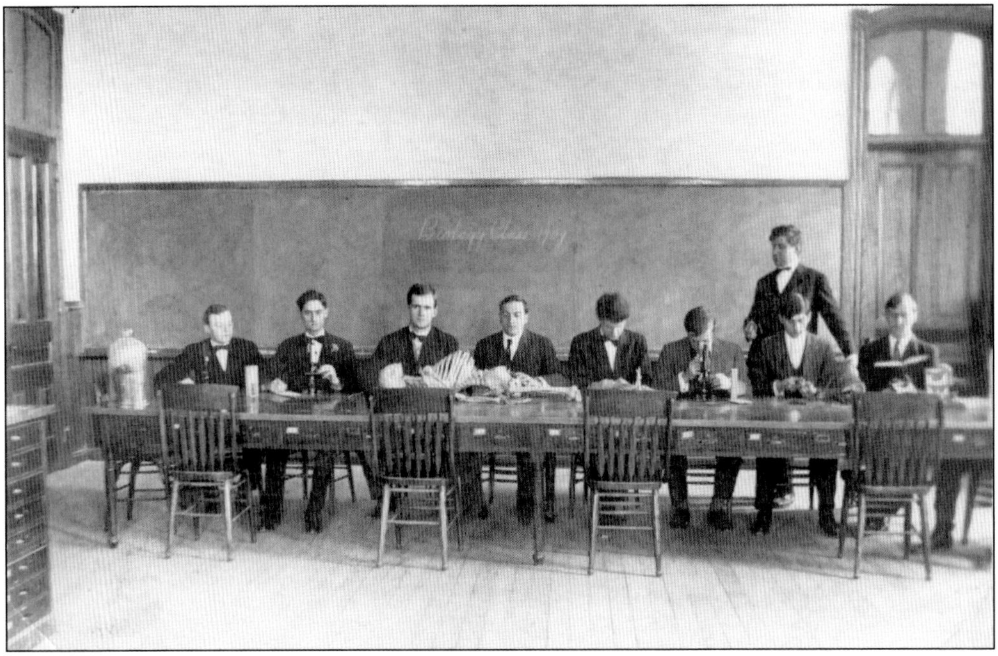

This biology class of 1909 is seen at work in one of the new laboratories designed by KSNS professor Dr. James Grim. In the photograph, some students are observing a human skeleton that has been laid out on the table, while others look through microscopes or read biology books. Their professor stands behind them, monitoring their progress.

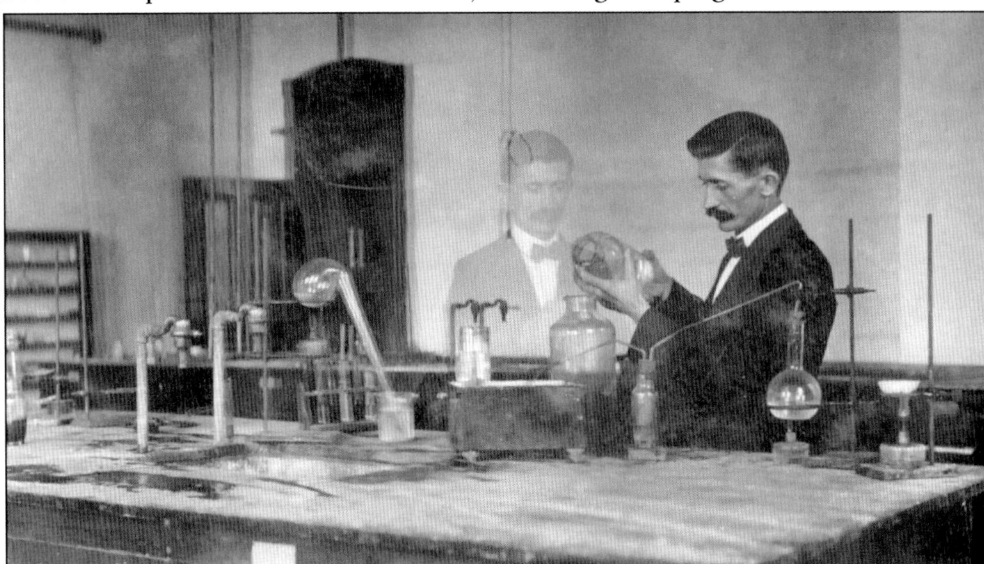

In 1872, when Abraham Reeser Horne became principal, a chemistry course was added to the curriculum. It is believed that Prof. Frank P. Miller, an 1893 graduate of Keystone State Normal School, is pictured here. Professor Miller was a physical science and German teacher at the school from around 1900 to 1907. Additions to Old Main in 1900 included science laboratories, such as the one pictured here. (Photograph by Werner E. DeTurk, courtesy of Jason Graver.)

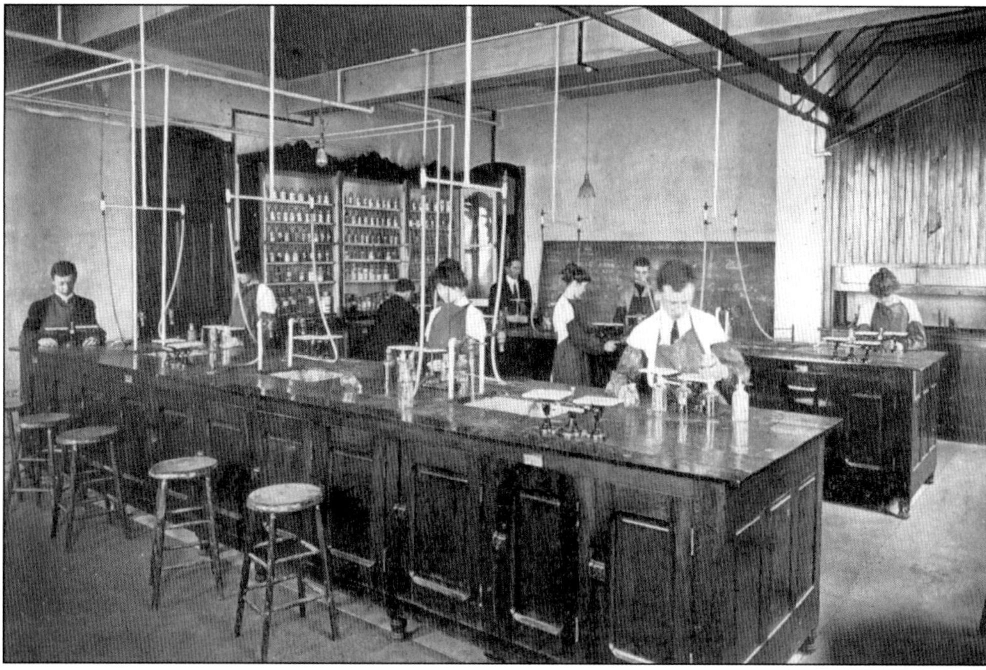

As the normal school curriculum evolved, the course of study required one year of general chemistry. The laboratory work consisted of individual exercises performed by the students, supplemented with demonstrations by the instructor. Gas, electricity, an ample supply of chemicals, and necessary apparatus made the work interesting as well as instructional. (Courtesy of KU.)

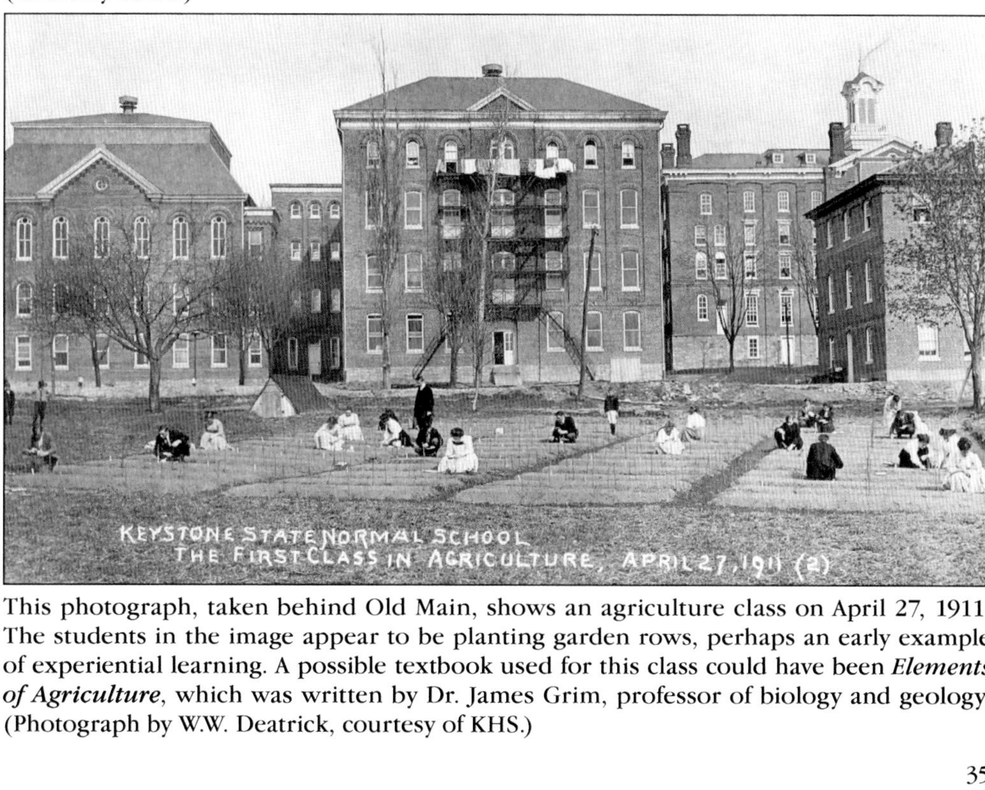

This photograph, taken behind Old Main, shows an agriculture class on April 27, 1911. The students in the image appear to be planting garden rows, perhaps an early example of experiential learning. A possible textbook used for this class could have been *Elements of Agriculture*, which was written by Dr. James Grim, professor of biology and geology. (Photograph by W.W. Deatrick, courtesy of KHS.)

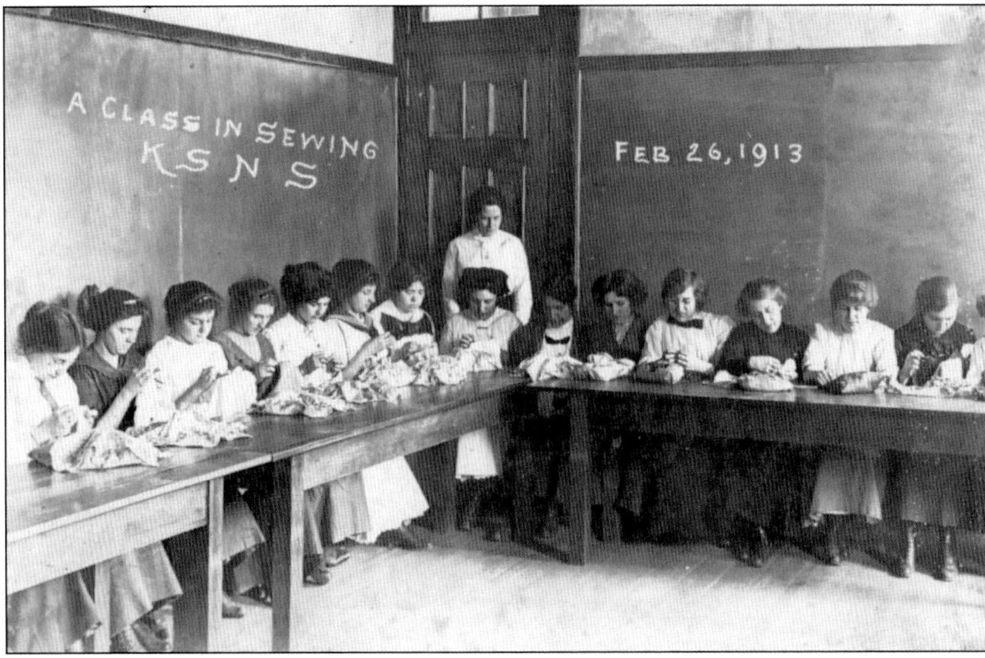

Part of the regular teacher curriculum of the normal school included electives such as sewing. The sewing class seen here occurred in Old Main on February 26, 1913. The woman standing in front of the door is Prof. Lillian Bull, who taught physical culture and sewing. (Photograph by W.W. Deatrick, courtesy of Jason Graver.)

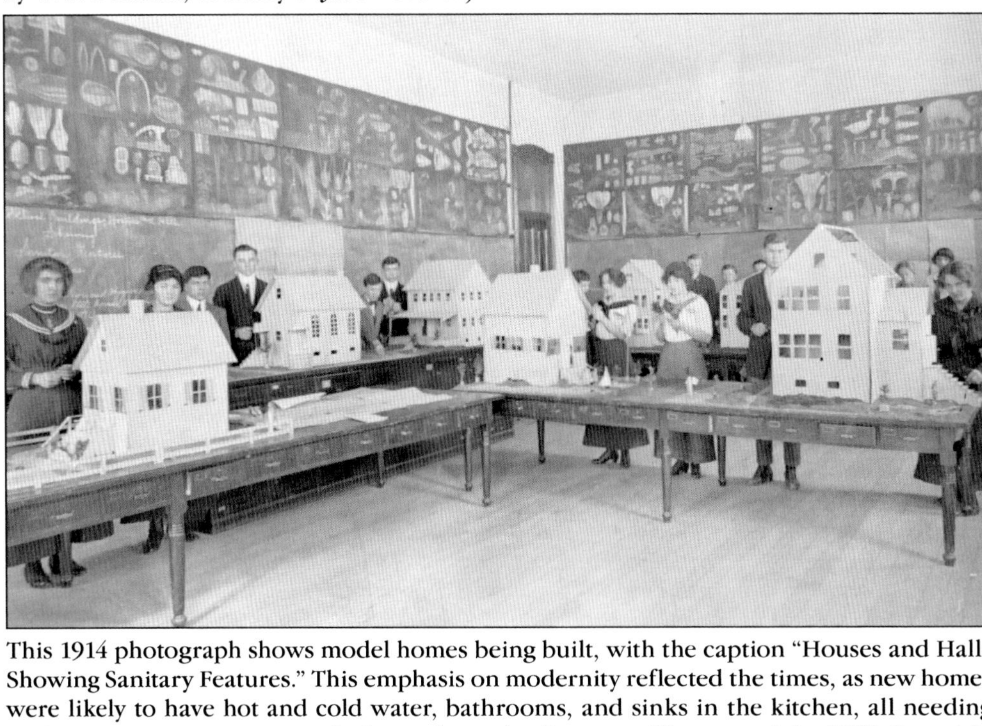

This 1914 photograph shows model homes being built, with the caption "Houses and Halls Showing Sanitary Features." This emphasis on modernity reflected the times, as new homes were likely to have hot and cold water, bathrooms, and sinks in the kitchen, all needing sanitary systems to manage drainage from the fixtures. (Photograph by W.W. Deatrick, courtesy of Jason Graver.)

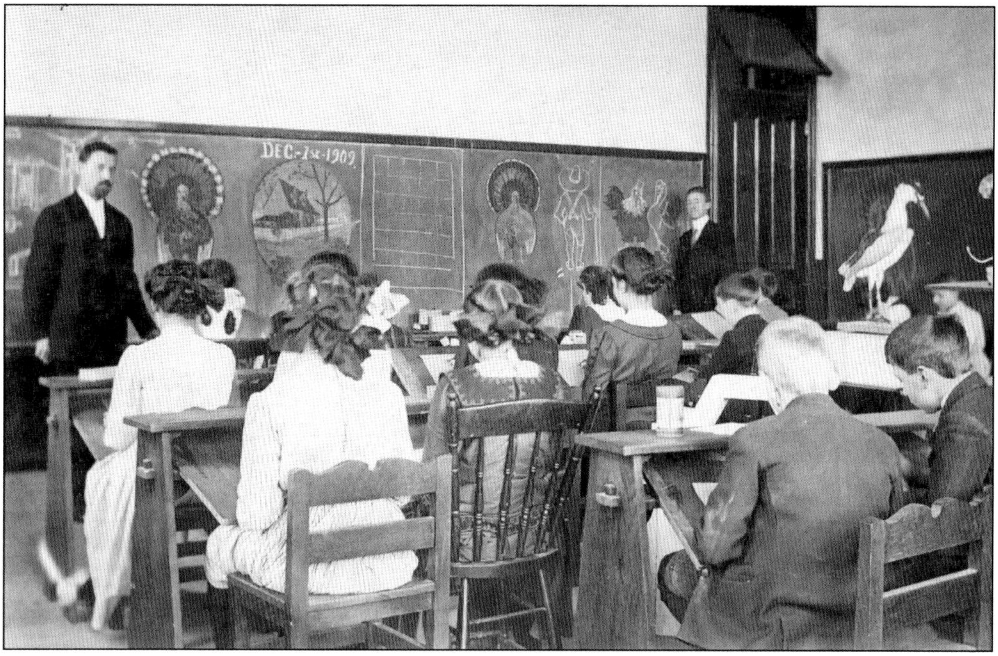

Here, students of an art class practice drawing on December 1, 1909. In the four-year normal school courses of 1910, drawing was taken during the second year. In 1924, the Keystone State Normal School was given permission to institute a three-year course of study for art teachers. Henry W. Sharadin, standing to the left, was considered qualified to introduce the new course. (Photograph by W.W. Deatrick.)

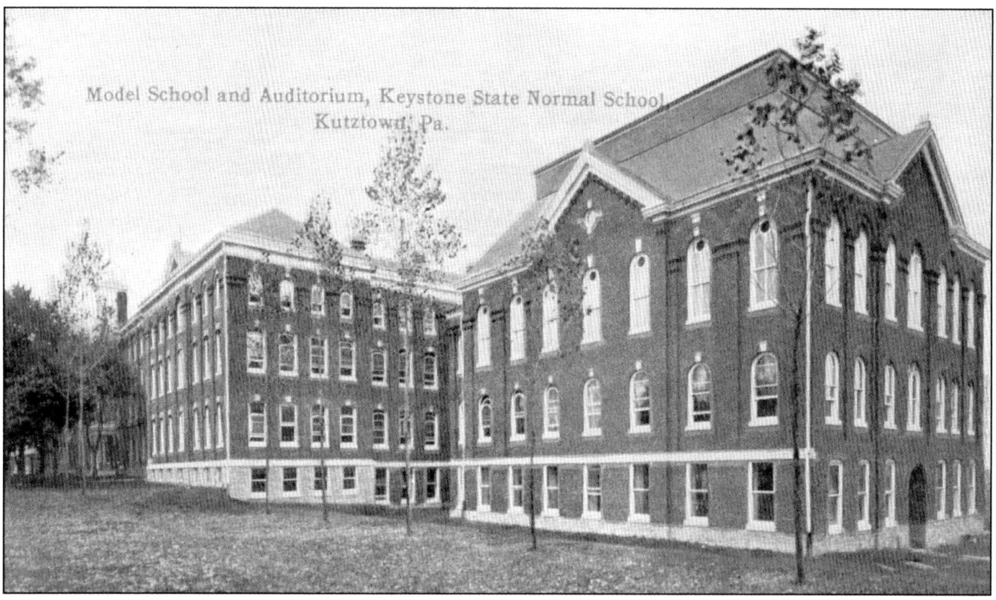

Beginning in 1900, additions were made to the west side of Old Main, designed by E.F. Durang. The project boasted a new model school, four science laboratories (including a biology lab designed by professor Dr. James Grim), several additional classrooms, dorm rooms, an auditorium that seated 500, and a new gymnasium area. Ground breaking occurred at commencement in 1900, and construction was completed in 1903. (Photograph by David Keck.)

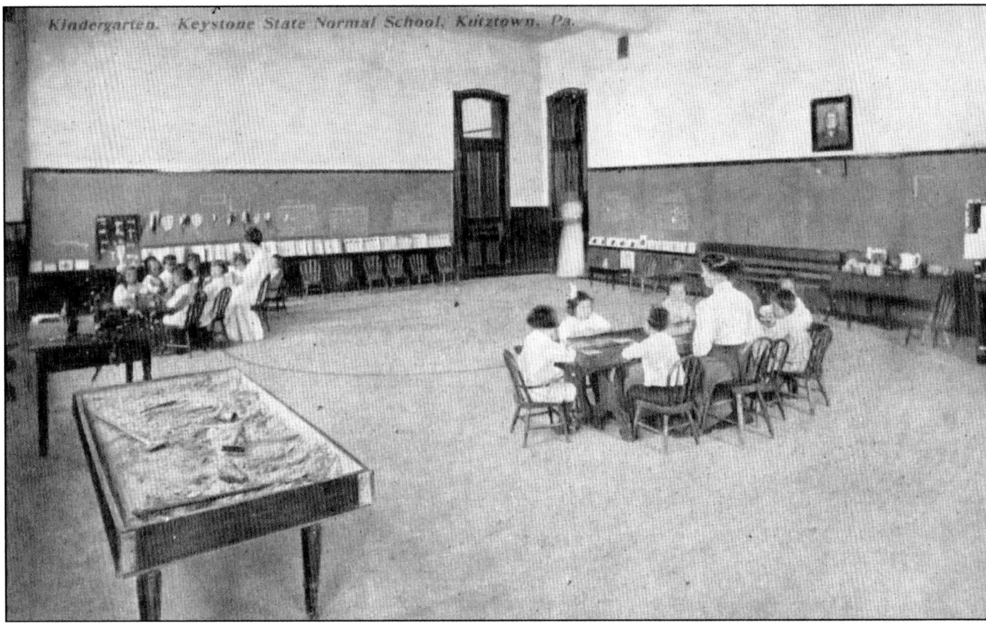

The implementation of a kindergarten class into the model school was a new idea for the Keystone State Normal School and the country. Based on the philosophy of Friedrich Froebel, children were taught through the use of games, songs, and play. The impressions children were given at an early age affected their character as they grew older. The first English-speaking kindergarten class was created in Boston in 1860.

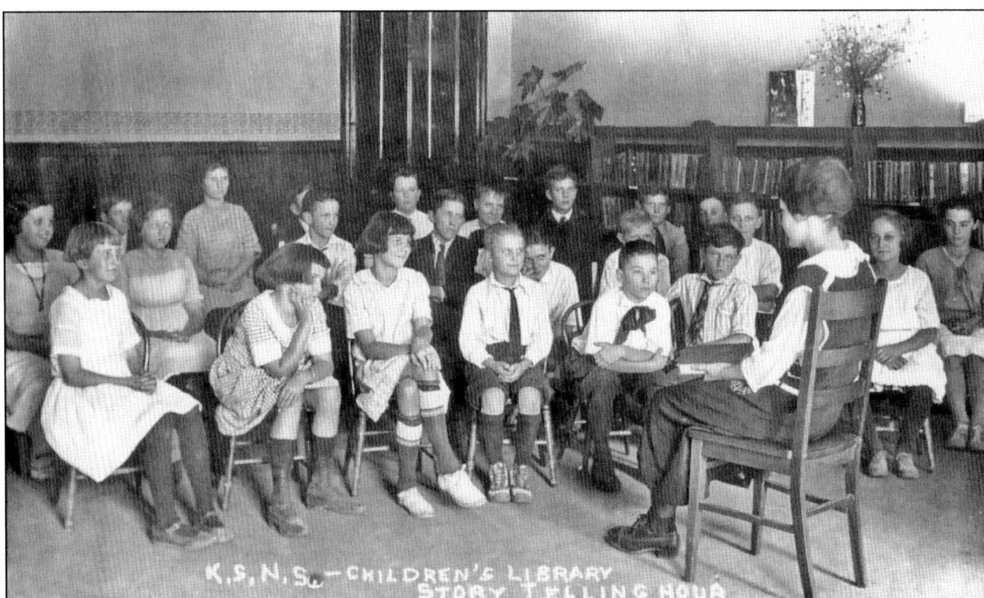

In the model school housed in the E wing of Old Main, students of the Keystone State Normal School taught children common school subjects as part of their teacher training education. KSNS students did the equivalent of today's student teaching in the model school that children from Kutztown attended. Here, a KSNS student is shown reading to some children who attended the model school. (Courtesy of KU.)

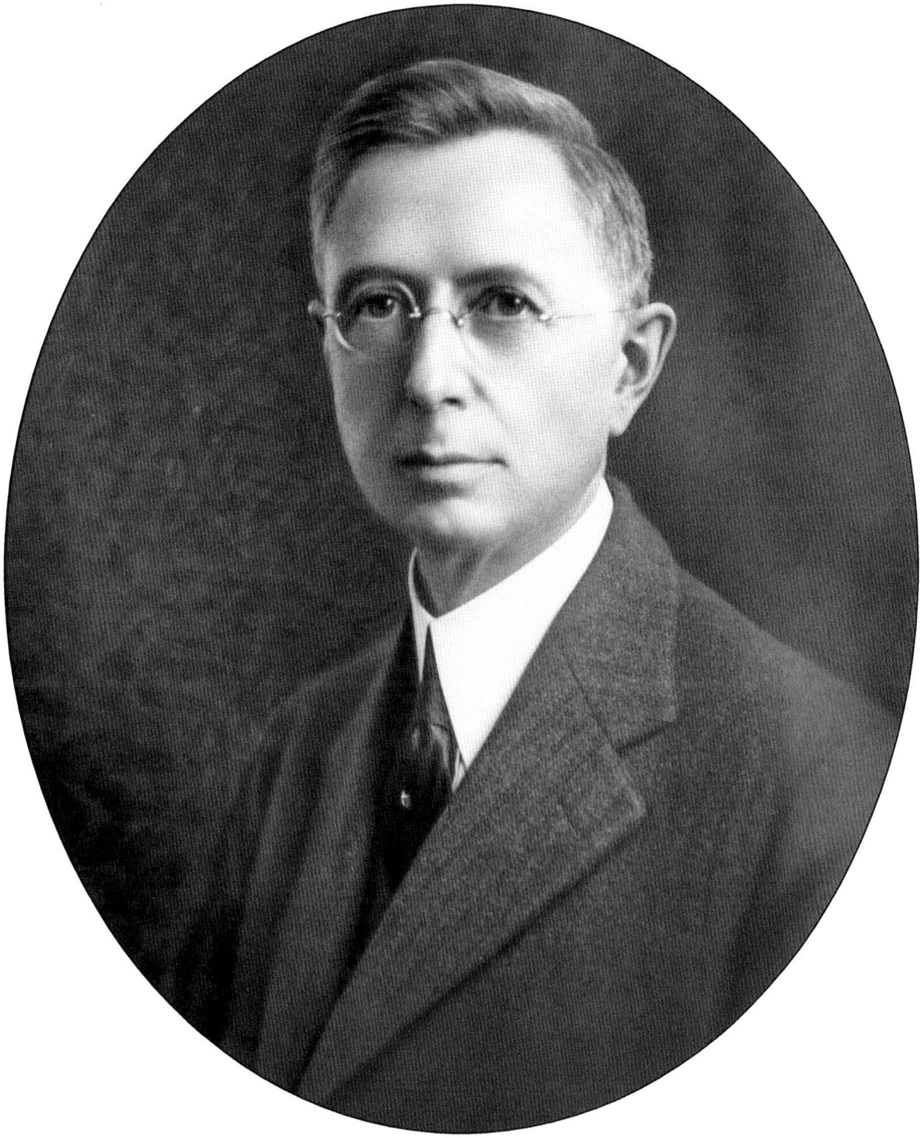

Dr. Amos C. Rothermel (1864–1946) graduated from Keystone State Normal School in 1886. In 1893, he was nominated to serve as vice principal. After Principal Hancher was dismissed in 1899, Dr. Rothermel was named acting principal for two years, before officially becoming principal. Highly religious, he was known as "the Reverend Doctor." During his era of leadership, the school became a state teachers college in 1928, and Dr. Rothermel became its first president. He remained president until his retirement in May 1934, having dedicated 45 years to the Keystone State Normal School and the Keystone State Teachers College. To honor his years of service, the students and faculty installed a bronze tablet at the entrance of the chapel building (today's Georgian Room) that is inscribed with his professional creed: "The perpetuity of free government, the security and progress of the future are in the hands of the teachers. The character of their work, their respect for law, their love for truth, their loyalty to home, school, and country—These leave their impress on the plastic minds of youth and are potent factors in molding the lives of the citizens of tomorrow." (Photograph by John Paul Endress, courtesy of KU.)

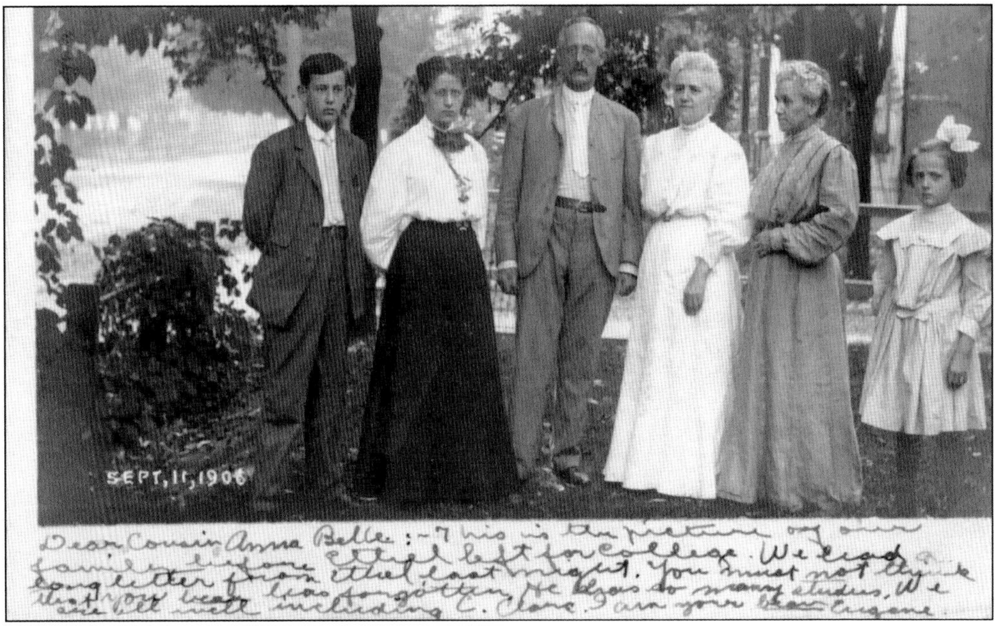

Dr. W.W. Deatrick (center), a faculty member of Keystone State Normal School, was married to Emma Jane Balliet Deatrick (1851–1933), pictured to the right of him. They had three children, all of whom graduated from Keystone State Normal School: Ethel Matilda Deatrick (1904), second from left; Eugene Peyton Deatrick (1906), far left; and Anna Louise Deatrick (1915), far right. The Deatrick Hall dormitory was named after the professor and prolific local photographer. The woman second from right is unidentified. (Courtesy of Jason Graver.)

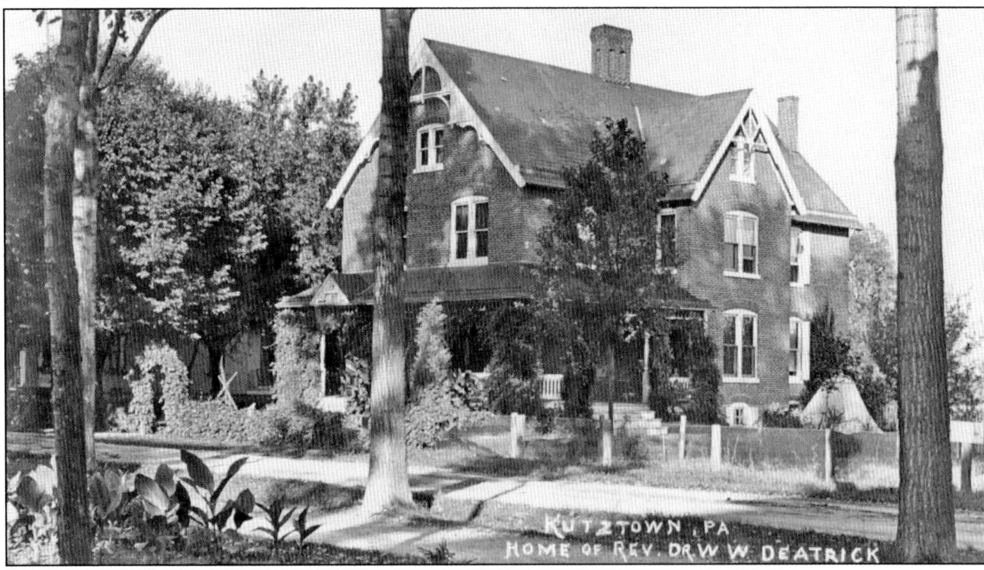

From 1902 to 1922, the Keystone State Normal School paid Deatrick to take photographs of the school to be made into postcards. These cards were used to communicate campus information to students and alumni of the school and served as the social media posts of their day. In 1898, Deatrick built a home on College Hill. Today, it is owned by the Kutztown University Foundation and is named Maple Manor. (Photograph by W.W. Deatrick, courtesy of Jason Graver.)

This Halloween-themed postcard shows decorations for the holiday, which was part of the fun for students of Keystone State Normal School during the fall. Halloween and Thanksgiving were reasons for fall social events. Students gathered in the chapel to act out small plays and challenge one another in charades. (Photograph by W.W. Deatrick, courtesy of Jason Graver.)

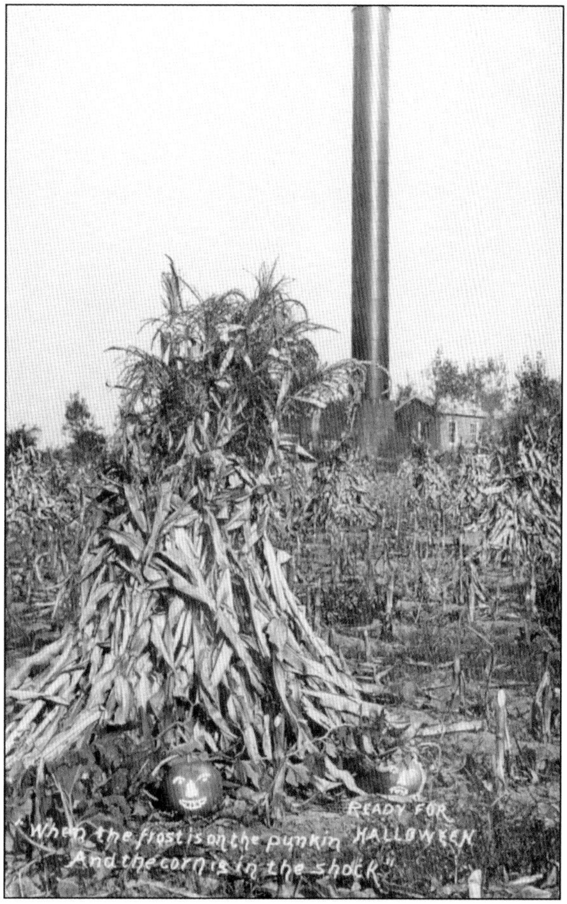

This 1912 mass-produced postcard does not depict Kutztown; rather, it was bought and sold in town. The caption reads, "How we do things at Kutztown, PA." A student at the Keystone State Normal School sent this humorous postcard in 1914. The message on the back reads, "Don't work too hard I am taking it good." (Photograph by Stanley Johnson, courtesy of Jason Graver.)

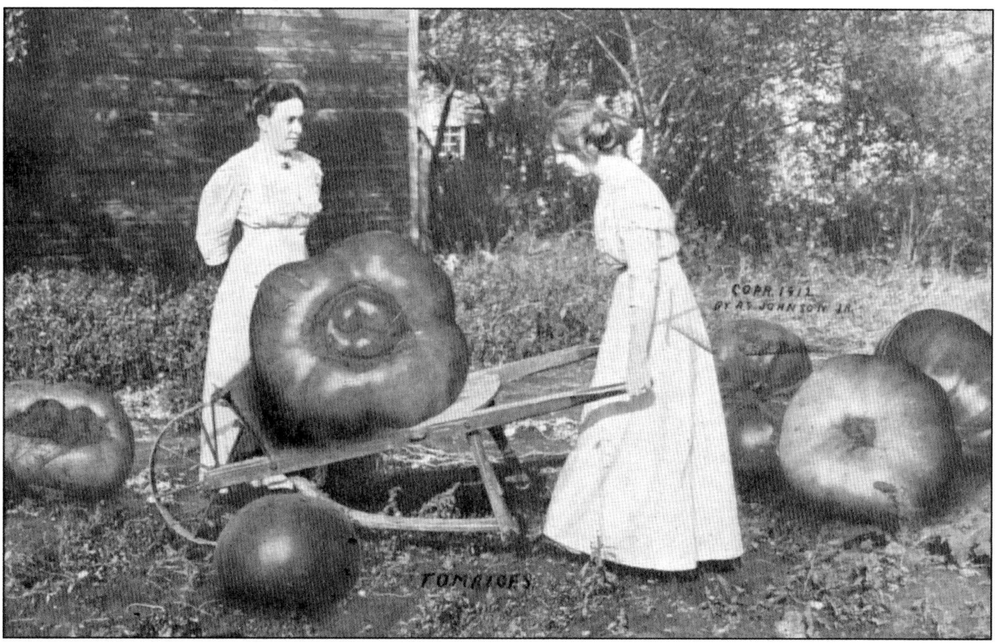

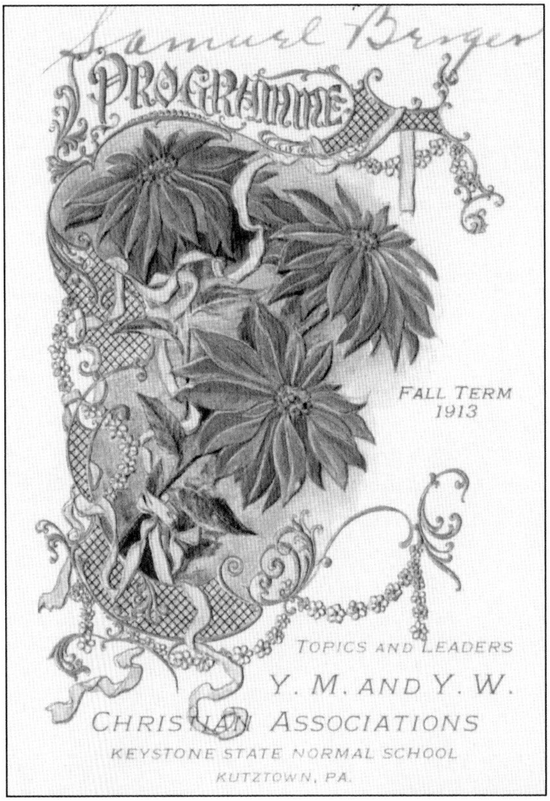

A Young Men's Christian Association and a Young Women's Christian Association were established at the Keystone State Normal School in 1887–1888. Both groups were active in promoting Bible study groups, and the YWCA was very active in sponsoring prayer meetings. The YMCA sponsored a lecture series. The highlight of the series was an 1895 humorous lecture by Robert J. Burdette on "The Rise and Fall of the Moustache." (Courtesy of Samuel Berger.)

Moral behavior and Christian values remained a significant aspect of the KSNS experience. This image depicts a YMCA sociable bazaar held in the gymnasium (today's Risley Hall) on February 20, 1915. The railing seen above encircled an elevated running track. (Courtesy of Jason Graver.)

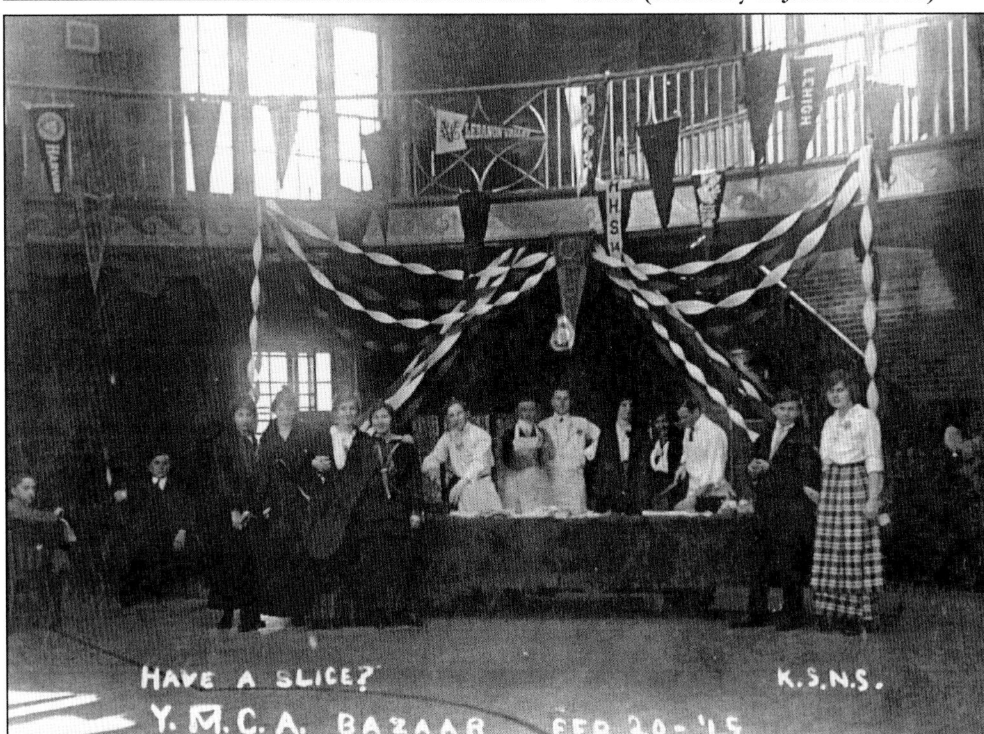

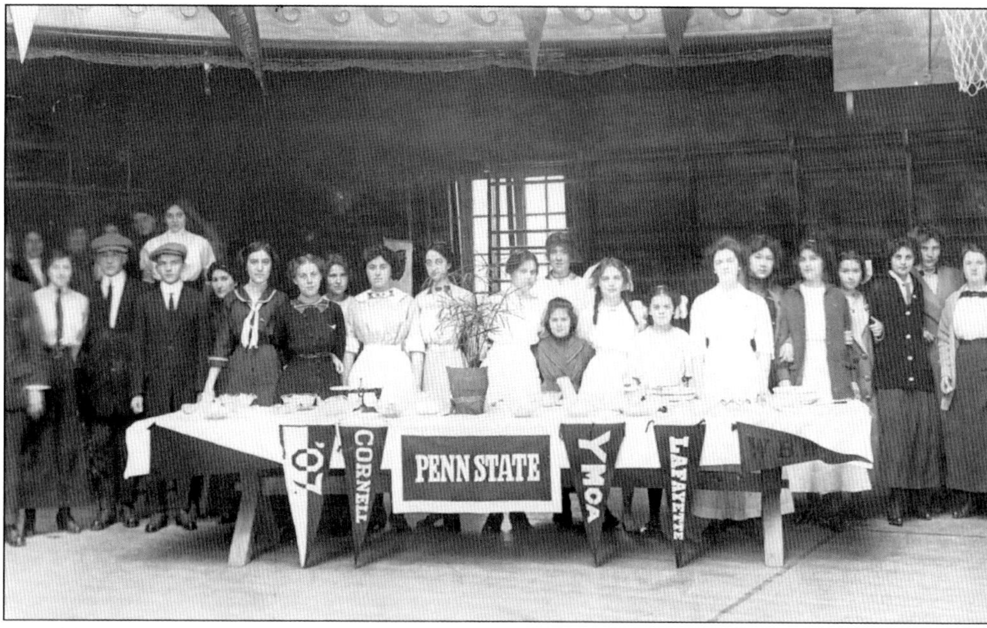

Sociables were prim and starchy affairs since the school had strict barriers between the sexes. When the Keystone State Normal School first opened, enrolled students were graduating from eighth grade at the age of 14, thus requiring a lot of oversight. As the age of entering students rose in later years, men and women were allowed to mingle at sociables, as seen in this image and the previous one. (Photographed by W.W. Deatrick.)

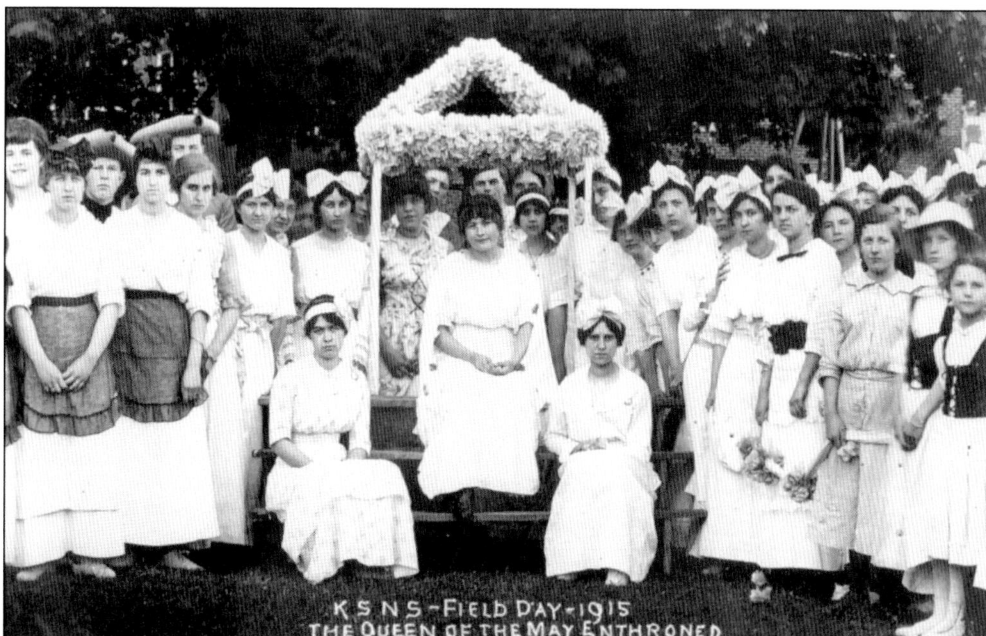

This 1915 photograph shows the crowning of the May Queen at Field Day. The May Day pageant was a campus tradition. "Pandora," a Greek pageant in which girls of the school play roles, was part of the Parents' Day celebration. The girl who played Pandora would then be crowned the Queen of the May. (Photograph by W.W. Deatrick, courtesy of Jason Graver.)

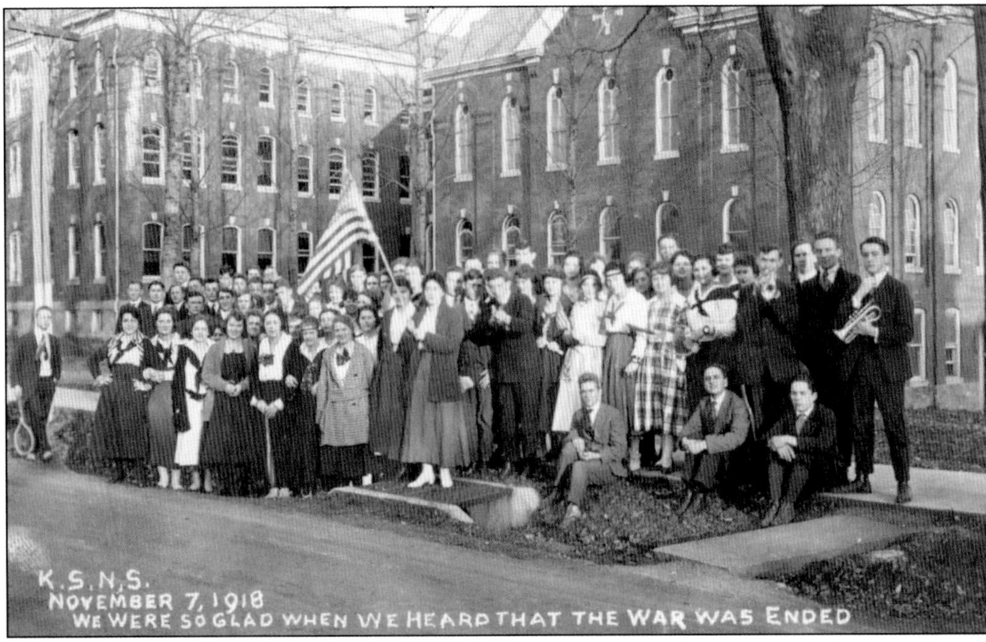

This photograph, taken on November 7, 1918, shows a group of students celebrating the end of World War I. The caption reads, "We were so glad when we heard that the war was ended." At this point in history, several newspapers prematurely announced that peace had been reached, triggering celebrations such as the one at the Keystone State Normal School. The real end of the war, the true armistice, went into effect at 6:00 a.m. (EST) on November 11, 1918. The photograph below documents the second postwar celebration at the Keystone State Normal School on Armistice Day. The caption states, "Celebrating the Armistice Declaration." (Both photographs by W.W. Deatrick, courtesy of Jason Graver.)

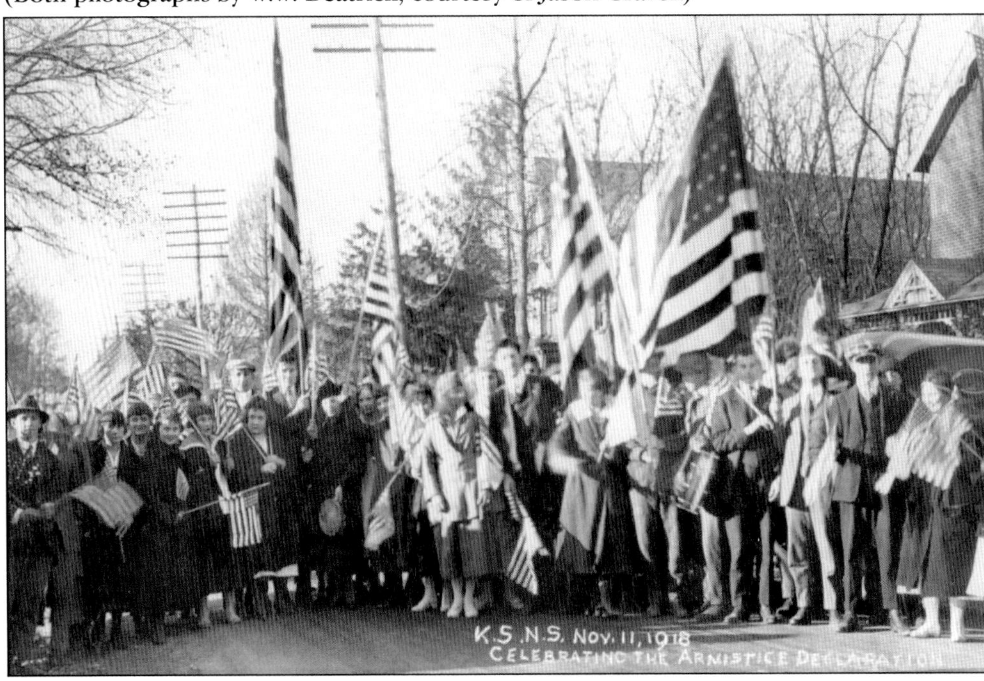

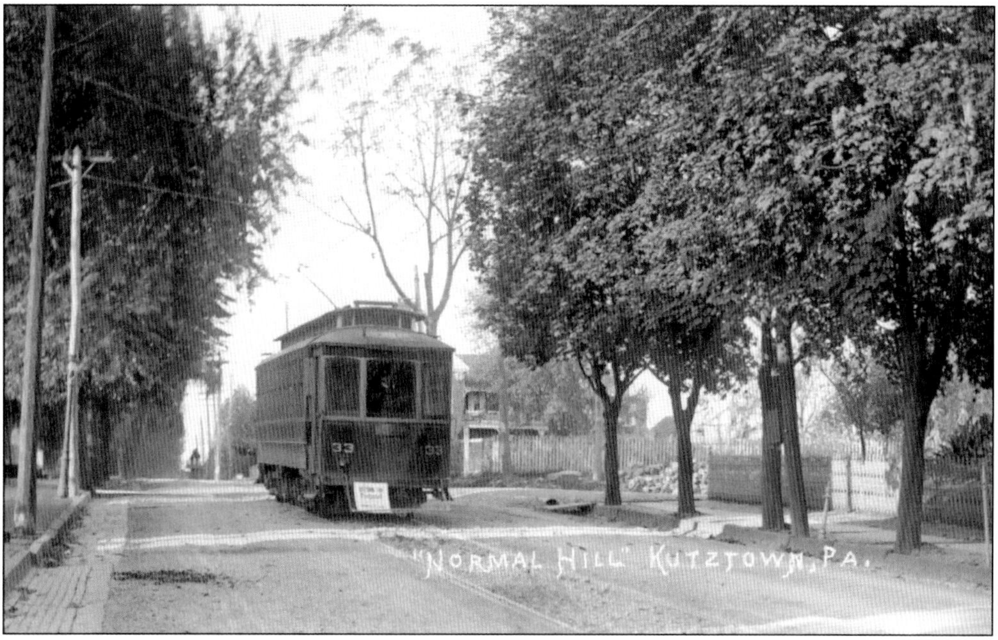

The trolley ran from Allentown to Reading. This 1905 photograph shows the trolley turning onto Main Street at College Hill on its way to Allentown. The electric trolley came in 1901 and proved to be helpful for weekend student activities at the school. Students who used the trolley were also given a discount. (Courtesy of Jason Graver.)

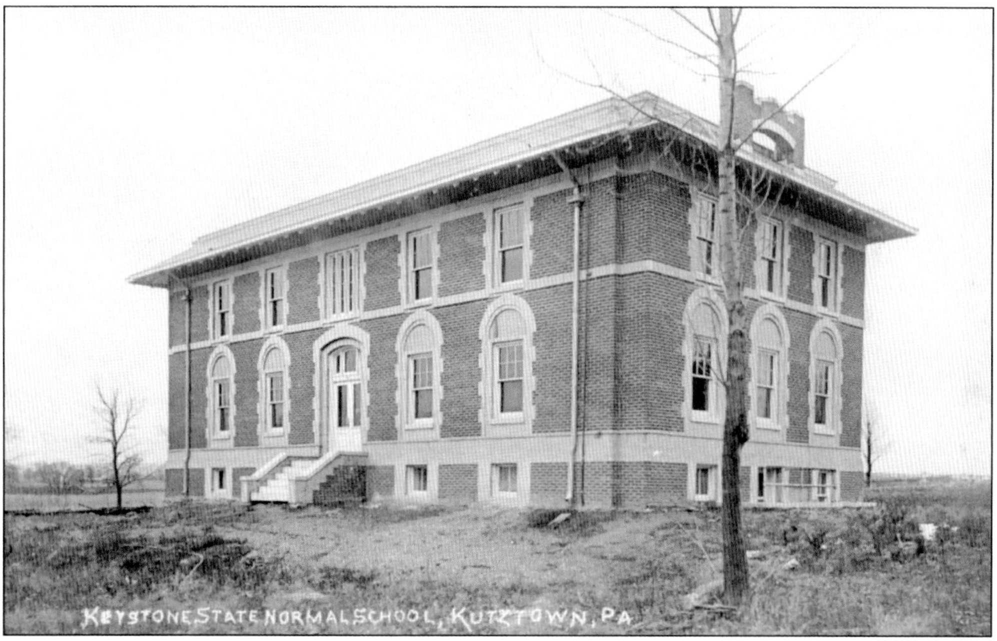

In 1908, construction began on a two-story infirmary building on the south side of campus. The building was used for health purposes until 1937, when it was converted into the first Sharadin Art Studio. In the early 1960s, the building became the Bear's Den student center. The building was repurposed in 1985 as the John B. White residence hall before becoming the KU multicultural center. (Photograph by W.W. Deatrick, courtesy of Jason Graver.)

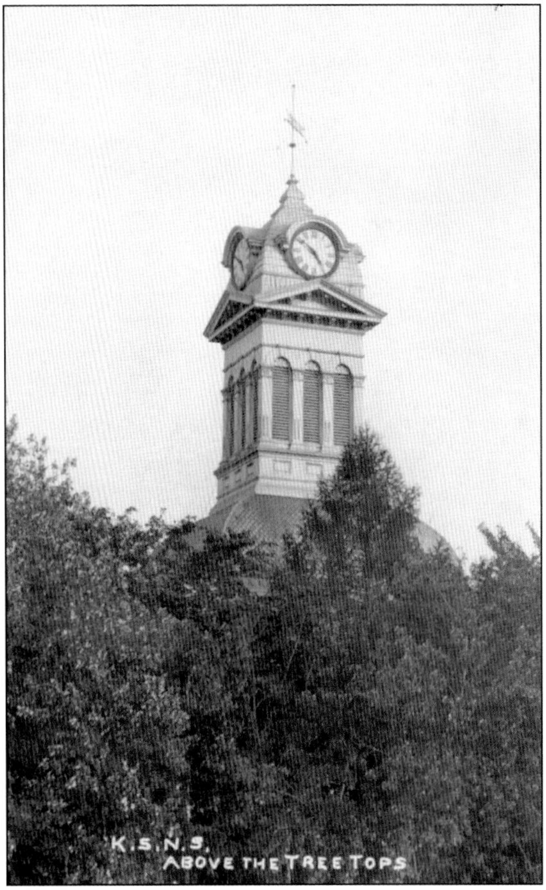

The clock tower is one of the most identifiable features of the campus. The clock faces were added as a gift from the class of 1910. The gift was managed by Harry Worley, the class representative. Spectacular views of Kutztown and Maxatawny Township can be seen from inside the tower. Long before the clock faces were added, Prof. Frank S. Krebs was known to take a powerful telescope into the tower to view the pairs of students supposedly looking for botanic specimens. Instead of conducting their fieldwork, the students were engaged in mingling between the sexes, which was forbidden. Professor Krebs said the way the students were "botanizing" had to stop, but it never really did. (Both photographs by W.W. Deatrick, courtesy of Jason Graver.)

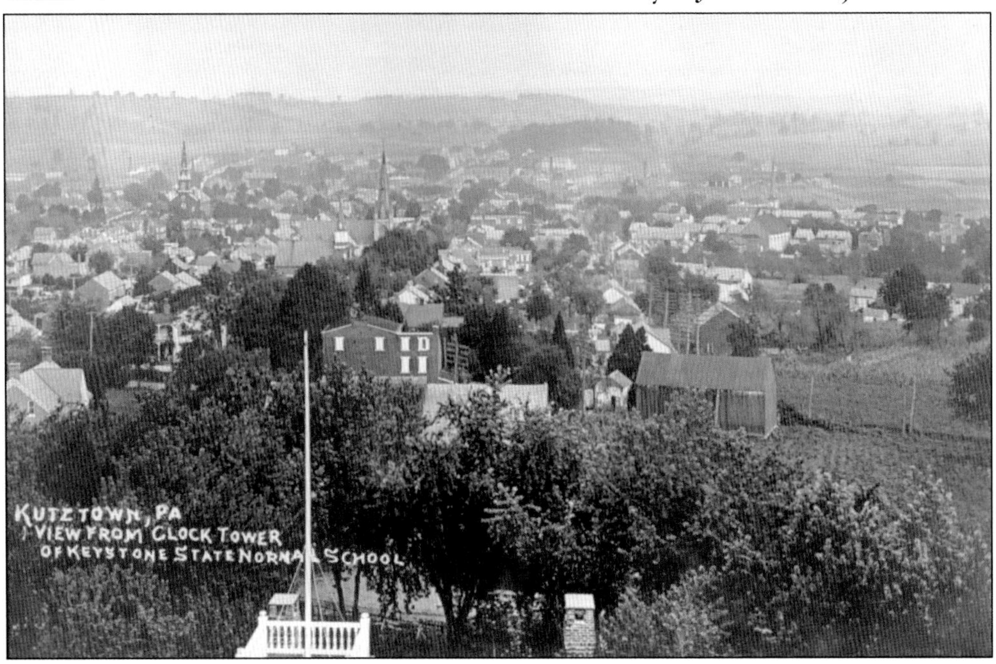

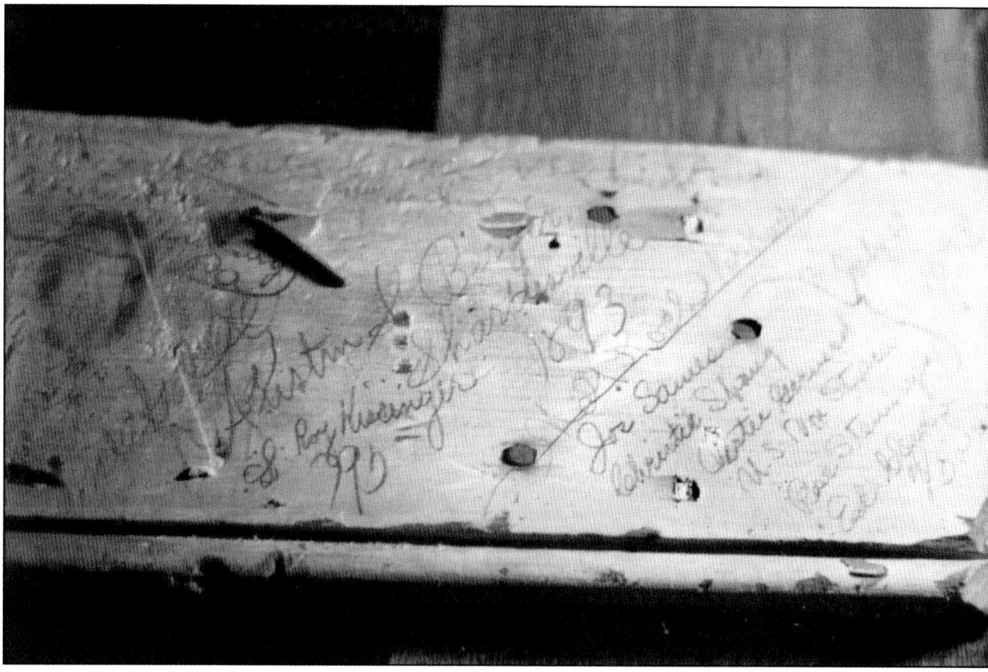

Featured inside the clock tower is the earliest signature, from 1893, the year the tower was completed. For decades, it was common for students to climb the stairs to the tower and add their signatures. Eventually, access to the tower was limited, and students were no longer allowed to venture to the top without special permission. (Courtesy of KU.)

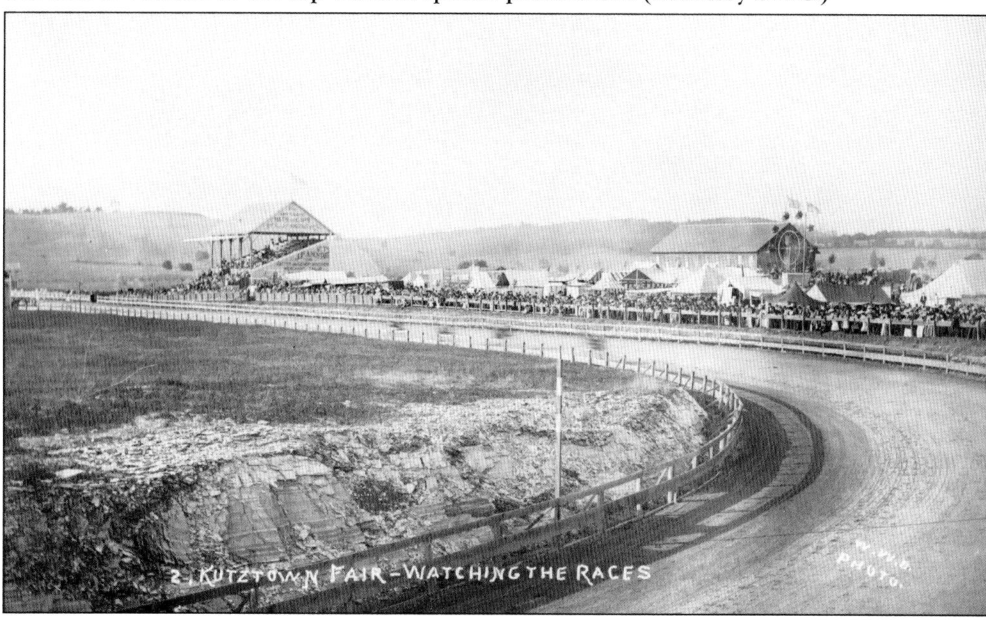

KSNS students often ventured down Main Street to frequent the stores and participate in numerous town events and public gatherings, such as the Kutztown Fair. Organized in 1870, the fair was well attended and enjoyed by the students. Land was purchased for the fairgrounds, where permanent facilities could be constructed, including a hotel and a half-mile track for the popular sport of horse racing. (Photograph by W.W. Deatrick, courtesy of KU.)

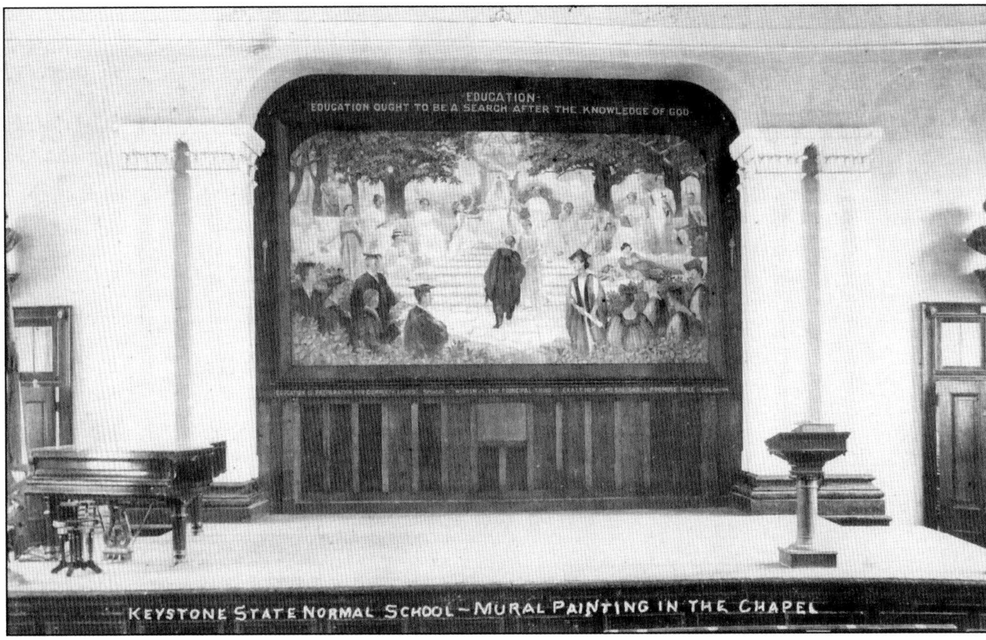

Prof. Henry W. Sharadin's mural titled *Education* was completed in the spring of 1914 as a gift from the class of 1913. The mural depicts characters that represent every branch of education. The painting was unveiled during chapel exercises, and both Principal Rothermel and Professor Sharadin addressed the students. This mural still graces the wall in the present-day Georgian Room. (Courtesy of KHS.)

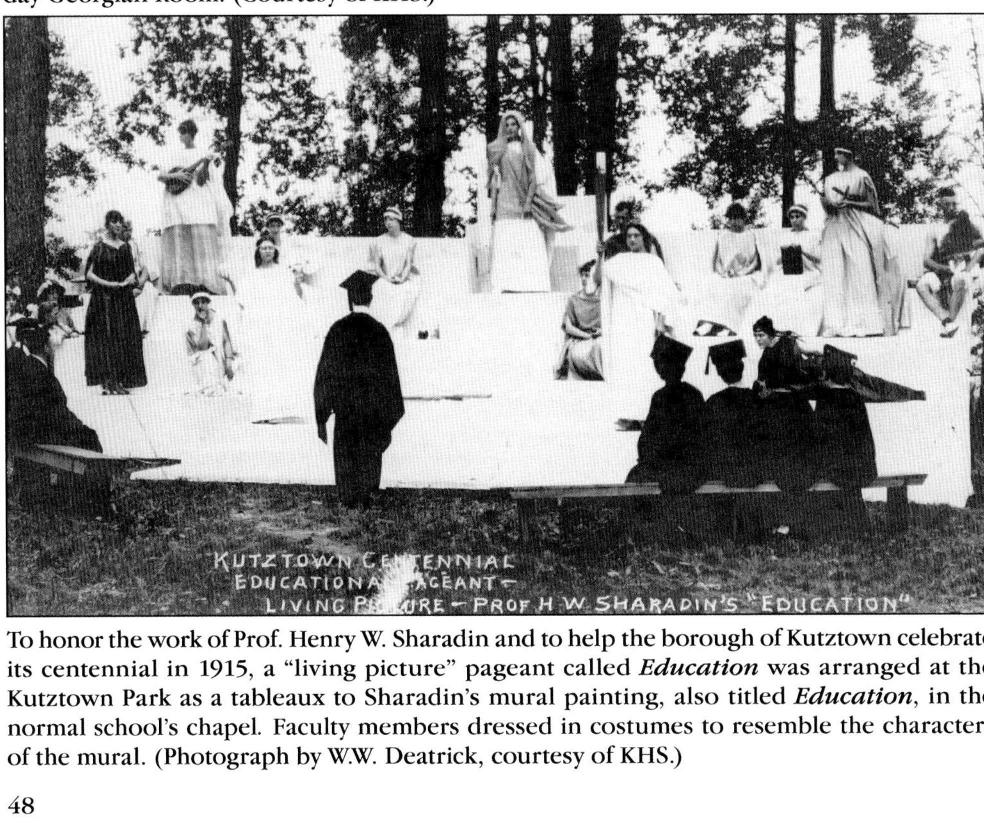

To honor the work of Prof. Henry W. Sharadin and to help the borough of Kutztown celebrate its centennial in 1915, a "living picture" pageant called *Education* was arranged at the Kutztown Park as a tableaux to Sharadin's mural painting, also titled *Education*, in the normal school's chapel. Faculty members dressed in costumes to resemble the characters of the mural. (Photograph by W.W. Deatrick, courtesy of KHS.)

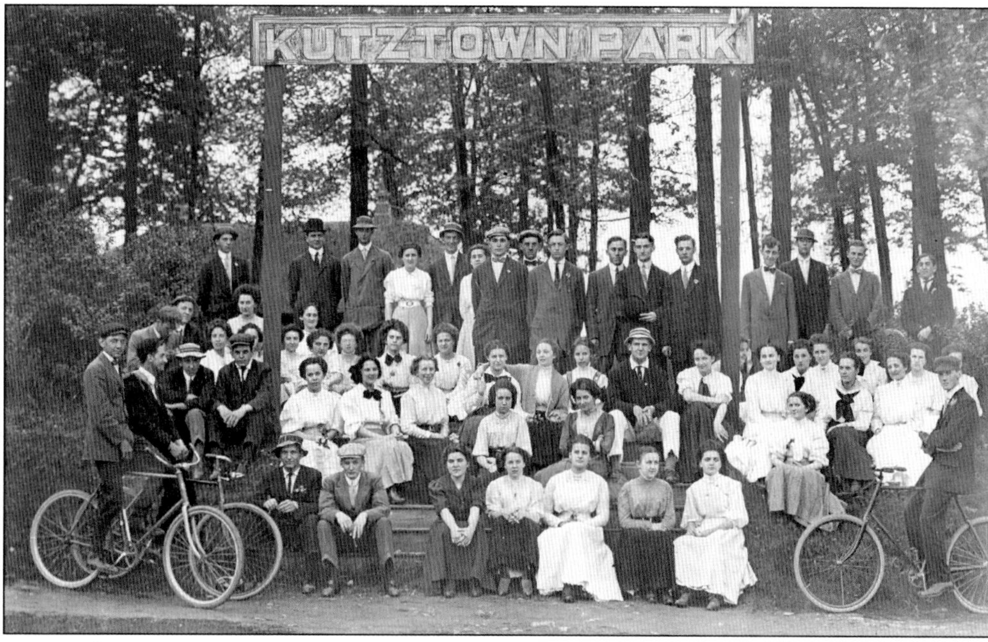

Originally 10 acres, Kutztown Park was established by a private corporation in 1903. A band shell, pavilions, a refreshment stand, recreational equipment, and a miniature railway were constructed for visitors. During the borough's centennial year of 1915, pageants were presented in Kutztown Park on Educational Day and Historical Day. The community was indebted to Lillian Bull, a faculty member of Keystone State Normal School, for arranging and directing these pageants.

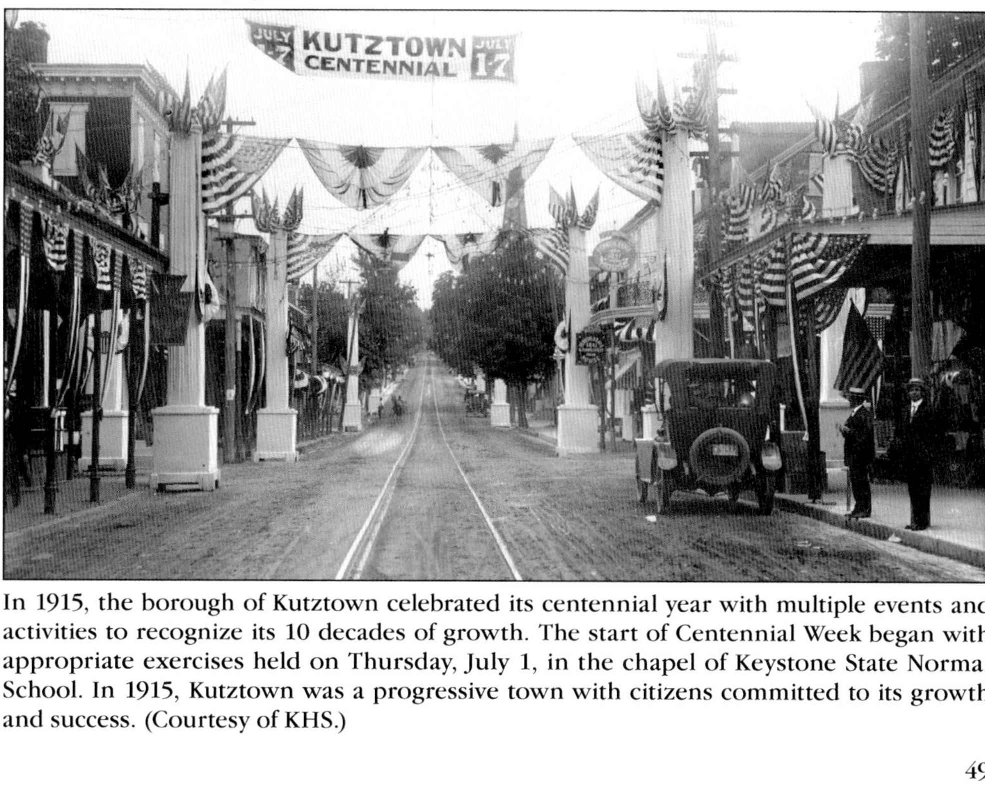

In 1915, the borough of Kutztown celebrated its centennial year with multiple events and activities to recognize its 10 decades of growth. The start of Centennial Week began with appropriate exercises held on Thursday, July 1, in the chapel of Keystone State Normal School. In 1915, Kutztown was a progressive town with citizens committed to its growth and success. (Courtesy of KHS.)

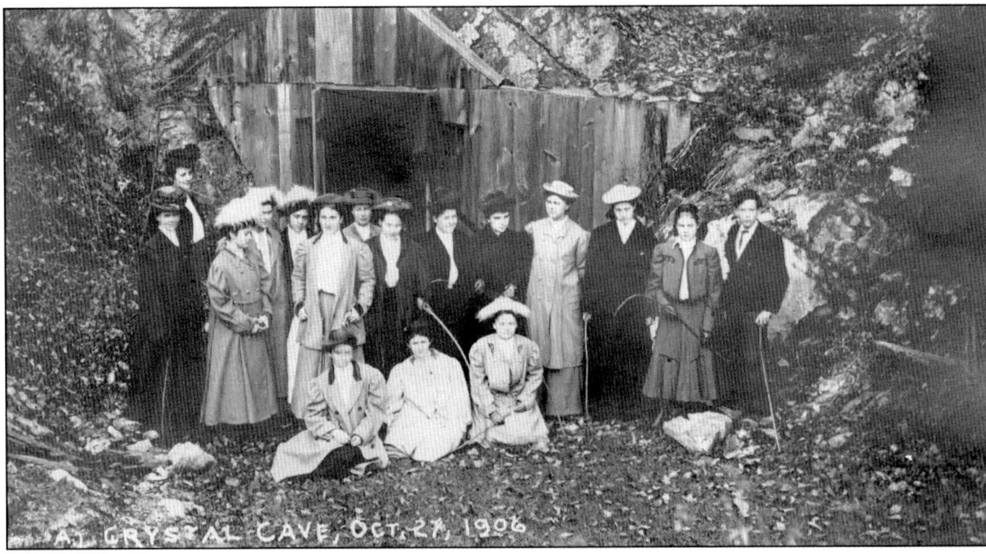

On October 27, 1906, a group of students went on a field trip to Crystal Cave. This underground wonder in Virginville was discovered in 1871 and opened as a tourist attraction the following year when it was purchased by Samuel Kohler. The group in the photograph might have traveled to the site in one of three stagecoaches owned by the cave operator, purchased to transport visitors from the train stations. (Photograph by W.W. Deatrick.)

CRYSTAL CAVE!

ONE OF AMERICA'S

Greatest of Natural Wonders!

This Natural Curiosity, located near Virginville, Pa., on the Schuylkill and Lehigh branch of the P. & R. R. R., during the past few seasons, entertained exceptionally large numbers of visitors. This proves the continued popularity of the Resort.

An Old Resort with Grand Attractions

Tourists, whether traveling for health, pleasure or knowledge, cannot consider their tour complete unless they have visited this—Berks County's Famous Cave. These grand and wonderful formations of nature have been seen and admired by people of all stations of life. Students will find its attractions to be instructive, unusual and unique.

A Picturesque, Quiet and Healthful Retreat

Surrounded by most beautiful and romantic mountain scenery, it would be difficult for anyone in quest of health, recreation or rest to find a place more pleasant. The neighboring streams afford good fishing, and their shady nooks and nearby mountains with their bracing atmosphere, offer to the overworked or the invalid a quiet and healthful retreat surpassed by few. Good roads make cycling a pleasure.

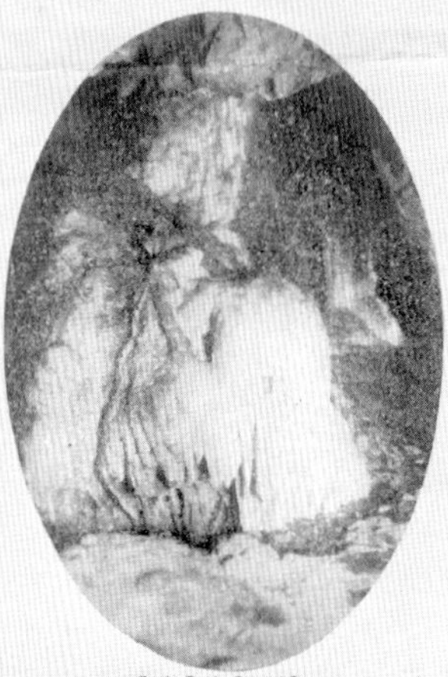
Eagle Rock, Crystal Cave

Testimonials

"The undersigned committee appointed by the Reading Society of Natural Sciences visited Crystal Cave and found it filled with very interesting curiosities; the stalactites, stalagmites and crystalline formations present a variety of beauty such as is seldom seen. Persons who visit the Cave will be amply repaid."

(Signed)
J. Schoenfeld, M. D.
R. S. Turner, M. D.
H. W. Hollenbush, Chemist.
D. B. Brunner, City Sup't.
A. R. Horne, Muhlenberg College.

"Niagara Falls and the Crystal Cave are the greatest Natural Wonders that we have seen in America."

(Signed)
F. Buisson, Commissioner of Sup'ts of Public Instruction in France, Paris, France.
B. Berger, Inspector of Schools, Paris, France.
Aug. Valens, Teacher, Paris, France.

Special Accommodations

Crystal Cave can be reached every hour of the day by Trolley from Reading or Allentown via Kutztown. Individuals or Clubs desiring transportation to the Cave from either Virginville or Kutztown, are requested to communicate particulars to the undersigned a day or two previous to the proposed visit to ensure prompt and satisfactory service.

Good hotel accommodations.

D. A. Kohler, Proprietor,

R. F. D. No. 3 *Kutztown, Berks Co., Pa.*

This pamphlet promotes Crystal Cave as "One of America's Greatest of Natural Wonders." Crystal Cave is portrayed as an established resort with grand attractions. A hotel built in 1876 accommodated visitors wishing to vacation in the country. Crystal Cave served as a picturesque, quiet, and healthful resort, accessible to visitors via trolleys from the Reading and Allentown areas every hour of the day.

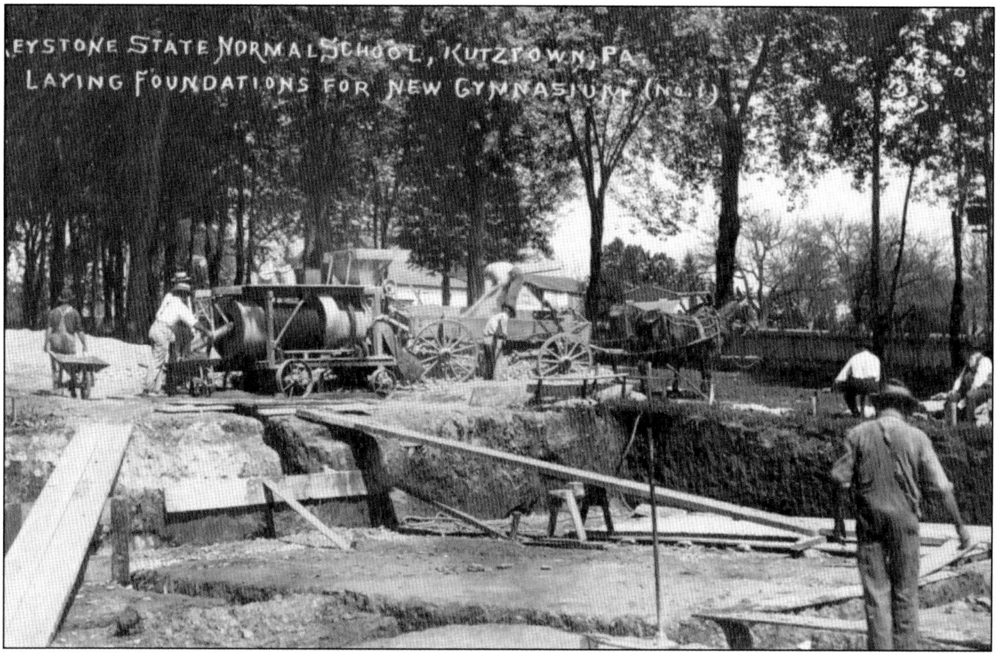

The original location of the gymnasium was on the fifth floor of the center section of Old Main. This was considered an ideal spot for the introduction of "striking bag," parallel bars, "jumping boards," and other pieces of equipment that ended up shaking the timbers and creating distracting noises. The gymnasium was moved from the attic to the basement and remained there until 1902. In June 1906, Dr. Amos C. Rothermel suggested a separate gymnasium building. The cornerstone was contributed by the class of 1908 and was laid on November 14, 1907. (Both photographs by W.W. Deatrick, courtesy of Jason Graver.)

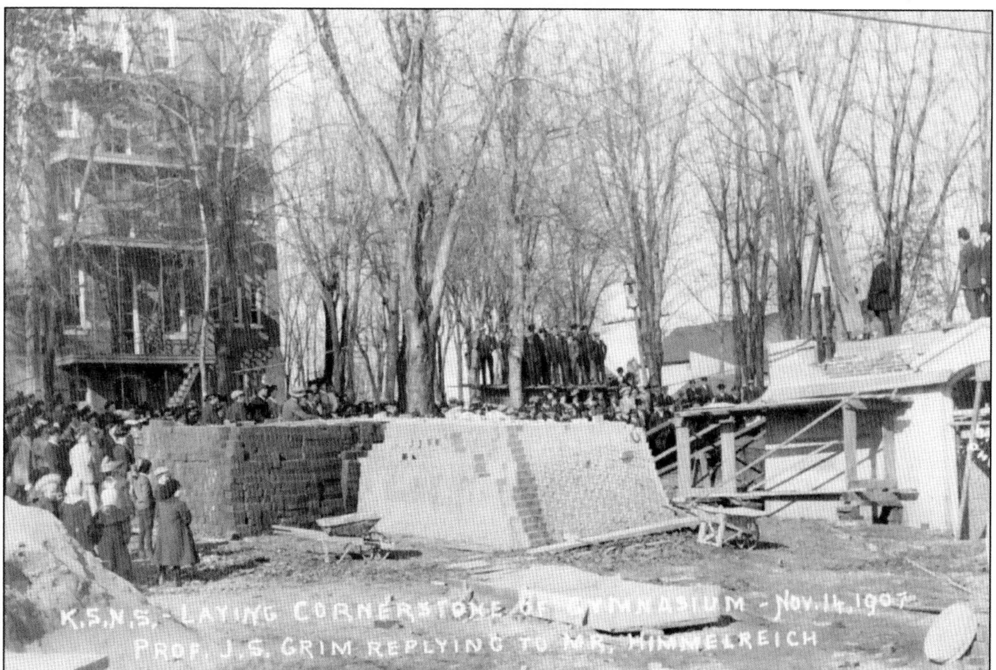

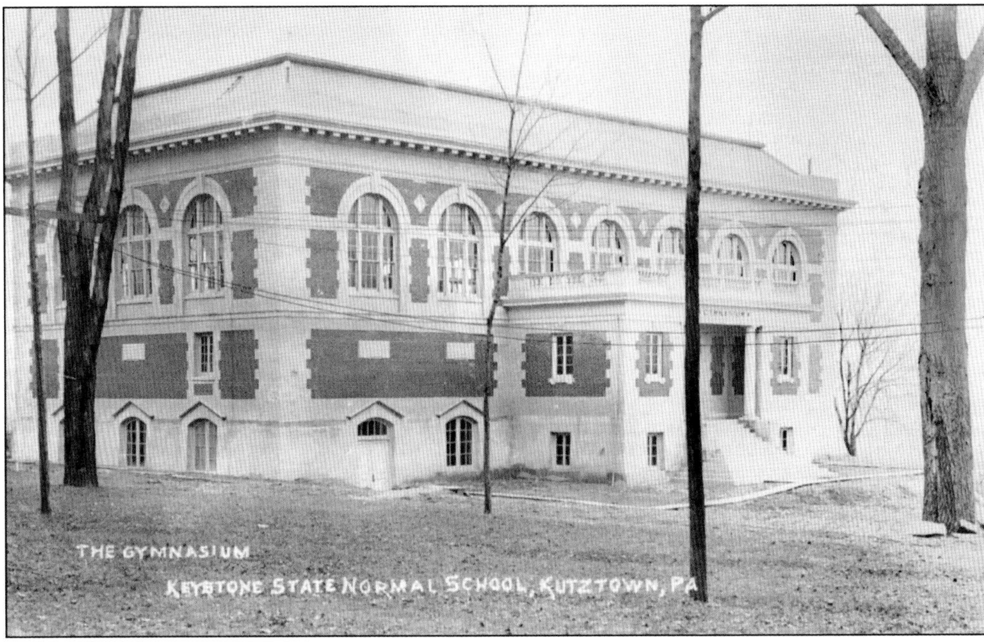

Professor Dr. James S. Grim proudly opened the new gymnasium and described the new facility as "second to none among the Normals of the country." Nearly 65 years later, on May 5, 1973, the gymnasium would be named Risley Hall in honor of Walter P. Risley, an assistant professor of health and physical education and a coach of intercollegiate athletics for more than 25 years. (Photograph by W.W. Deatrick, courtesy of Jason Graver.)

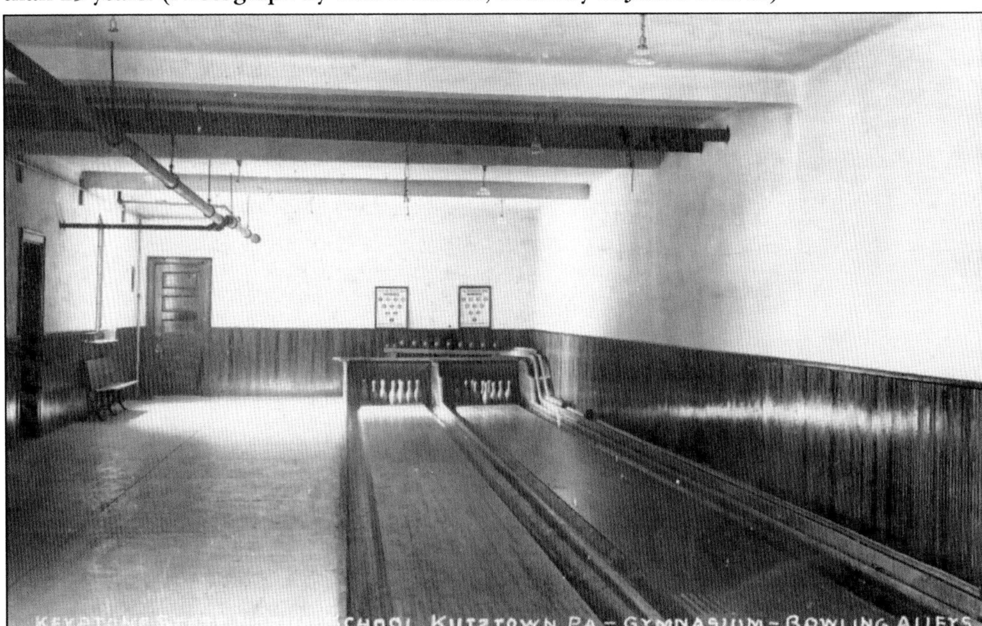

Pleasing not only in appearance but also in facilities, the gymnasium was a fine building and location for physical education. With an elevated running gallery, tiled bathing and swimming pool, and two bowling alleys that cost in excess of $800, this new addition was considered prestigious and competitive. (Photograph by W.W. Deatrick, courtesy of Jason Graver.)

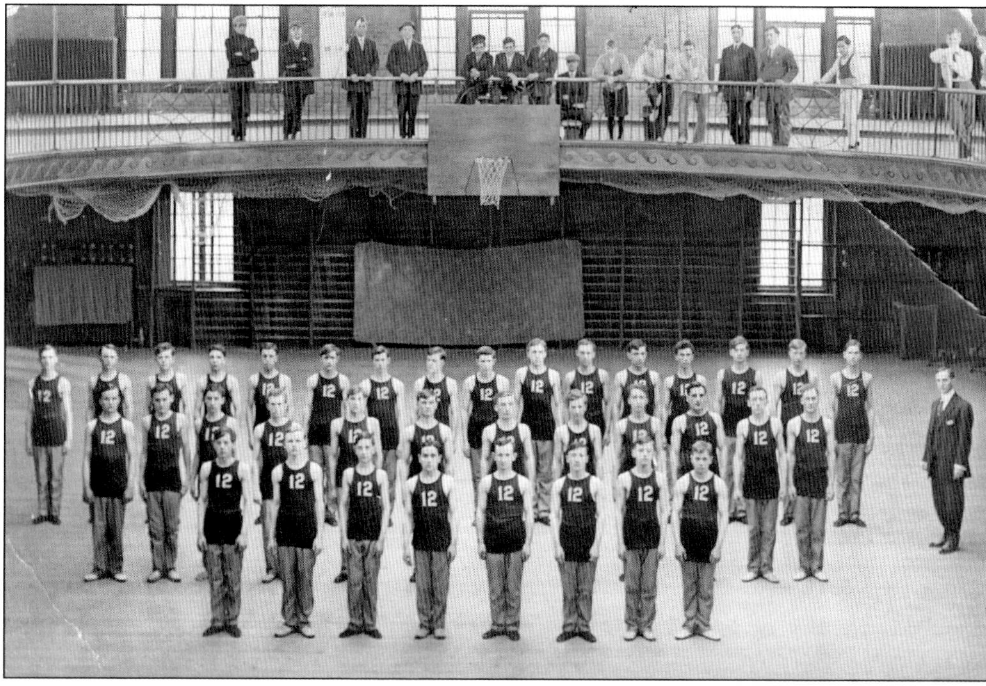

This photograph shows 36 male students performing drills in the newly finished gymnasium. They are all wearing athletic tank tops and pants with the No. 12 on the front, which indicates these students are members of the KSNS class of 1912. The new gymnasium was utilized by both male and female students for daily physical training classes, which were required every year of attendance.

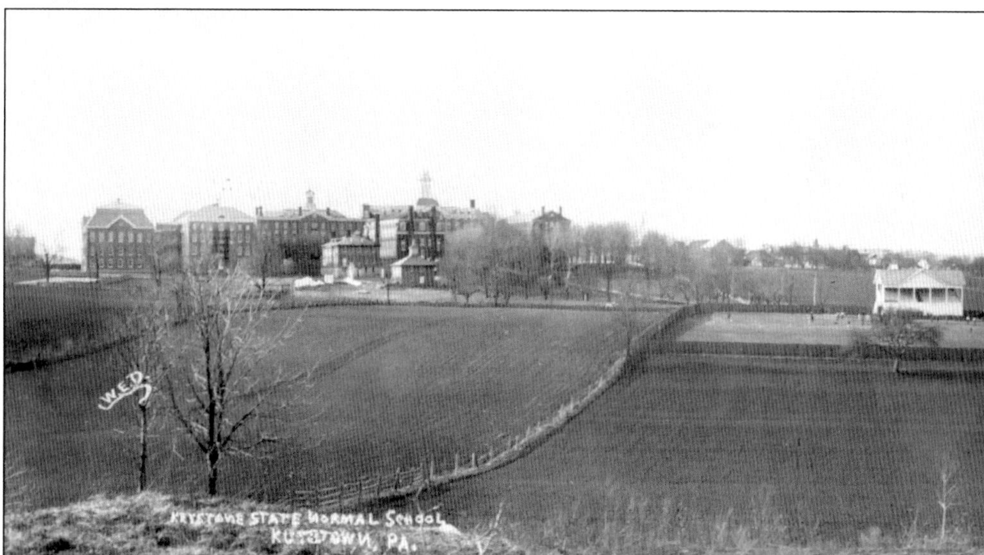

This image captures the rear side of Keystone State Normal School. Besides the main building, the athletic fields can be seen. This photograph was taken sometime between 1903 and 1907. At this time, the area behind Old Main remained farmland. Today, this land area makes up what is now the south side of campus, which houses residence halls. (Photograph by Werner E. DeTurk, courtesy of Jason Graver.)

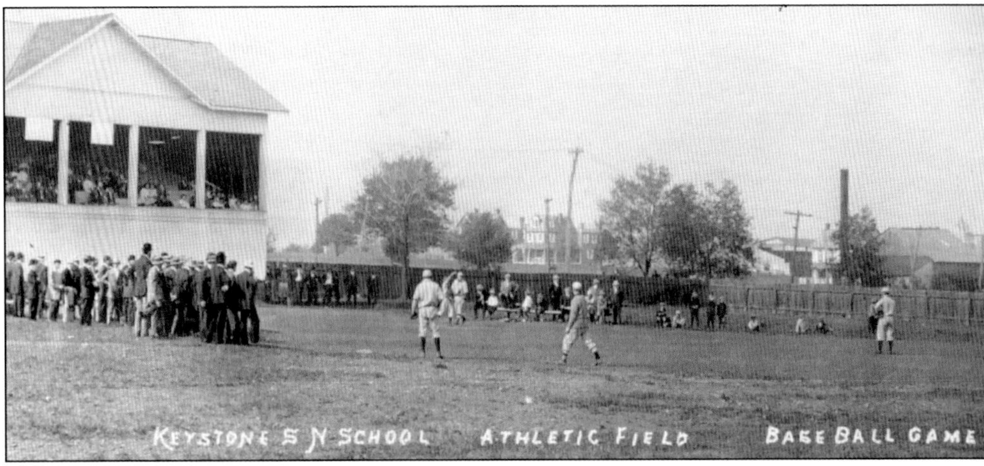

The early 20th century brought a stronger interest in organized sports, although athletics had always been in place at the Keystone State Normal School. The first official faculty coach was George B. Ely, whose name appears on the 1905–1906 roster. Coach Ely not only coached the baseball team but also played second base. In the early 1900s, it was decided that uniforms and more forms of athletic organization from the principal of each normal school needed to happen. Sports in this era included basketball, baseball, football, lawn tennis, and croquet. The group photograph captures the 1907 baseball team, known as the Clippers. (Above, photograph by W.W. Deatrick, courtesy of Jason Graver; below, photograph by W.W. Deatrick.)

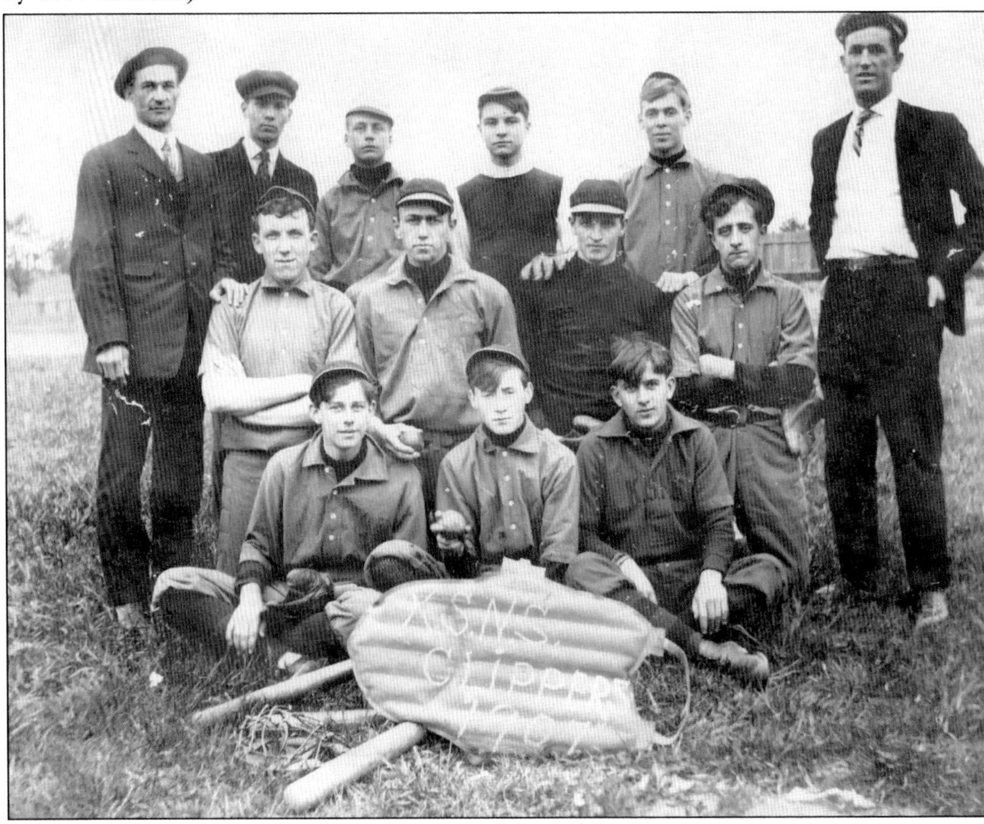

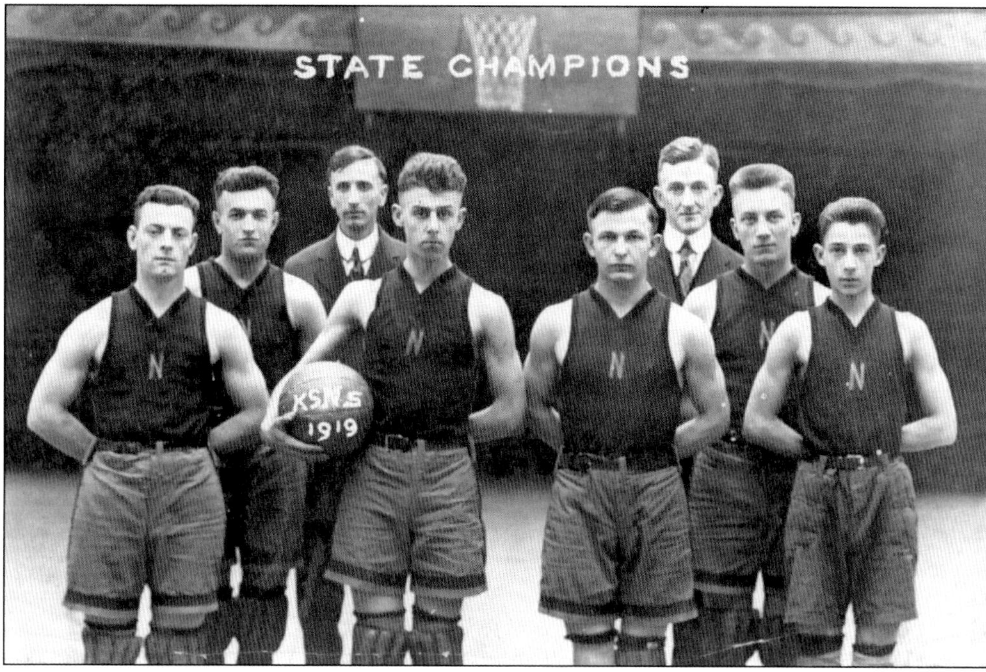

In 1919, the KSNS basketball team took home the Pennsylvania State Normal School championship title. This great honor was nearly curtailed by a flu epidemic. Even though the season started late and ended in March 1919, coach Bert Bohler and team captain Earl Lesher led Kutztown to win every game but one. Coach Bohler was later inducted into the Kutztown University Athletics Hall of Fame in 1999.

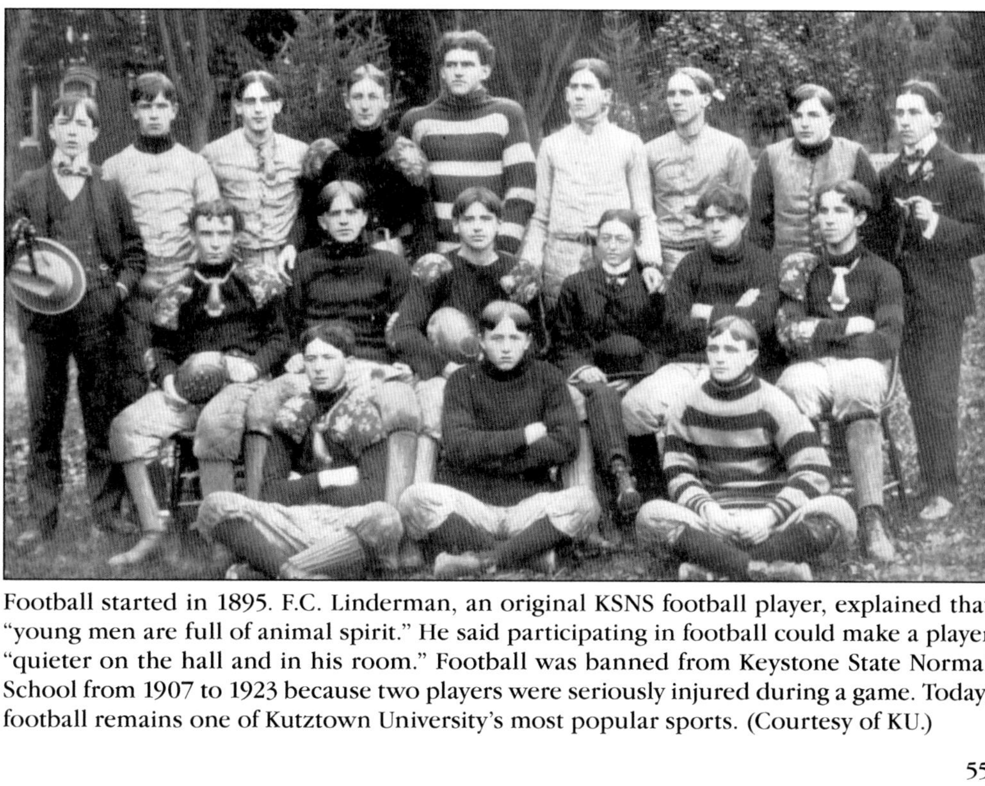

Football started in 1895. F.C. Linderman, an original KSNS football player, explained that "young men are full of animal spirit." He said participating in football could make a player "quieter on the hall and in his room." Football was banned from Keystone State Normal School from 1907 to 1923 because two players were seriously injured during a game. Today, football remains one of Kutztown University's most popular sports. (Courtesy of KU.)

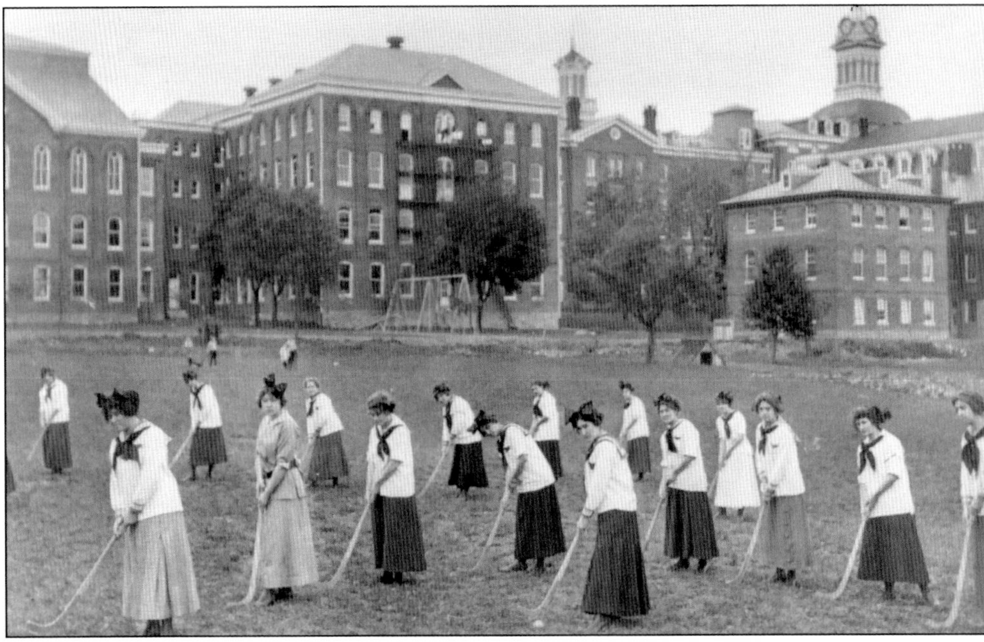

The hockey field was located near the southwest side of the main buildings. The interclass games of field hockey aroused a lot of enthusiasm. The vigorous exercise derived from this game put the students in good condition for mental work. The sport went mainstream in 1908 when it was included in the Summer Olympics in London. Outdoor exercise proved as good for the girls as it did for the boys. (Courtesy of KU.)

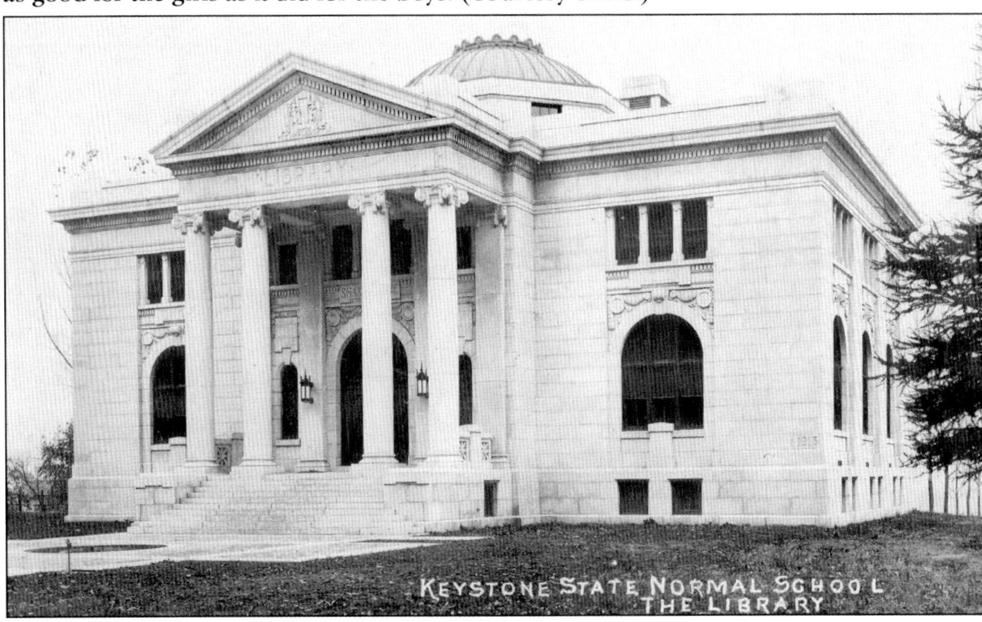

As early as 1902, Dr. Amos C. Rothermel suggested a library association to solicit funds for a dedicated library building that would combine the separate libraries of Old Main into one collection. On March 17, 1913, ground was broken for the school's new library. The initial library was built to house 60,000 volumes at the cost of $110,000. Today, this monumental and ornately designed building serves as the Graduate Center. (Courtesy of KHS.)

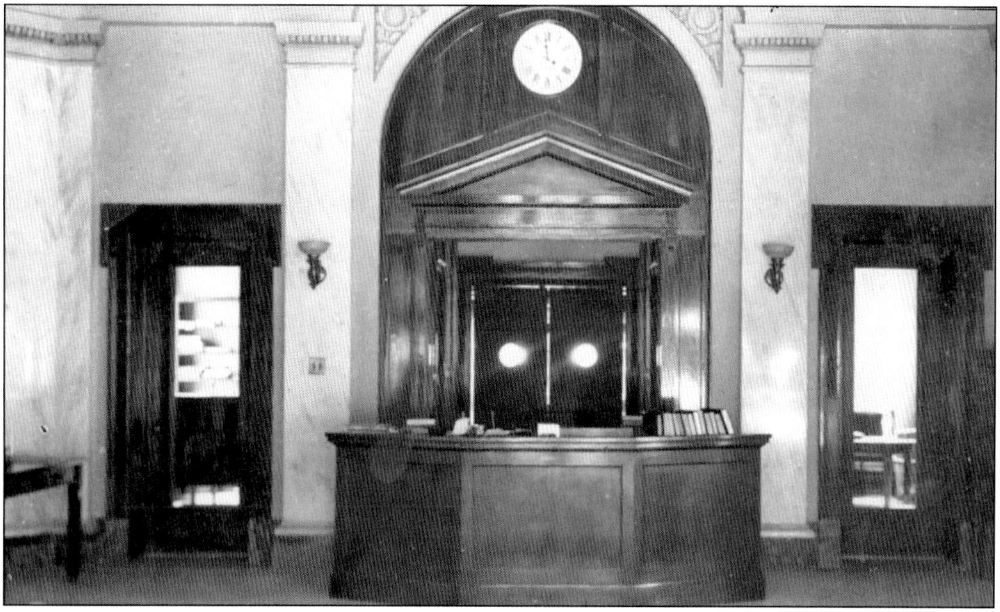

Special attention was directed toward the "superb rotunda" paneled with polished marble. Completed in 1915, the building was used as the library for 53 years. On May 19, 1960, it was renamed the Rohrbach Library after Dr. Quincy A.W. Rohrbach, who was a 1912 graduate of Keystone State Normal School and Kutztown's sixth president. The completed structure was regarded as one of the finest buildings of its kind in the state. (Photograph by W.W. Deatrick, courtesy of Jason Graver.)

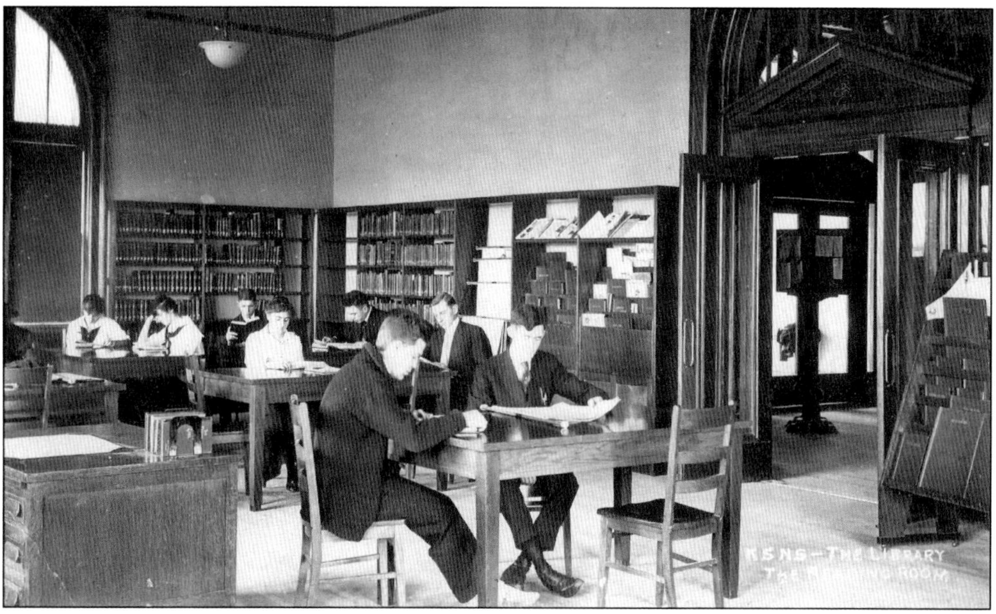

Both students and professors used the 1915 library to research, study, relax, and read. Originally, there were separate reading rooms for boys and girls so the opposite sexes would not mingle. Several students are shown reading and focusing on schoolwork. Though the handwritten caption refers to the normal school, this room was still in use decades later. (Photograph by W.W. Deatrick, courtesy of KHS.)

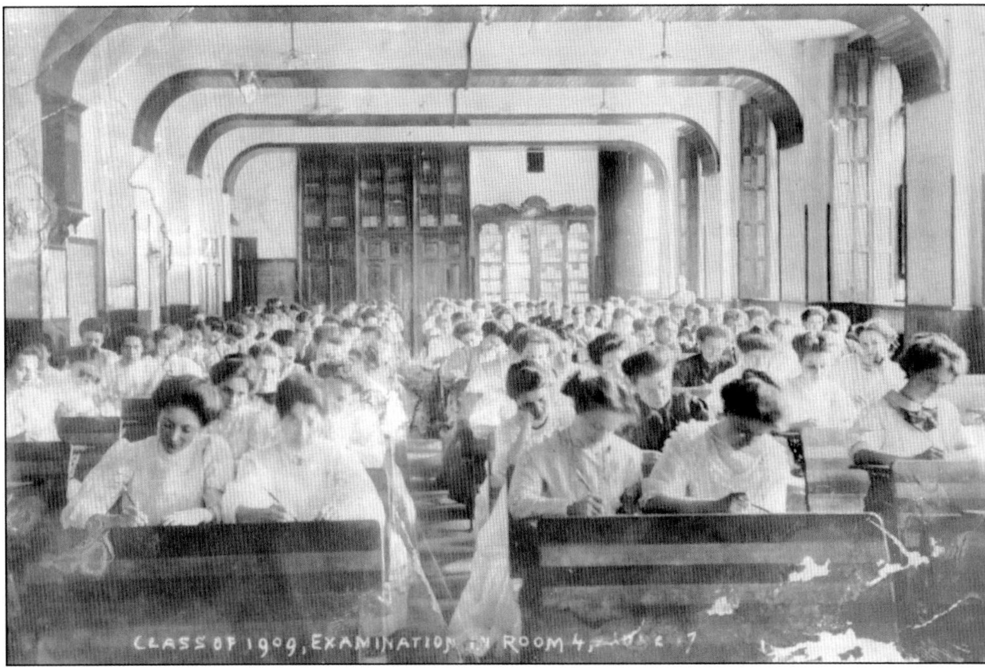

Above, the class of 1909 is shown taking an examination in Room 4 on June 7, 1909; below, the students are seen receiving their examination report in the chapel on June 18, 1909. The photograph below clearly shows the separation of the sexes, with women sitting on one side and men on the other. It was not until later in the 20th century that the rules regarding gender separation were relaxed. Dr. Rothermel's first year as head (not acting) principal was the end of the rule that forbade students of opposite genders from talking in the lecture rooms and the halls. (Both photographs by W.W. Deatrick, courtesy of Jason Graver.)

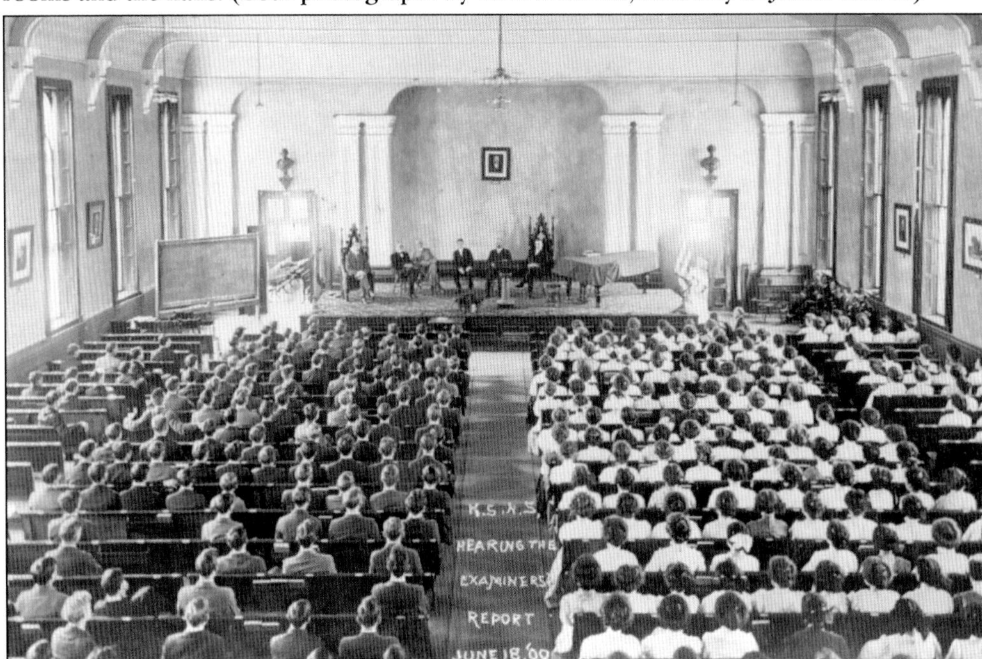

Letter writing kept students connected to their parents. Fatherly advice traveled to Isaac Heller via this letter, dated June 9, 1868. Mr. Heller instructs his son to obey his professors so they will learn to like him and his time at school will be more pleasant. He also expresses how proud he is of his son. Isaac Heller attended the Keystone State Normal School from 1867 to 1868 and likely came from Wapwallopen, Pennsylvania.

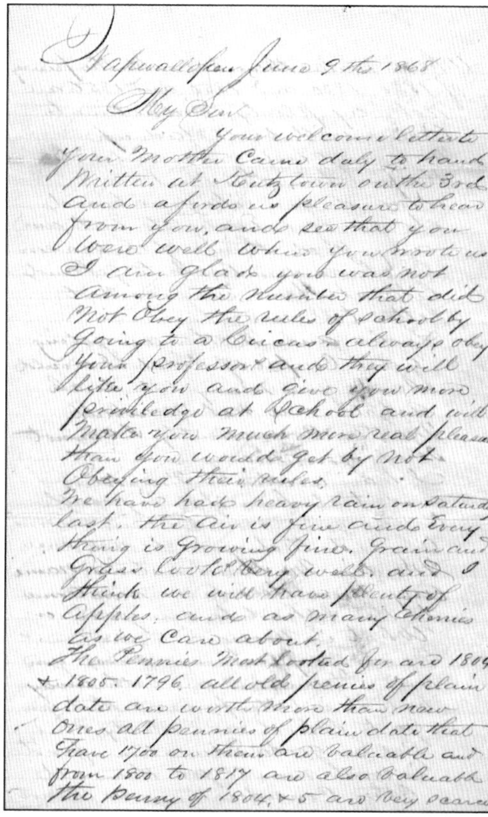

Wapwallopen June 9th 1868

My Son

Your welcome letter to your Mother Came duly to hand Written at Kutztown on the 3rd and afords us pleasure to hear from you, and see that you were well when you wrote us I am glad you was not among the number that did not Obey the rules of school by going to a Circus always obey your professors and they will like you and give you more priviledge at School and will make you much more real pleasure than you would get by not Obeying their rules.

We have had heavy rain on Saturday last. the air is fine and Every thing is growing fine. grain and Grass Looks very well. and I think we will have plenty of apples, and as many Cherries as we Care about.

The Pennies most looked for are 1804 + 1805. 1796. all old pennies of plain date are worth more than new ones all pennies of plain date that have 1700 on them are valuable and from 1800 to 1817 are also valuable the Penny of 1804, + 5 are very scarce

Pictured below is the Keystone State Normal School class of 1909. The class photograph includes all 123 graduates. The ratio of men to women in this particular class was 1:3.5. This image was donated by the family of Charles H. Esser, who is seen in the third row, fifth man from left.

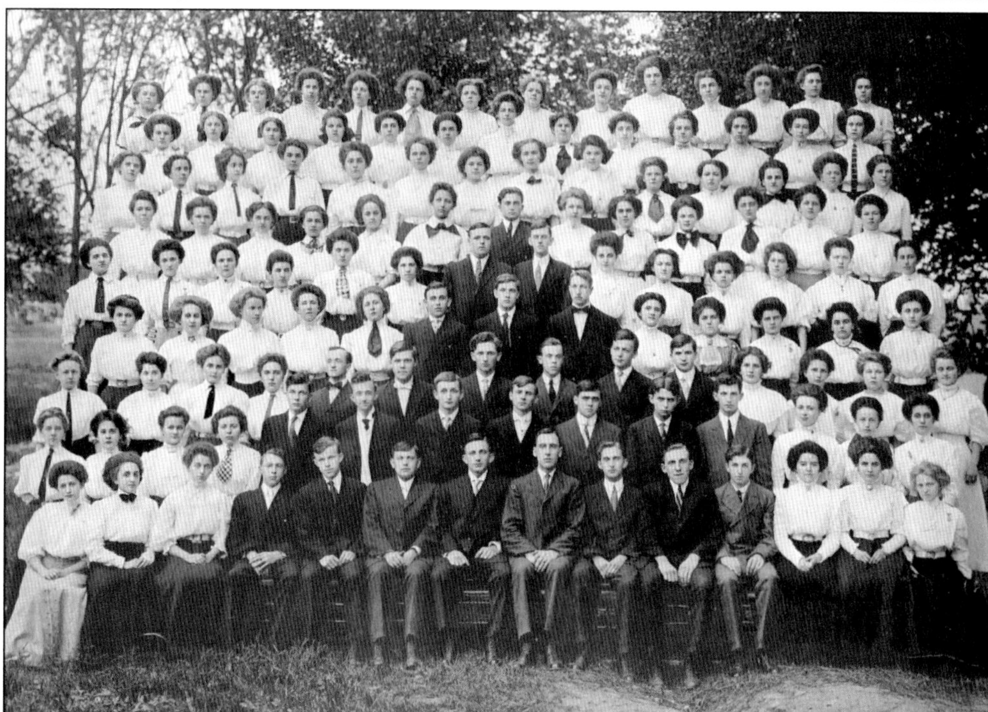

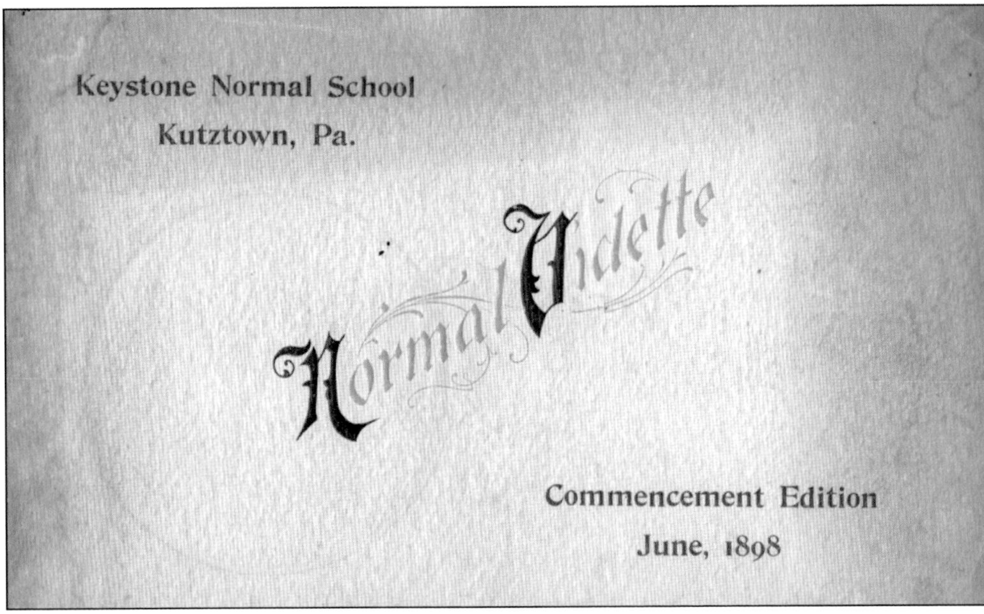

The word *vidette* was a radical metaphor that meant "bearer of important news." Four times a year, the *Normal Vidette* was sent to inform alumni about the goings-on at their alma mater. This promotional mailing was made in hopes of bringing information to more people who might not know about the Keystone State Normal School.

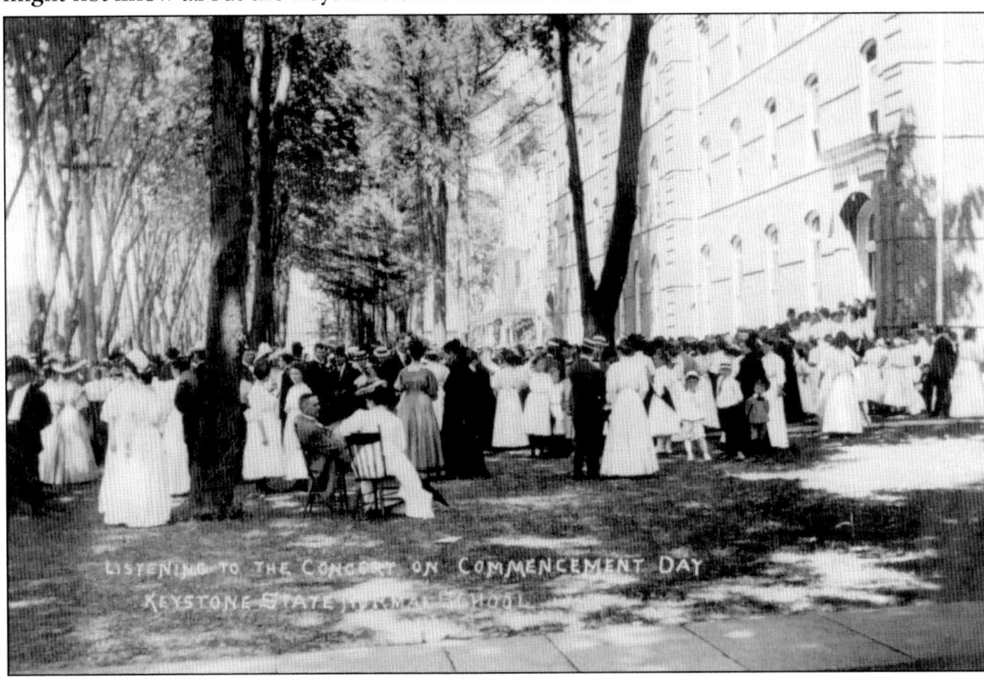

Commencement, the biggest occasion of the year, was usually an incessantly long affair as speaker after speaker was presented. In 1880, the commencement exercises were broken into two sessions: one from 9:00 a.m. to 11:30 a.m. and another from 2:00 p.m. to late in the afternoon. With growth in the size of graduation classes, the faculty had reduced the number of student commencement speakers to 14 by 1884.

Two

KUTZTOWN STATE TEACHERS COLLEGE 1928–1960

On December 3, 1926, the state council of education declared the Keystone State Normal School a degree-granting institution. Representing the commonwealth, Dr. Henry Klonower presented the certificate that conferred degree-granting authority to the Honorable James E. Norton, president of the board of trustees. It was not until two years later that the name of Keystone State Normal School was officially changed to Kutztown State Teachers College (KSTC). The school had to wait for the first students to graduate with their bachelor of science degrees. On May 29, 1928, six students earned their bachelor of science degrees, one of whom was Dr. James Grim's daughter, Margaret. Dr. Grim was a graduate, professor, and advocate for science and agriculture at the Keystone State Normal School. Dr. Amos C. Rothermel, who was principal at the time of the changeover, became the first president of the state teachers college.

With the start of the Great Depression in 1929, the fight to retain the state teachers colleges began. The administrative code placed teachers colleges in a financial straitjacket. On February 10, 1933, with the threat of having to disband four schools, the trustees of the school took a stand against the elimination of any state teachers colleges.

In 1934, Dr. Rothermel reluctantly retired upon reaching the mandatory age of 70, and Dr. Quincy A.W. Rohrbach (class of 1912) was picked to be his successor. The Kutztown State Teachers College had successfully passed through a very critical period, but with the Great Depression and the start of World War II, enrollment declined. The low point of 243 students in 1943, including just a dozen men, forced President Rohrbach to bring Army Air Forces students to train at the Kutztown State Teachers College as part of the war effort and to boost enrollment to keep the school from closing.

With the increase in enrollment, Dr. Rohrbach got to work renovating and improving the Kutztown State Teachers College, including constructing the new laboratory school in 1929 and the Nathan C. Schaeffer Auditorium by 1940. A dignified concourse was developed. The Georgian Dining Room emerged from the old chapel and auditorium. A new athletic field and a greenhouse were built. In 1948, Dr. Rohrbach was still reminding the trustees that, after 14 years of service, he did not have a garage for his car.

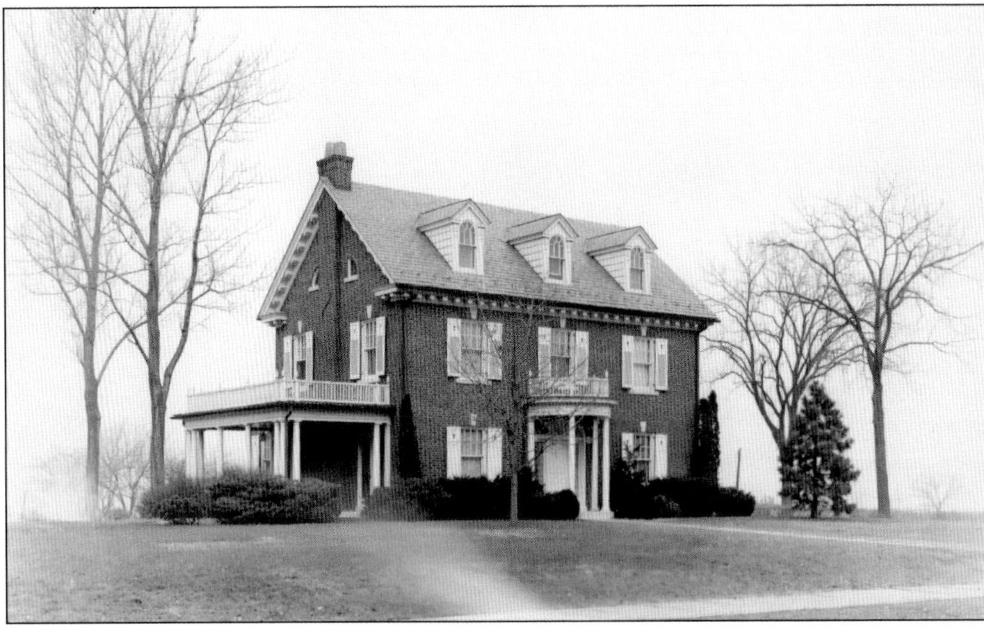

In 1929, the new president's house was built on a plot of land near the 1915 library, today's Graduate Center. Dr. Amos C. Rothermel was the first president to reside in the home. Since then, every president of the college has lived there. The house was built in the Colonial Revival style with a mixture of Georgian and Federal details. The newest resident is Dr. Kenneth S. Hawkinson, Kutztown University's 12th president.

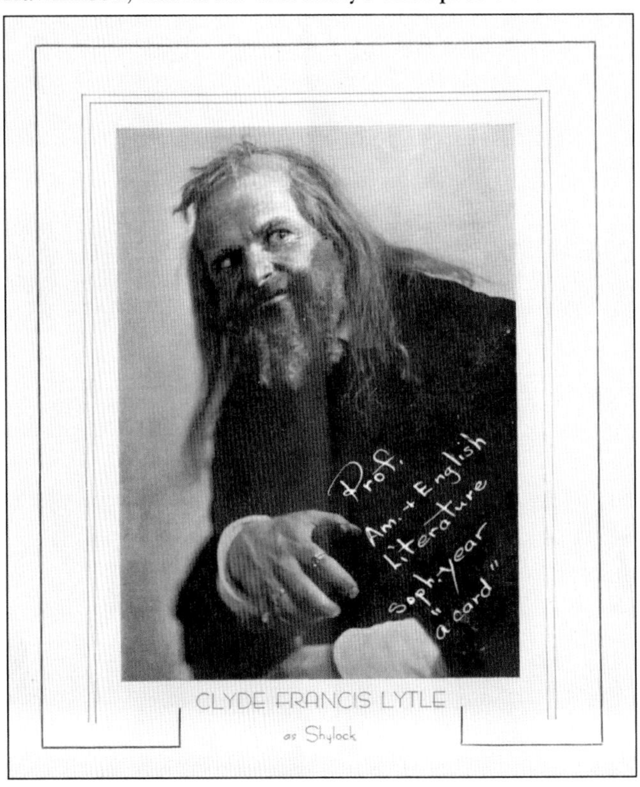

Dr. Clyde Francis Lytle joined the KSNS faculty as an English teacher in 1922, before becoming chairman of the English department only a year later. He dedicated 35 years of his life to the Keystone State Normal School and the Kutztown State Teachers College as a teacher, scholar, adviser, writer, actor, and administrator. He retired from the Kutztown State Teachers College in 1956. Lytle Hall, built in 1970, was named in his honor and currently houses the English, history, and math departments.

In 1929, a group of students acted out some of the most dramatic scenes from Shakespeare's plays. Despite an improvised stage, the public performance proved successful, and the group grew in members and renown. According the 1942 *Keystonia*, the Shakespearean Players club had an "established reputation for successful performances . . . presentations for off-campus audiences . . . [and] this year's contribution—'Julius Caesar.'"

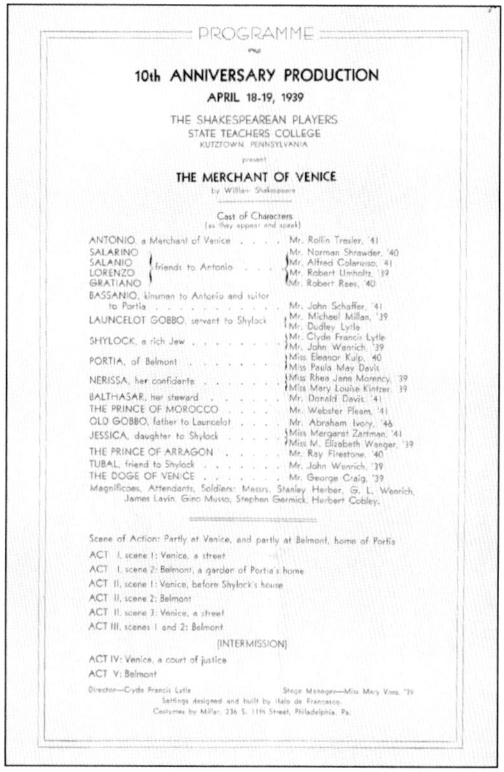

PROGRAMME

10th ANNIVERSARY PRODUCTION

APRIL 18-19, 1939

THE SHAKESPEAREAN PLAYERS
STATE TEACHERS COLLEGE
KUTZTOWN, PENNSYLVANIA

present

THE MERCHANT OF VENICE

by William Shakespeare

Cast of Characters
(as they appear and speak)

ANTONIO, a Merchant of Venice	Mr. Rollin Trexler, '41
SALARINO, SALANIO, LORENZO, GRATIANO — friends to Antonio	Mr. Norman Shrawder, '40; Mr. Alfred Colarusso, '41; Mr. Robert Umholtz, '39; Mr. Robert Rees, '40
BASSANIO, kinsman to Antonio and suitor to Portia	Mr. John Schaffer, '41
LAUNCELOT GOBBO, servant to Shylock	Mr. Michael Millan, '39; Mr. Dudley Lytle
SHYLOCK, a rich Jew	Mr. Clyde Francis Lytle; Mr. John Wenrich, '39
PORTIA, of Belmont	Miss Eleanor Kulp, '40; Miss Paula May Davis
NERISSA, her confidante	Miss Rhea Jane Morency, '39; Miss Mary Louise Kintzer, '39
BALTHASAR, her steward	Mr. Donald Davis, '41
THE PRINCE OF MOROCCO	Mr. Webster Pleam, '41
OLD GOBBO, father to Launcelot	Mr. Abraham Ivory, '46
JESSICA, daughter to Shylock	Miss Margaret Zartman, '41; Miss M. Elizabeth Wenger, '39
THE PRINCE OF ARRAGON	Mr. Ray Firestone, '40
TUBAL, friend to Shylock	Mr. John Wenrich, '39
THE DOGE OF VENICE	Mr. George Craig, '39

Magnificoes, Attendants, Soldiers: Messrs. Stanley Herber, G. L. Wenrich, James Lavin, Gino Musso, Stephen Germick, Herbert Cobley.

Scene of Action: Partly at Venice, and partly at Belmont, home of Portia

ACT I, scene 1: Venice, a street
ACT I, scene 2: Belmont, a garden of Portia's home
ACT II, scene 1: Venice, before Shylock's house
ACT II, scene 2: Belmont
ACT II, scene 3: Venice, a street
ACT III, scenes 1 and 2: Belmont

(INTERMISSION)

ACT IV: Venice, a court of justice
ACT V: Belmont

Director—Clyde Francis Lytle   Stage Manager—Miss Mary Voss, '39
Settings designed and built by Italo de Francesco.
Costumes by Miller, 236 S. 11th Street, Philadelphia, Pa.

This image from the 1942 *Keystonia* yearbook features the Shakespearean Players. The president, a senior, was Roland Trexler, who worked with the club's sponsor, Clyde Francis Lytle, a professor of English who later had an academic building named after him. Shakespearean production rehearsals at Kutztown began in the classroom.

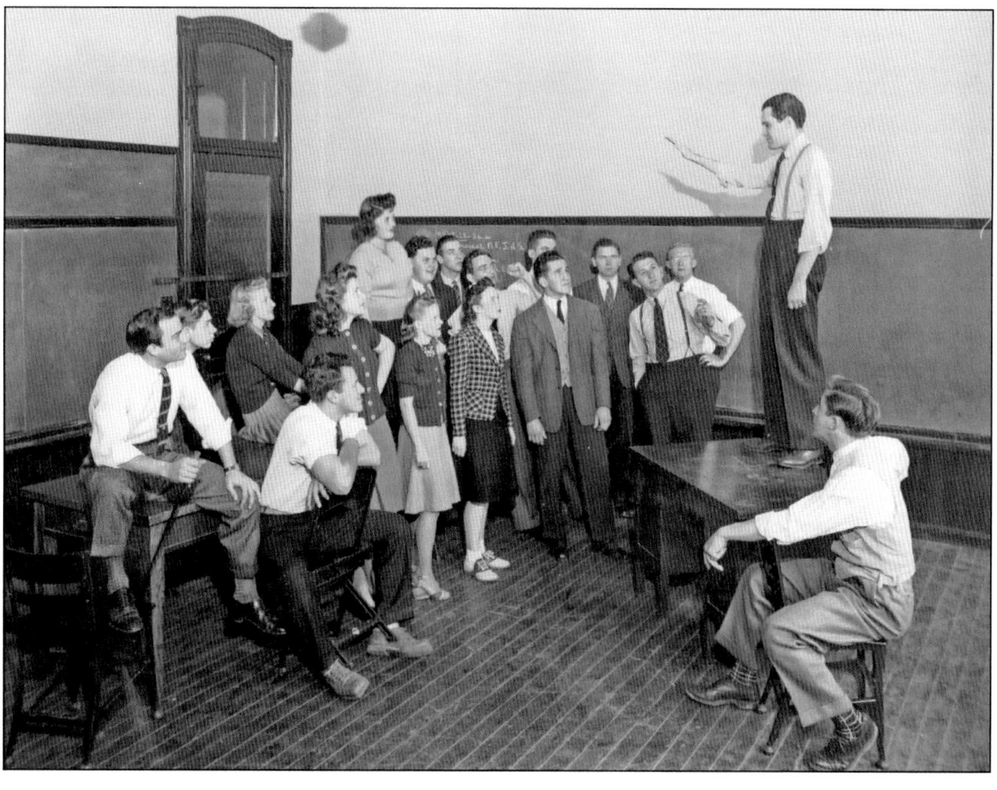

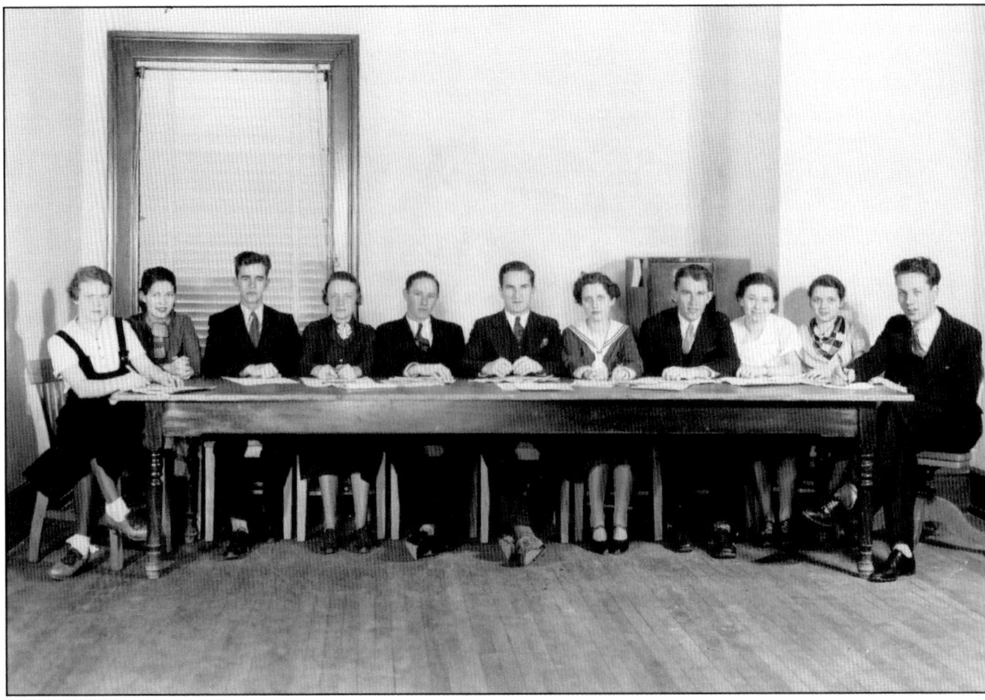

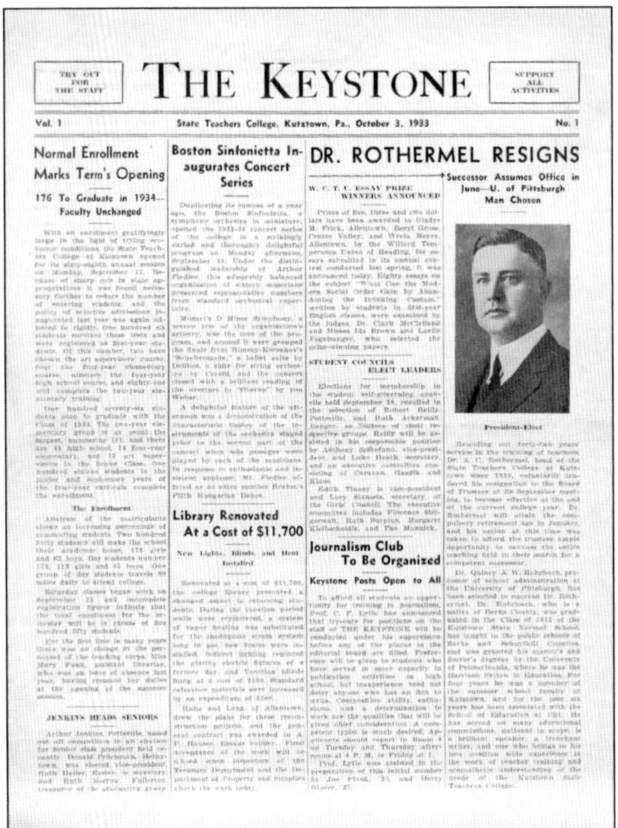

TRY OUT FOR THE STAFF

THE KEYSTONE

SUPPORT ALL ACTIVITIES

Vol. 1 State Teachers College, Kutztown, Pa., October 3, 1933 No. 1

Normal Enrollment Marks Term's Opening

176 To Graduate in 1934—Faculty Unchanged

Boston Sinfonietta Inaugurates Concert Series

DR. ROTHERMEL RESIGNS

Successor Assumes Office in June—U. of Pittsburgh Man Chosen

President-Elect

Library Renovated At a Cost of $11,700

Journalism Club To Be Organized

Keystone Posts Open to All

Dr. Clyde F. Lytle and a group of students began publishing the school's first newspaper, the *Keystone*, in 1933. Dr. Lytle served as the adviser for several years, while the Keystone staff ran the biweekly school newspaper. Among the Keystone staff members of 1934–1935 included in the photograph are Blanche Fox, William Bartholomew, Ronald MacAdam, Joe Hagameyer, Ruth Freyberger, Fred Hess, Grace Yoder, and Joseph Plank.

On October 3, 1933, the first issue of the *Keystone*, Kutztown's biweekly student newspaper, was published under the leadership of Dr. Clyde F. Lytle, editor. The top story of volume 1, issue 1, was the upcoming retirement of Dr. A.C. Rothermel as president and the appointment of Dr. Quincy A.W. Rohrbach (class of 1912) as his successor.

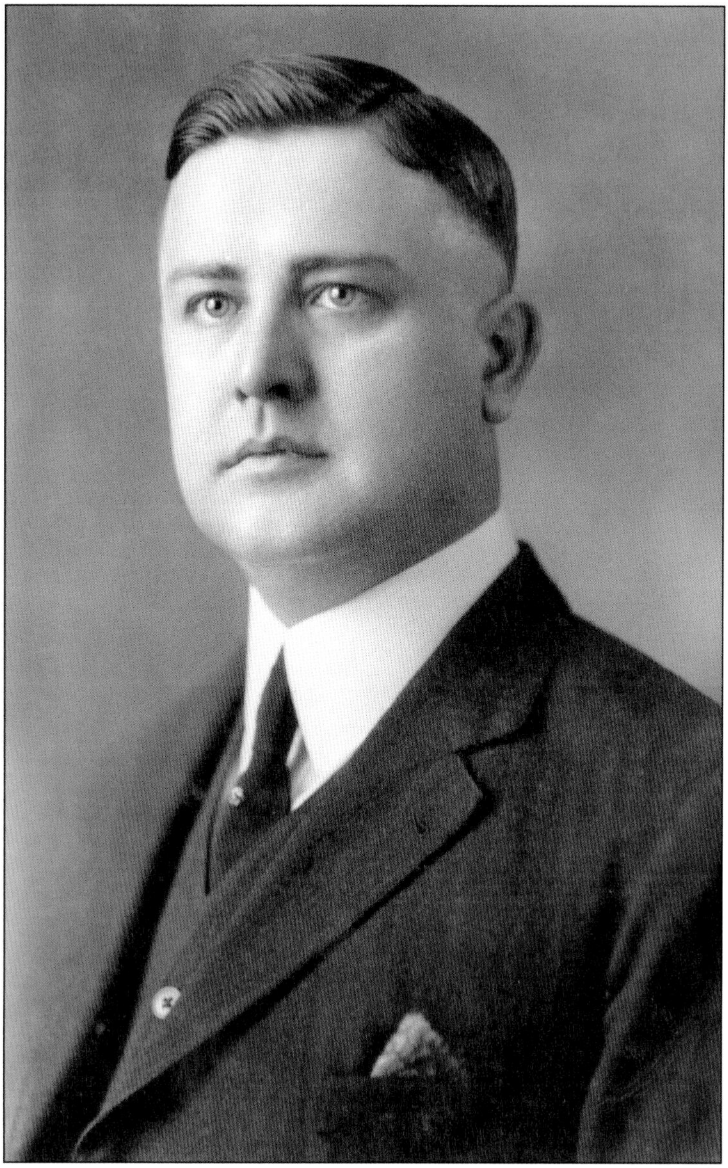

On October 19, 1934, Dr. Quincy Alvin W. Rohrbach (1894–1988) was inaugurated as the sixth president of Kutztown State Teachers College. A 1912 graduate of Keystone State Normal School, he served Kutztown State Teachers College as president during some of the school's most trying times, including the Great Depression and World War II. Dr. Rohrbach transformed the faculty during his time as president. In 1934, when Rohrbach started, there were 38 members of the faculty, including only one with an earned doctorate. By the time Rohrbach retired, the faculty had grown to 62 people, with 20 of them holding doctoral degrees. After he retired in 1959 with 25 years of service to his alma mater, the school named its original library (today's Graduate Center) in his honor in 1960. By 1969, the new Rohrbach Library had been completed and dedicated to Dr. Rohrbach. He and his wife promoted the study of library science at Kutztown State College by providing the Quincy and Laura Rohrbach Award in Librarianship, which was presented annually to a graduate in the library education curriculum.

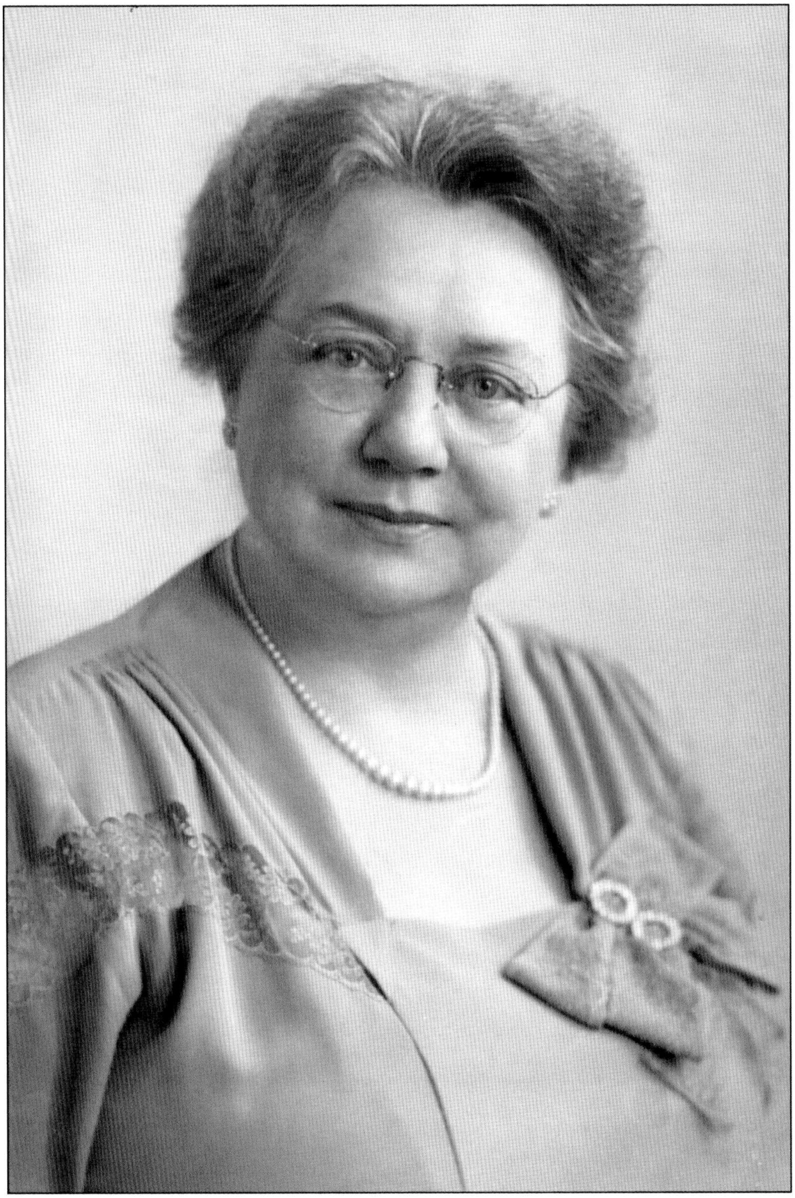

Mary Rickenbach graduated from the Keystone State Normal School in 1912. After serving as an elementary school principal for several years, she returned to the Keystone State Normal School in 1919 as a critic teacher and supervisor in the model school. From the fall of 1922 until 1925, she served as the director of the model school and reorganized it into the training school. After taking a year's absence to continue her education at Columbia University, she returned to the Keystone State Normal School in 1926 as the head of the Department of Psychology and Sociology. She also served as the assistant dean of women. Later in her career, she was appointed dean of women and taught as a professor in the social studies department. In 1960, Kutztown State College dedicated the campus laboratory school (today's south side of the Stratton Administration Building) to Mary Rickenbach. Later, the Mary Rickenbach Research and Learning Center on the north side of campus was dedicated to her on May 24, 1969.

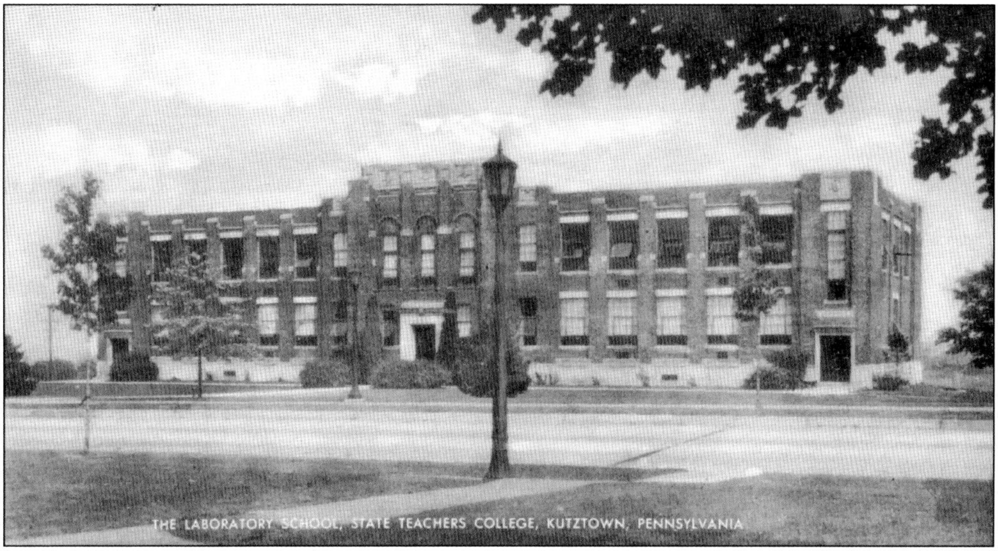

In 1929, the Kutztown State Teachers College constructed the training school, later known as the laboratory school. The school served as the borough of Kutztown's elementary school, and its faculty were members of the college. The school allowed KSTC elementary education majors the chance to see new educational theories and methods put into practice. In 1977, extensive renovations were made to the building to convert it into the Kutztown State College's administration building, today's Stratton Administration Building.

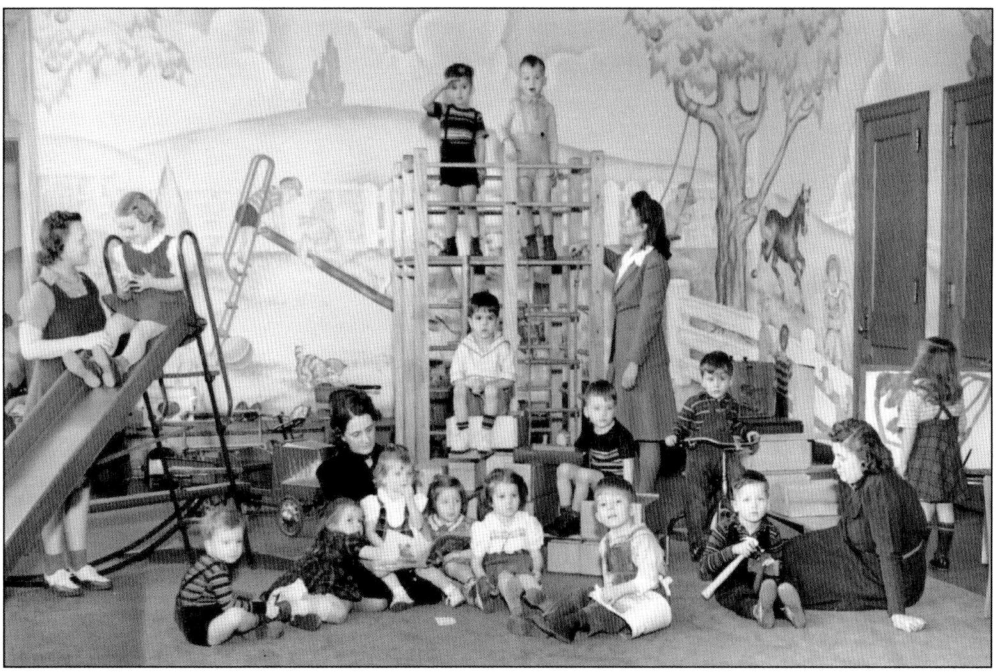

The average day in the life of a model school student started with opening exercises. After morning devotions, children broke up into small classes with different teachers for each subject. Full-time training school teachers were KSTC faculty members. KSTC seniors, who were elementary education majors, completed their student teaching in the laboratory training school.

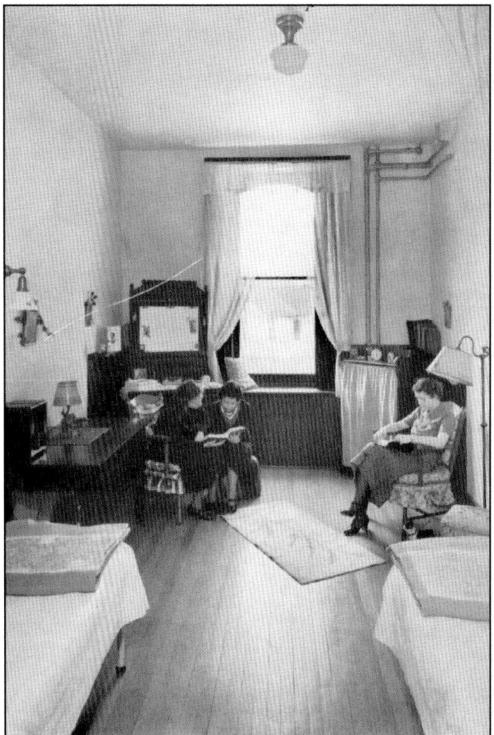

All residence halls for girls have been renovated. Each room has single beds, two closets, including trunk space, and wiring for a radio.

Gaining entry to the Kutztown State Teachers College was regarded as a pledge to follow the rules of the school. In the 1930s, all residence halls for girls were renovated. Each room had two single beds, two closets with trunk space, and wiring for a radio. With these new renovations came strict housing regulations that all students living in the dormitories had to follow. The list of 12 housing standards was to be followed strictly, and inspections by the dean of women were required weekly. The underlined rules were the most explicit ones to be followed and breaking them carried a heavy penalty. (Both, courtesy of KU.)

HOUSING STANDARDS
KUTZTOWN STATE COLLEGE
OLD MAIN

Kindly observe these regulations:

1. To preserve the paint please do not use scotch tape or thumb tacks on these walls. Moore pushless hangers are permissible. Occupants of this room are held responsible for any damage.
2. On the door place nothing but your name cards.
3. Furniture may not be moved from one room to another; nor is room exchange permitted.
4. Bureau scarves must be used to protect the bureau tops.
5. Under no circumstances are screens to be removed from the windows.
6. Beds must be made by 10 A.M.
7. Your room must be tidy. A weekly cleaning is required, to be followed by inspections.
8. For cleaning, use the mops in the Broom Closets.
9. Shake out mops and rugs into your wastebasket or use the large waste cans in the hall.
10. Smoking in this room is forbidden.
11. The use of unauthorized electrical appliances is forbidden. Violators of this regulation will automatically forfeit their choice of a room for next semester and may possibly be dismissed from the residence hall.
12. Upon leaving your room, LOCK THE DOOR.

The *Key*, directed by Mary Rickenbach, began in 1934. The KSTC student handbook was distributed to every incoming and new student. Listed inside were the rules that needed to be followed while on school grounds. The guide also gave students a look at an average day in college. Today's electronic version of the *Key* is now available online for KU students.

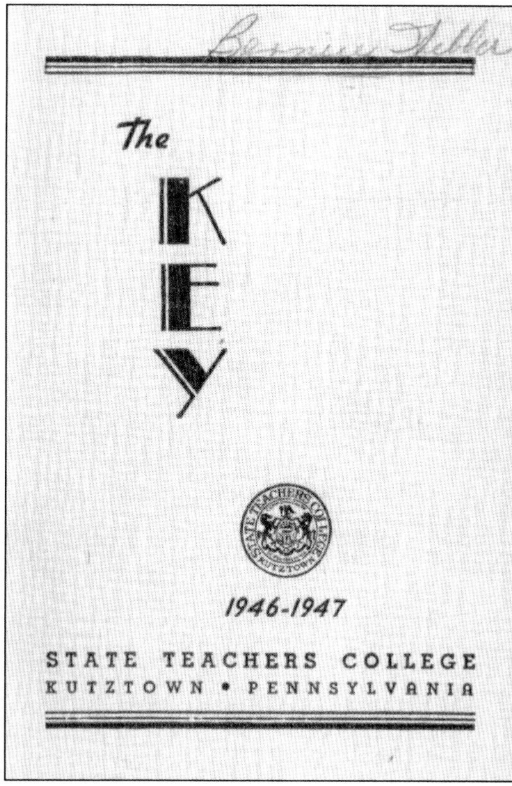

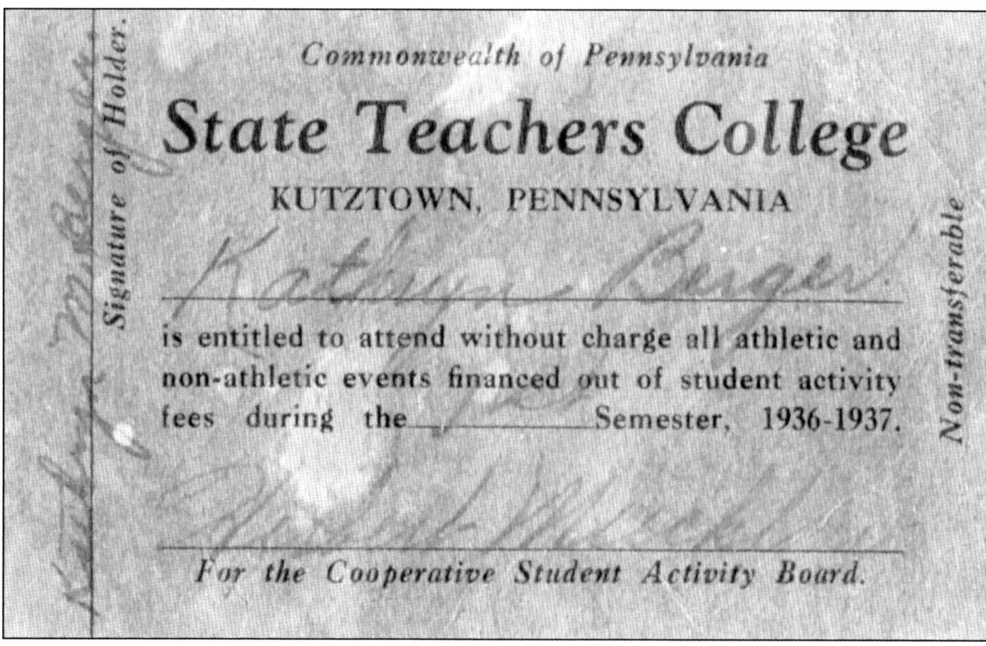
Commonwealth of Pennsylvania

State Teachers College

KUTZTOWN, PENNSYLVANIA

is entitled to attend without charge all athletic and non-athletic events financed out of student activity fees during the ______ Semester, 1936-1937.

For the Cooperative Student Activity Board.

Signature of Holder.

Non-transferable

All students of Kutztown State Teachers College were given a season ticket to the athletic and nonathletic events held at the school, which was paid for out of their student activity fees. This nontransferable pass was issued to Kathryn Berger (class of 1940) for her first semester of the 1936–1937 school year.

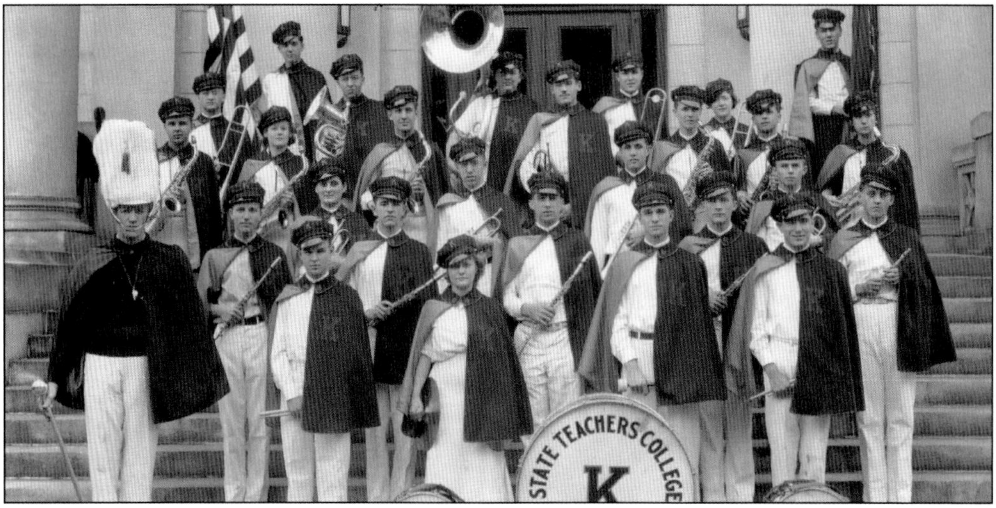

On September 29, 1934, Kutztown State Teachers College debuted its first marching band at a football game versus Mansfield. The school spent nearly $1,000 (more than $17,000 in today's currency) to purchase instruments and uniforms for the 31 band members. The first rehearsal was held on September 17 under the direction of Bessie Waldrop.

ALMA MATER

Where stately trees are bending,
Where Nature's glories shine,
And loveliness unending
In beauty rare combine,
There rise the Kutztown towers,
And there the College stands,
The well-spring of our powers—
The shrine our love commands.

About our happy hall-ways
Our fondest memories cling,
Of days that we shall always
In joyous rapture sing:
Firm as a keystone they stand,
Round which we shared life's span.
She taught the source of all good:
Who serves God must serve man.

And we will ever love her
And live to spread her fame;
Our lives shall add new lustre
Unto her glorious name;
As guardians of her new day
Our work will even be,
To labor so that she may
Achieve her destiny.

—CLYDE FRANCIS LYTLE

In 1933, Dr. Clyde F. Lytle, head of the English department, composed the school's alma mater for its first presentation at the convocation honoring retiring president Dr. Amos C. Rothermel. Dr. Lytle's alma mater is recited at KU events and graduation ceremonies to this day. During the 2015–2016 school year, music of the school's alma mater was scheduled to play each afternoon from the Old Main clock tower in celebration of the sesquicentennial.

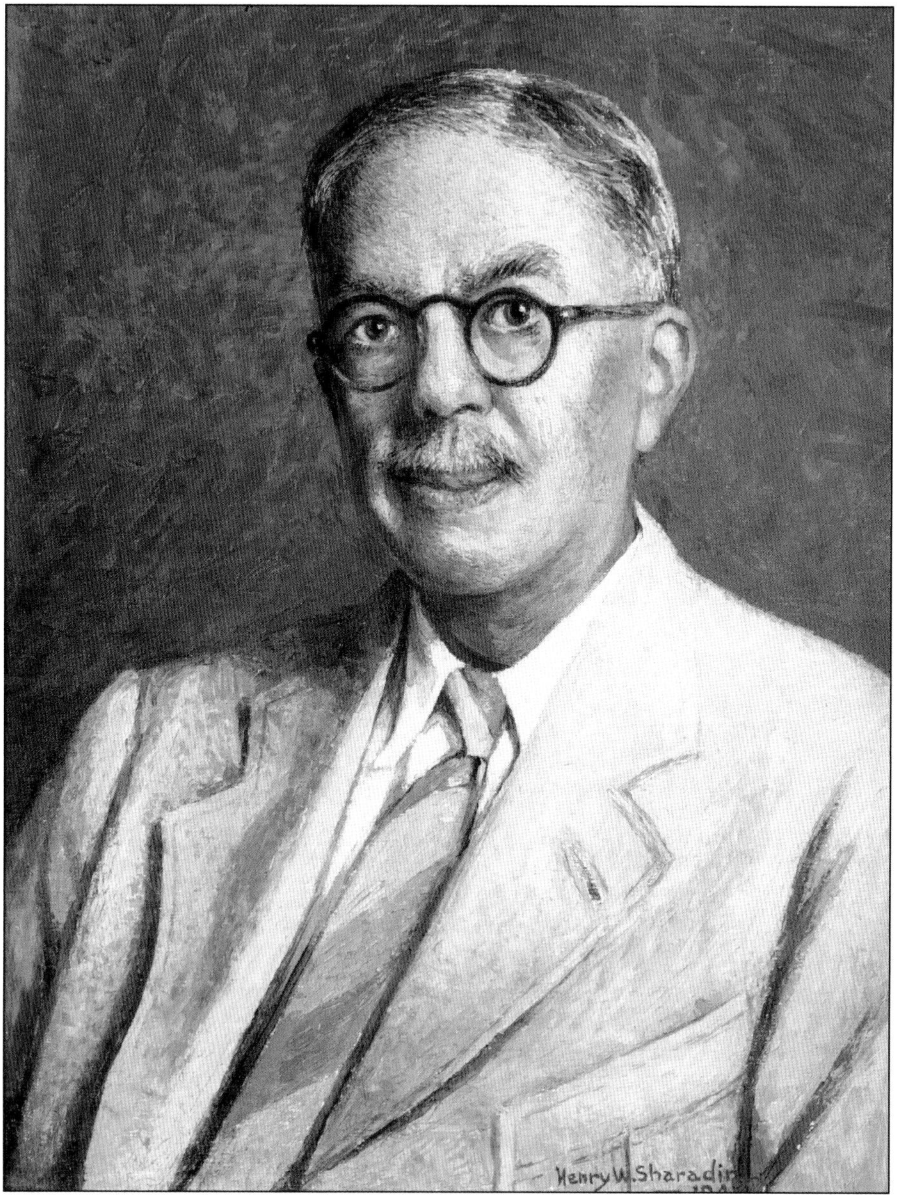

Henry William Sharadin (1872–1966) graduated from Keystone State Normal School in 1891. In 1907, he accepted the chair of art and drawing at the school, where he taught until 1916. He left in 1916 to teach at Allentown High School but returned to the Keystone State Normal School in 1919, not only to teach art, but also to head the department where he worked until his retirement in 1939. In 1937, the school converted the infirmary into a new art studio. The Sharadin Art Studio was the first building named for an individual. His most famous painting is the mural titled *Education* that he created in 1913. Sharadin's grandfather once owned the farm that became the Pennsylvania German Cultural Heritage Center, and he grew up spending lots of time on the farm during his formative years. This is a photograph of a self-portrait Sharadin painted later in life. Sharadin died in 1966 at the age of 93 and was the last surviving member of his KSNS class. (Photograph by John Paul Endress, courtesy of Kutztown University Foundation.)

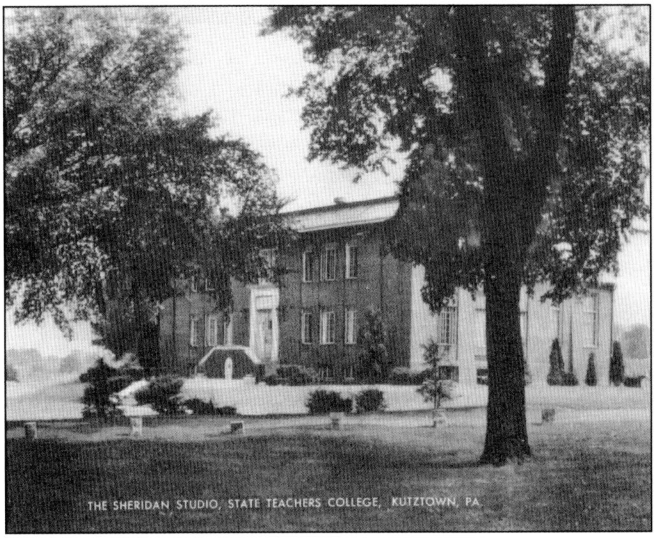

The original Sharadin Art Studio was named after Prof. Henry Sharadin in 1937. Arts, crafts, and drawing courses were taken in this building during a student's second and fourth years of study. On June 28, 1929, the state council of education granted the Kutztown State Teachers College the power to confer the bachelor of science degree in public school art. In 1960, the new Sharadin Art Building was completed on the north side of campus to house the growing art program.

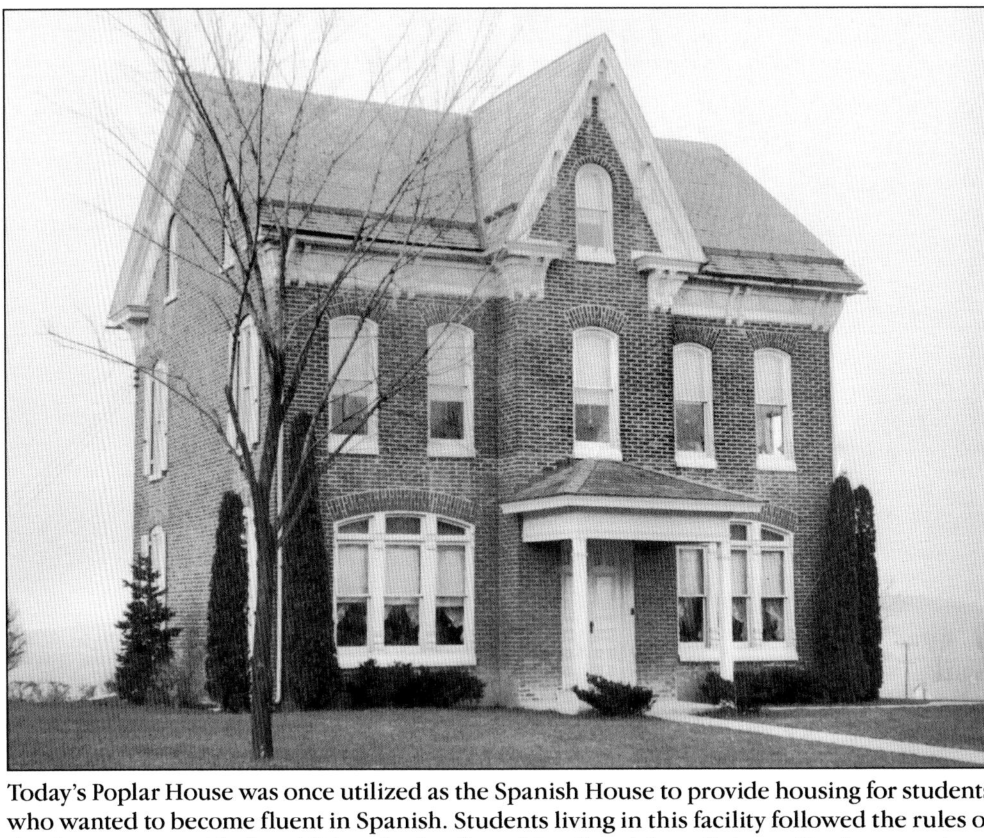

Today's Poplar House was once utilized as the Spanish House to provide housing for students who wanted to become fluent in Spanish. Students living in this facility followed the rules of the dormitories, with the additional rule of speaking Spanish at all times. Graduate students were put in charge to ensure Spanish was always spoken. The house remained popular into the 1980s.

The Nathan C. Schaeffer Auditorium, named for Keystone State Normal School's third principal, was completed in late 1940. Along with an auditorium that could seat 1,200, the building included several music classrooms. At the time, one of the required classes for students was vocal music. Musical, theatrical, and dance performances continue to be held in the auditorium today.

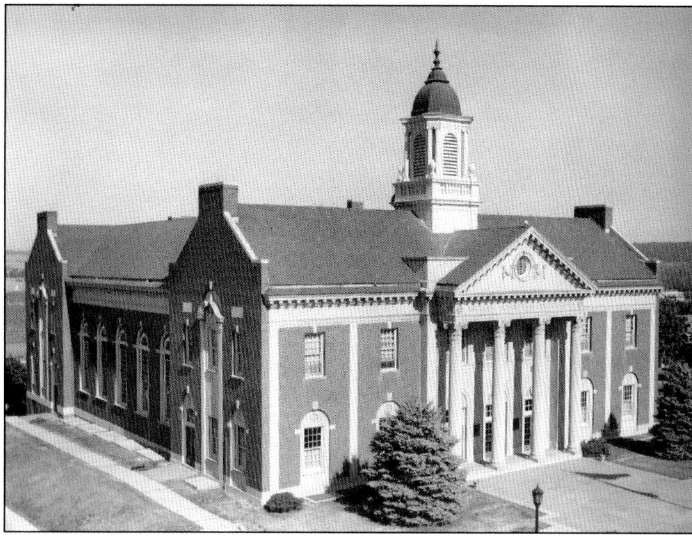

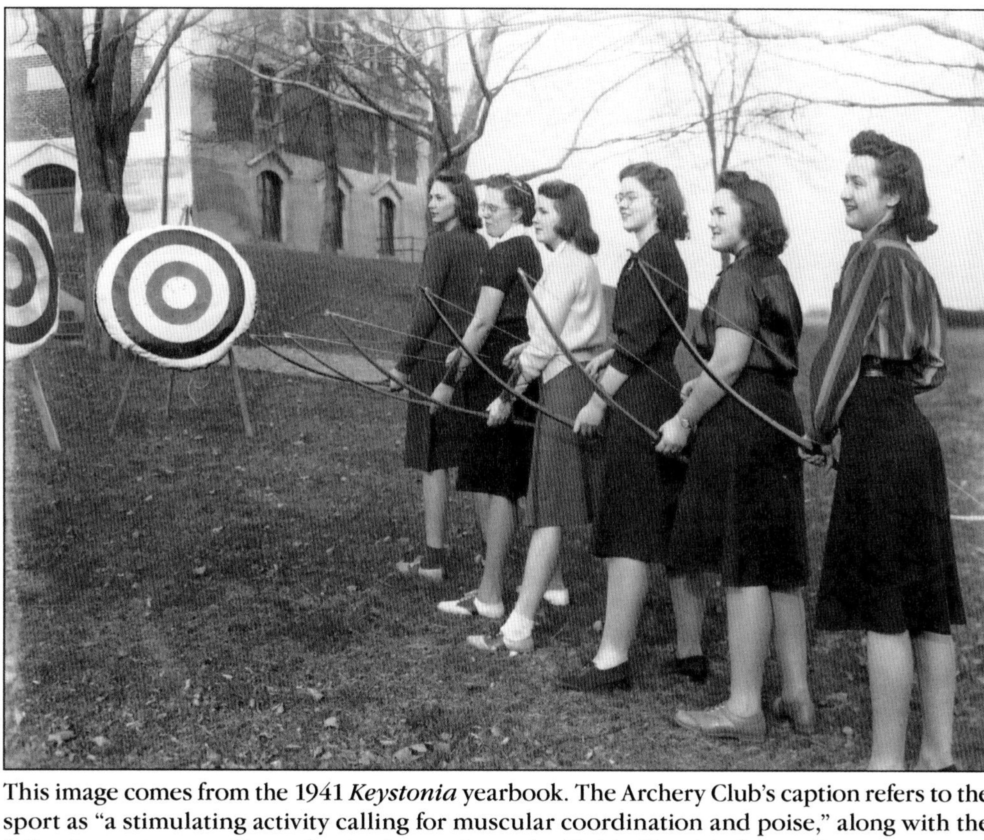

This image comes from the 1941 *Keystonia* yearbook. The Archery Club's caption refers to the sport as "a stimulating activity calling for muscular coordination and poise," along with the following statement: "Its enthusiastic members, the 'Robin Hoods' of the college, encourage the pursuits of this activity to add that extra zest to after-class hours." The manager was Marguerite Holland, who worked with the club's sponsor, Minerva Stern.

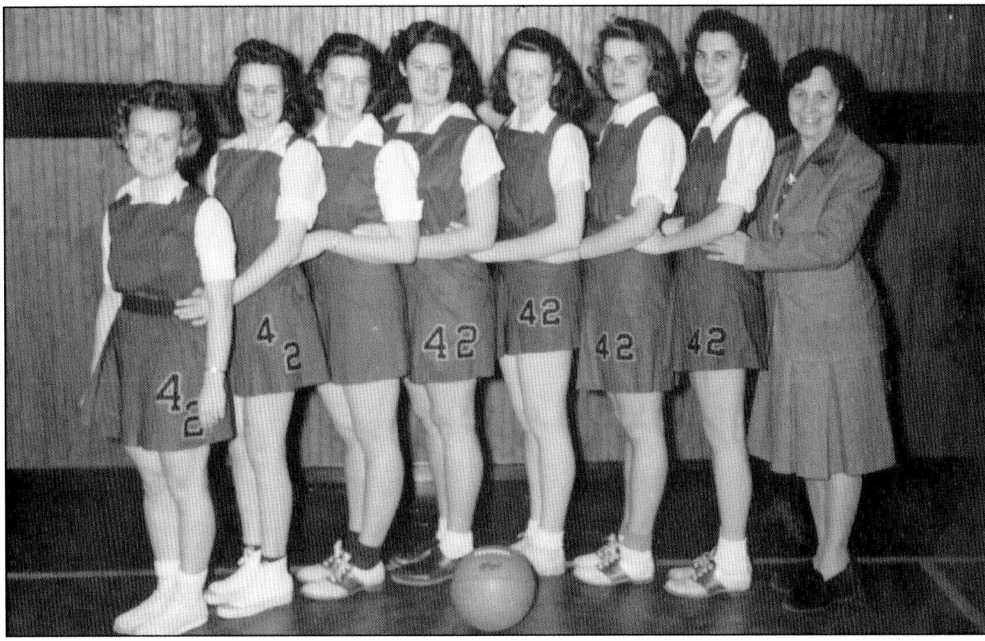

The seniors on the 1942 women's basketball team include, from left to right, Marcia Zechman, Gladys Spatz, Ruth Brown, Emma Lentz, Bettina Brubaker, Margaret Hittell, and Mildred Klingaman—plus Peg Preaton (not pictured). They made their own uniforms (some were still pinned the first night they played). Their coach, Minerva Stern (right), led women's athletics from 1928 to 1952 and is a member of the Kutztown University Athletics Hall of Fame.

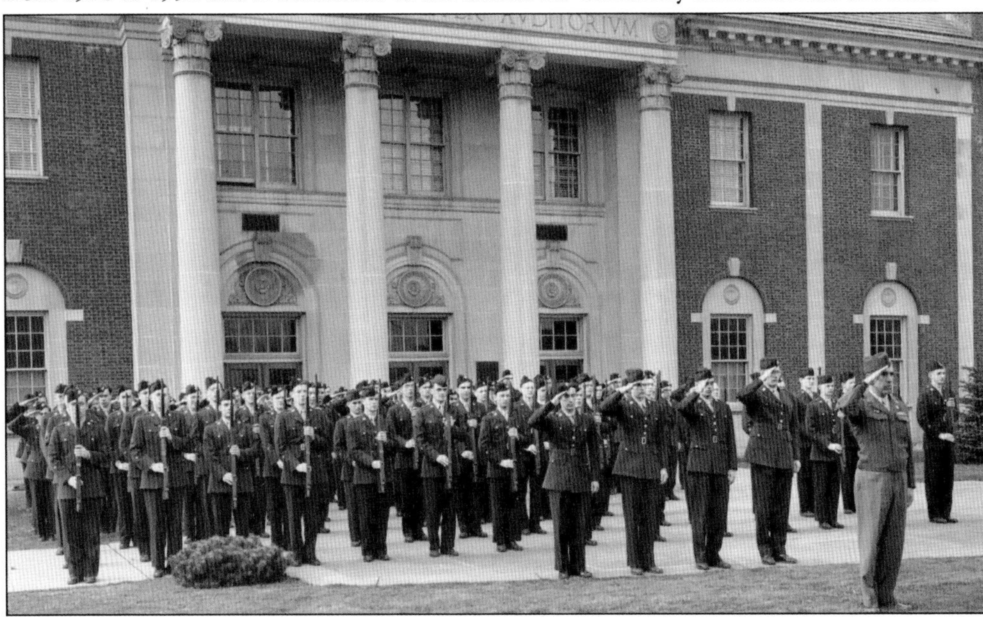

On December 7, 1942, the KSTC community gathered for a service to commemorate the one-year anniversary of the bombing of Pearl Harbor. During the ceremony, which had the theme "Work-Fight-Sacrifice," those in attendance heard a firsthand account of the war from neighboring Fleetwood resident Lt. Paul Schlegel, who was home on leave. Students and faculty also discussed how they could support the war effort and protect the campus.

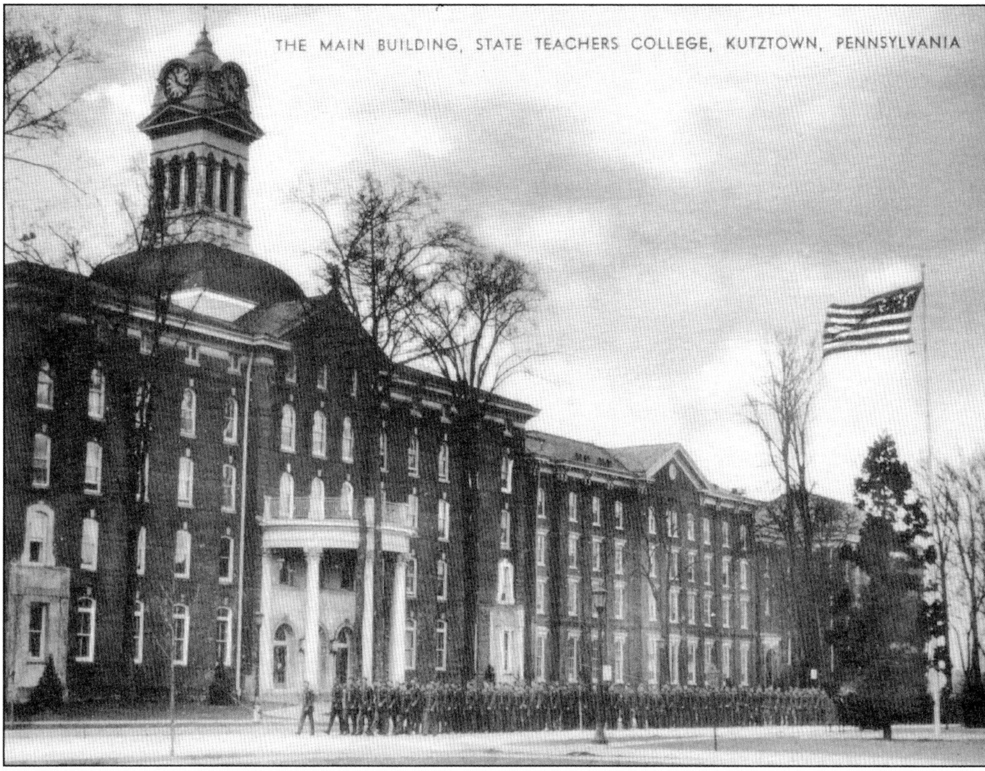

When World War II arrived, student enrollment at the Kutztown State Teachers College declined drastically. The low point reached 243 students, which included only a dozen men. Dr. Quincy A.W. Rohrbach secured contingents of Army Air Forces students to bolster enrollment and keep the school open. For several years beginning in 1943, students from the US Army Air Forces studied at the college to prepare for their service in World War II. These soldiers are shown marching in front of Old Main.

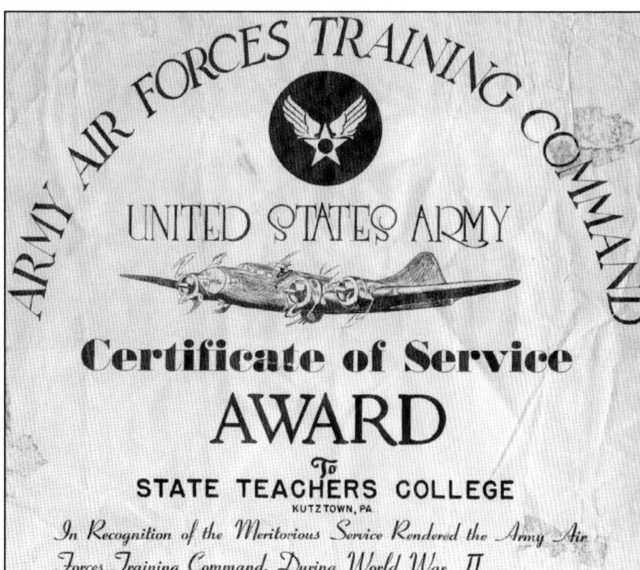
ARMY AIR FORCES TRAINING COMMAND

UNITED STATES ARMY

Certificate of Service

AWARD

To

STATE TEACHERS COLLEGE

KUTZTOWN, PA

In Recognition of the Meritorious Service Rendered the Army Air Forces Training Command, During World War II...

This Certificate of Service Award was given to the Kutztown State Teachers College for allowing the recruits of the Army Air Forces college training program to study and train at the school from 1943 to 1944. The citation came from the headquarters of the Army Air Forces Training Command in Fort Worth, Texas. It is signed by Maj. Gen. William O. Butler and Lt. Gen. B.K. Yount.

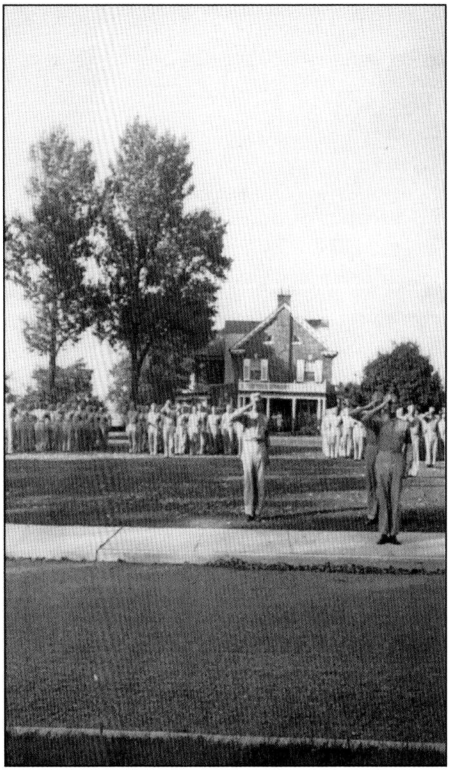

Army Air Forces students were trained at the Kutztown State Teachers College as part of the war effort and to help augment the school's enrollment. In 1943, Ted Strater was the wing commander in charge of the July retreat. Soldiers at drill stand beside the president's residence, facing toward the library. (Courtesy of KU.)

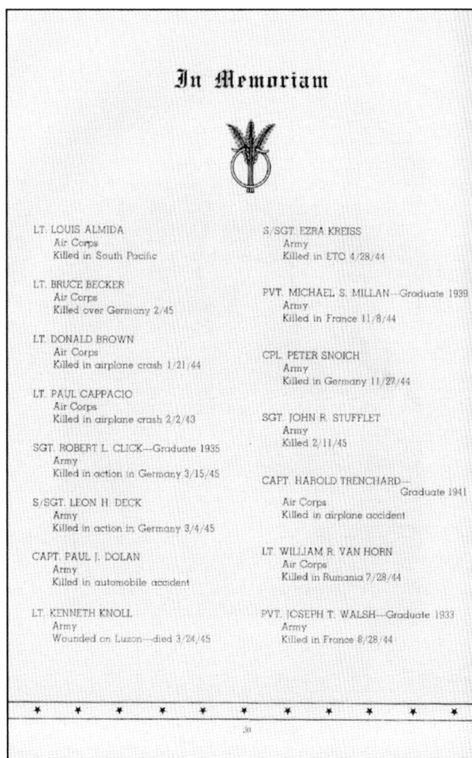

In Memoriam

LT. LOUIS ALMIDA
Air Corps
Killed in South Pacific

LT. BRUCE BECKER
Air Corps
Killed over Germany 2/45

LT. DONALD BROWN
Air Corps
Killed in airplane crash 1/21/44

LT. PAUL CAPPACIO
Air Corps
Killed in airplane crash 2/2/43

SGT. ROBERT L. CLICK—Graduate 1935
Army
Killed in action in Germany 3/15/45

S/SGT. LEON H. DECK
Army
Killed in action in Germany 3/4/45

CAPT. PAUL J. DOLAN
Army
Killed in automobile accident

LT. KENNETH KNOLL
Army
Wounded on Luzon—died 3/24/45

S/SGT. EZRA KREISS
Army
Killed in ETO 4/28/44

PVT. MICHAEL S. MILLAN—Graduate 1939
Army
Killed in France 11/8/44

CPL. PETER SNOICH
Army
Killed in Germany 11/27/44

SGT. JOHN R. STUFFLET
Army
Killed 2/11/45

CAPT. HAROLD TRENCHARD—Graduate 1941
Air Corps
Killed in airplane accident

LT. WILLIAM R. VAN HORN
Air Corps
Killed in Rumania 7/28/44

PVT. JOSEPH T. WALSH—Graduate 1933
Army
Killed in France 8/28/44

30

The compilers of the 1946 *Keystonia* yearbook dedicated a page to the Kutztown students who had fought and died for their country during World War II. The list included 15 names, along with each person's rank and fighting unit, time and place of death, and graduation year, if applicable.

Starting as a freshman in 1946, Bessie Reese Crenshaw stood out as the only African American student enrolled at the Kutztown State Teachers College. Although she encountered numerous situations of unease, she busied herself with her studies and extracurricular activities. In 1950, she became the first African American student to graduate from the college. (Courtesy of KUR.)

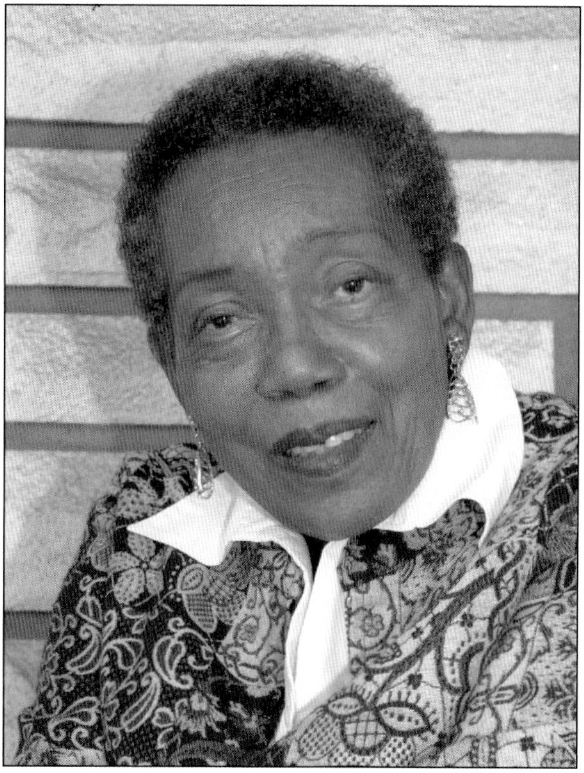

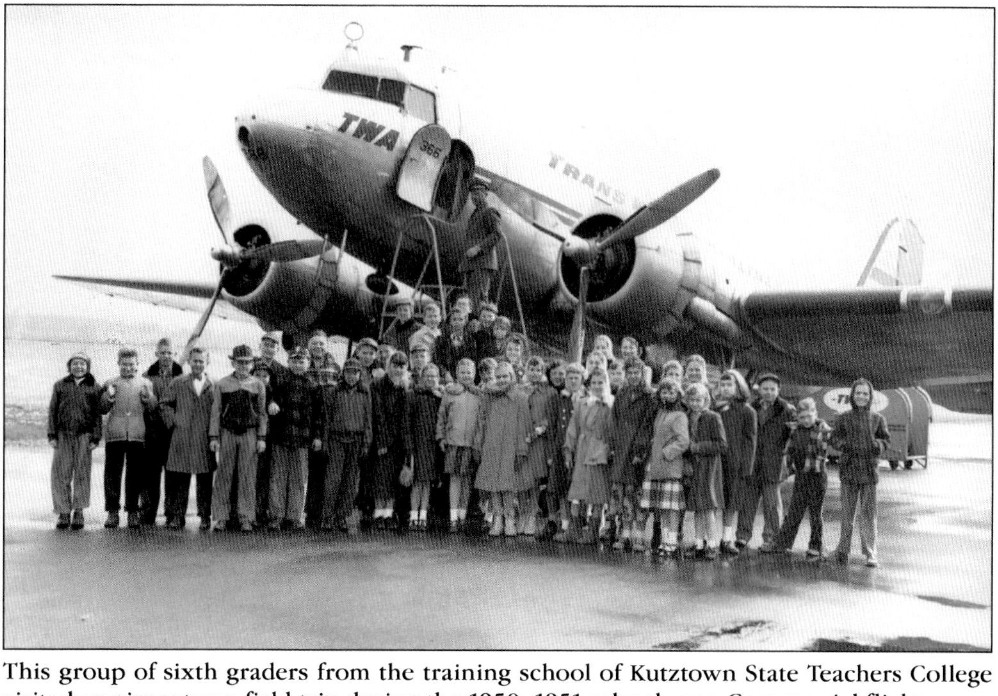

This group of sixth graders from the training school of Kutztown State Teachers College visited an airport as a field trip during the 1950–1951 school year. Commercial flights were a relatively new phenomenon in the early 1950s. The children viewed a Trans World Airlines (TWA) commercial airplane while on their trip. (Courtesy of KU.)

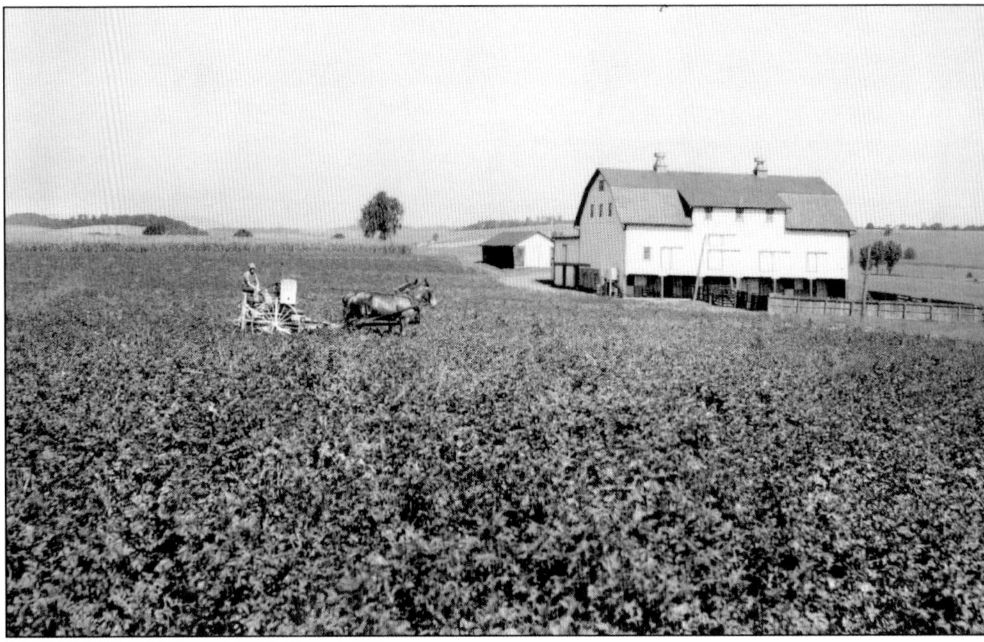

In 1917, the Keystone State Normal School purchased the 77-acre Kutz farm after 20 years of negotiations. The newly acquired farmland required the construction of a new barn and poultry house. In the 1940s, another farm was utilized on the northern side of campus. The second farm had 126 acres overall, with 30 acres dedicated to potatoes, yielding an estimated 10,000 bushels. The college owned and operated the large fertile farm where fine foods were grown for the college menus. The school farmer, Harvey Reidenhauer, with assistant Mr. Meitzler, used two teams of mules and the power of an F-30 Farmall tractor to plow and sow the fields. In November 1948, farming on campus was abandoned. The Pennsylvania Department of Forests and Waters planted a tree farm on portions of the land. Today, softball and baseball fields, as well as several academic buildings, occupy the former fields.

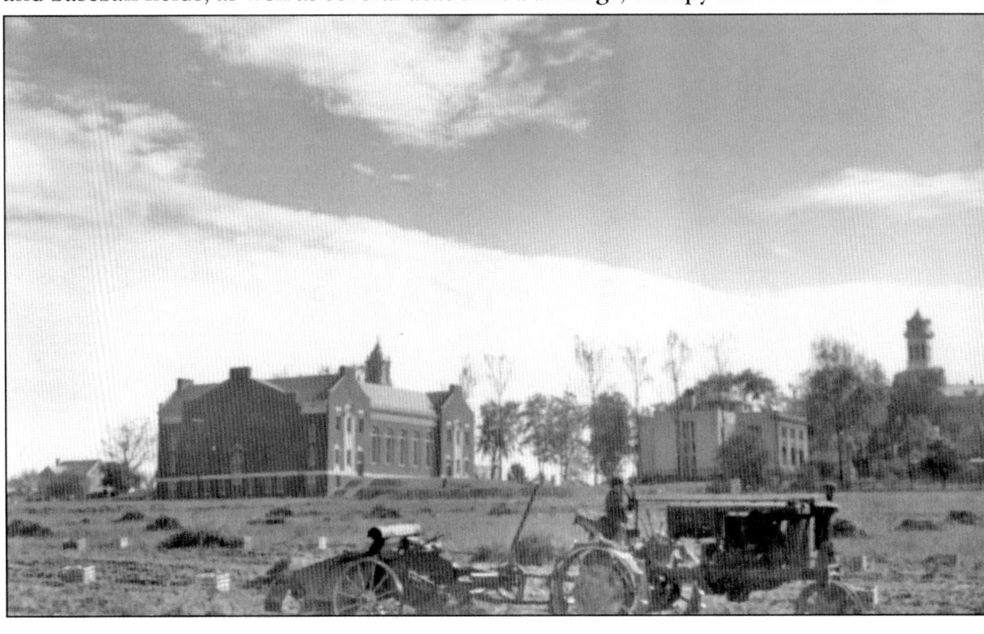

On November 19, 1948, the *Keystone* staff proposed a new mascot for the college, Krushin' Korky the Kutztown Kangaroo. They even welcomed Korky with a song: "Welcome to Korky! Long may he leap. There lies the Avalanche, All in a heap. Let's carry away, The Avalanche bear, and shout to the heavens, 'Cause Korky is here." The proposed idea was not accepted, and the school mascot remained a bear. (Courtesy of KU.)

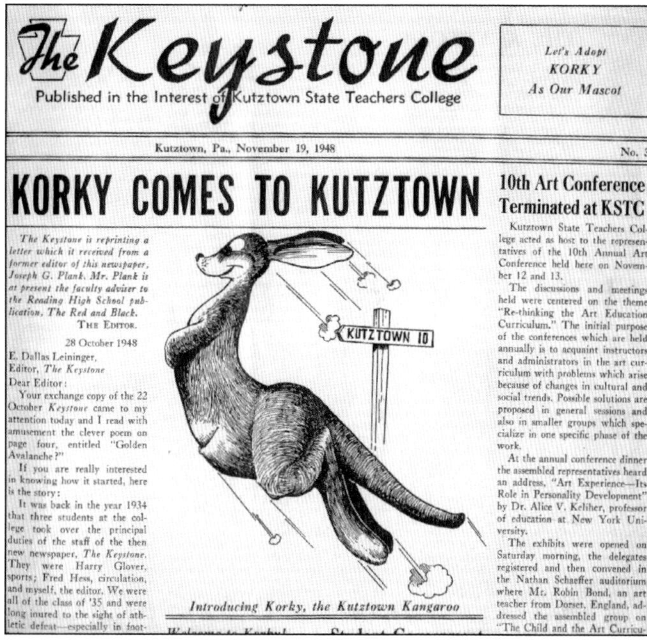

The Keystone

Published in the Interest of Kutztown State Teachers College

Let's Adopt KORKY As Our Mascot

Kutztown, Pa., November 19, 1948 — No. 3

KORKY COMES TO KUTZTOWN

The Keystone is reprinting a letter which it received from a former editor of this newspaper, Joseph G. Plank. Mr. Plank is at present the faculty adviser to the Reading High School publication, The Red and Black.
THE EDITOR.

28 October 1948

E. Dallas Leininger,
Editor, *The Keystone*
Dear Editor:

Your exchange copy of the 22 October *Keystone* came to my attention today and I read with amusement the clever poem on page four, entitled "Golden Avalanche?"

If you are really interested in knowing how it started, here is the story:

It was back in the year 1934 that three students at the college took over the principal duties of the staff of the then new newspaper, *The Keystone*. They were Harry Glover, sports; Fred Hess, circulation, and myself, the editor. We were all of the class of '35 and were long inured to the sight of athletic defeat—especially in foot-

Introducing Korky, the Kutztown Kangaroo

10th Art Conference Terminated at KSTC

Kutztown State Teachers College acted as host to the representatives of the 10th Annual Art Conference held here on November 12 and 13.

The discussions and meetings held were centered on the theme "Re-thinking the Art Education Curriculum." The initial purpose of the conferences which are held annually is to acquaint instructors and administrators in the art curriculum with problems which arise because of changes in cultural and social trends. Possible solutions are proposed in general sessions and also in smaller groups which specialize in one specific phase of the work.

At the annual conference dinner the assembled representatives heard an address, "Art Experience—Its Role in Personality Development" by Dr. Alice V. Keliher, professor of education at New York University.

The exhibits were opened on Saturday morning, the delegates registered and then convened in the Nathan Schaeffer auditorium where Mr. Robin Bond, an art teacher from Dorset, England, addressed the assembled group on "The Child and the Art Curricu-

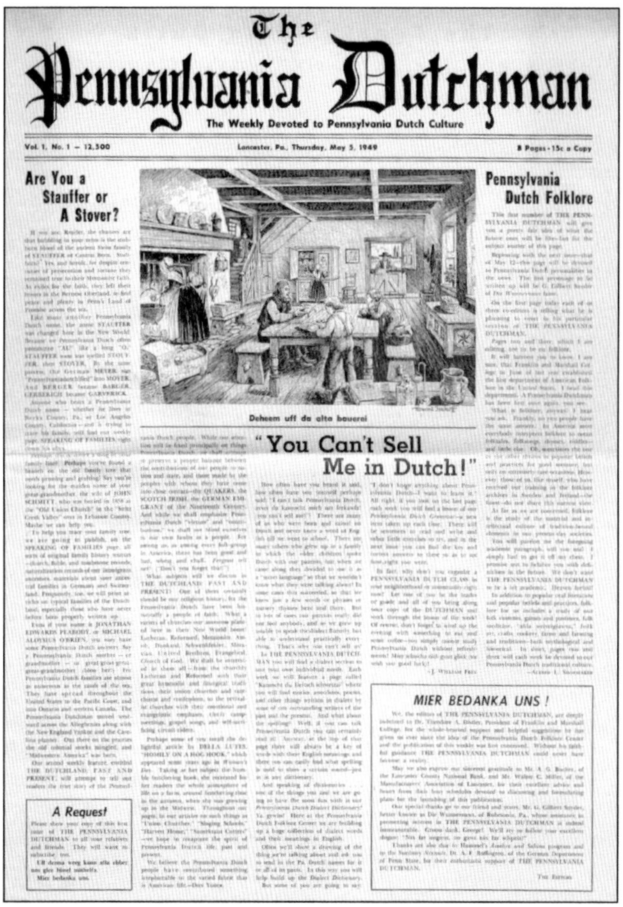

The Pennsylvania Dutchman

The Weekly Devoted to Pennsylvania Dutch Culture

Vol. 1, No. 1 — 12,500 — Lancaster, Pa., Thursday, May 5, 1949 — 8 Pages - 15c a Copy

Are You a Stauffer or A Stover?

Pennsylvania Dutch Folklore

Deheem uff da alta bauerei

"You Can't Sell Me in Dutch!"

MIER BEDANKA UNS!

A Request

The *Pennsylvania Dutchman* weekly newspaper began in 1949, then evolved into a magazine format before becoming *Pennsylvania Folklife* in 1958. The periodical's founders were instrumental in establishing the Kutztown Folk Festival in 1950. Don Yoder (1921–2015), one of the scholars and the preeminent authority on Pennsylvania German folklore at the time of his death, provided significant donations and archival materials to the collections of the Pennsylvania German Cultural Heritage Center.

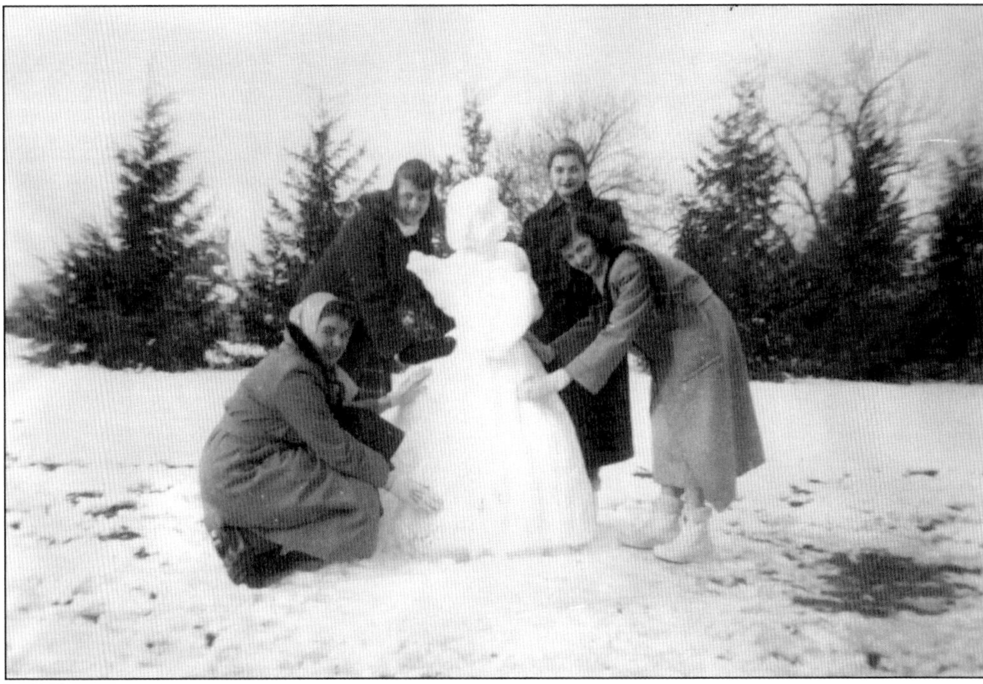

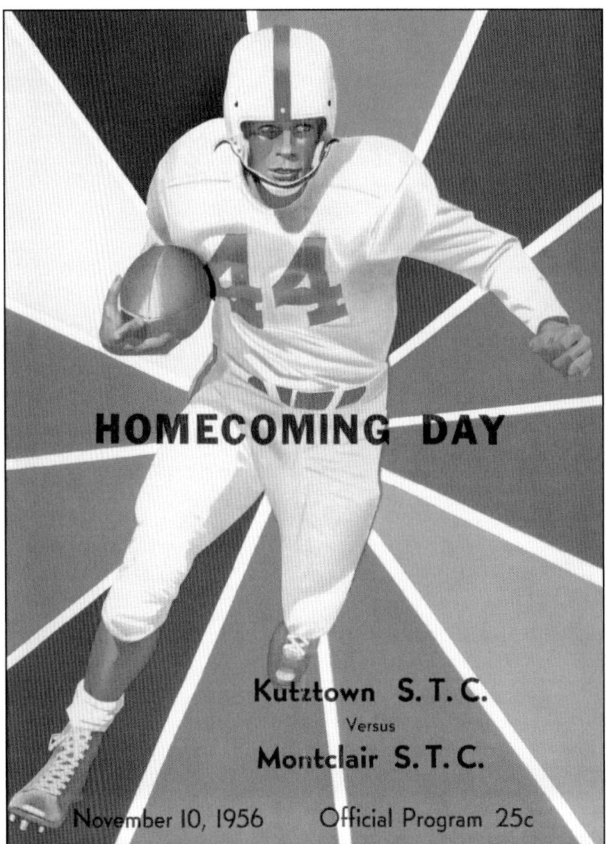

Photographs similar to this one appear in the 1953 *Keystonia* yearbook. Here, a group of freshman roommates and friends are building a snow angel during a winter session. Clockwise from left are Joyce Worthington (class of 1955), Mary Ann Koch (class of 1955), Jeanne Schank, and Barbara Ruh (class of 1955), an art major. This image was later featured in two issues of the *Tower*.

Homecoming Day was planned each year for alumni and parents. Guests were given guided tours of the campus, and as a highlight of the day, floats were presented at the football game. On November 10, 1956, Kutztown State Teachers College hosted Montclair State Teachers College; unfortunately, Kutztown lost 35-7. The evening activities centered around the homecoming queen and her court at an informal dance. (Courtesy of KU.)

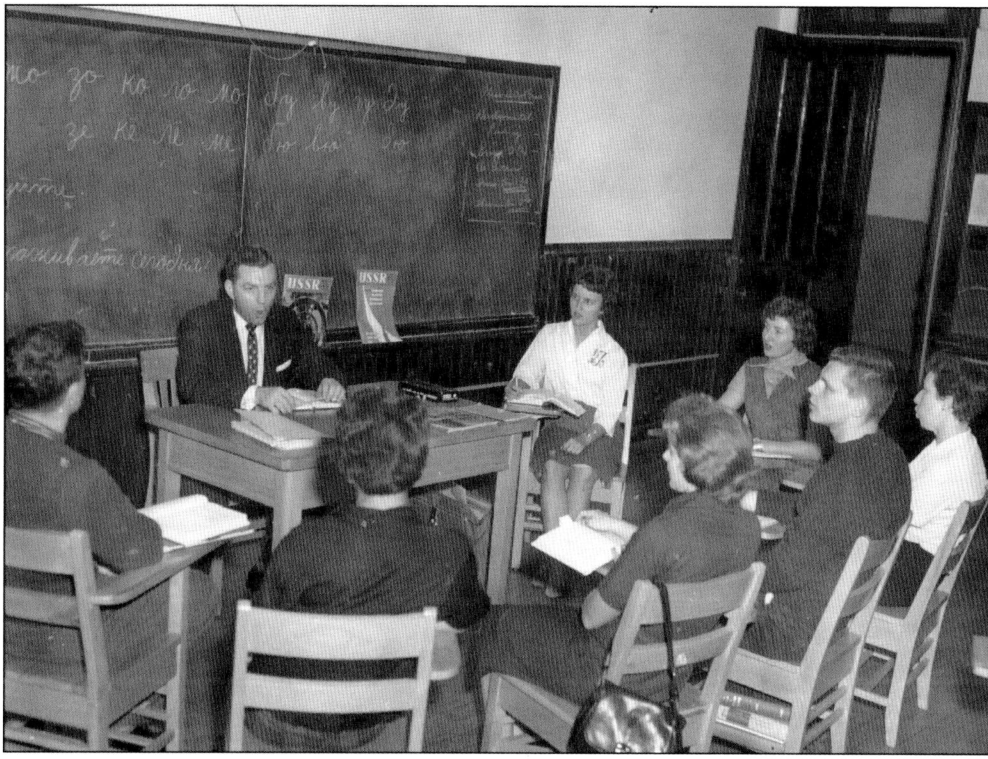

The Russian language was introduced in 1958 when President Rohrbach expanded the modern language studies. Russian was a major language offered in conjunction with the liberal arts degree, which was granted on May 23, 1962. Other languages offered as part of the degree were French, Spanish, and German. On November 10, 1964, Italo L. deFrancesco, who took over as president after Dr. Rohrbach, successfully implemented a graduate teachers program in Russian.

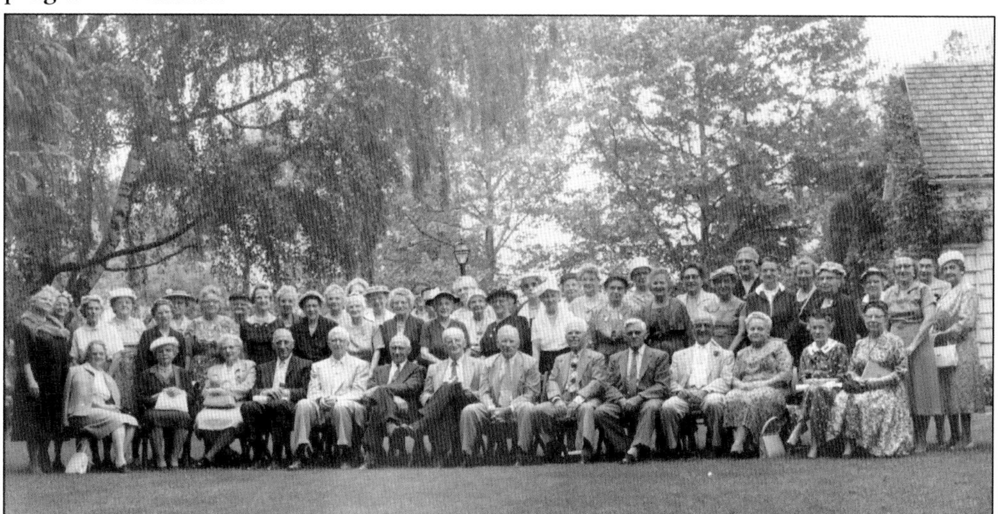

This photograph features the reunion of the KSNS class of 1909. The exact date of this reunion is unknown, but it is estimated to have happened 50 years after their graduation from the normal school. Out of the original 123 classmates, 52 alumni attended this reunion.

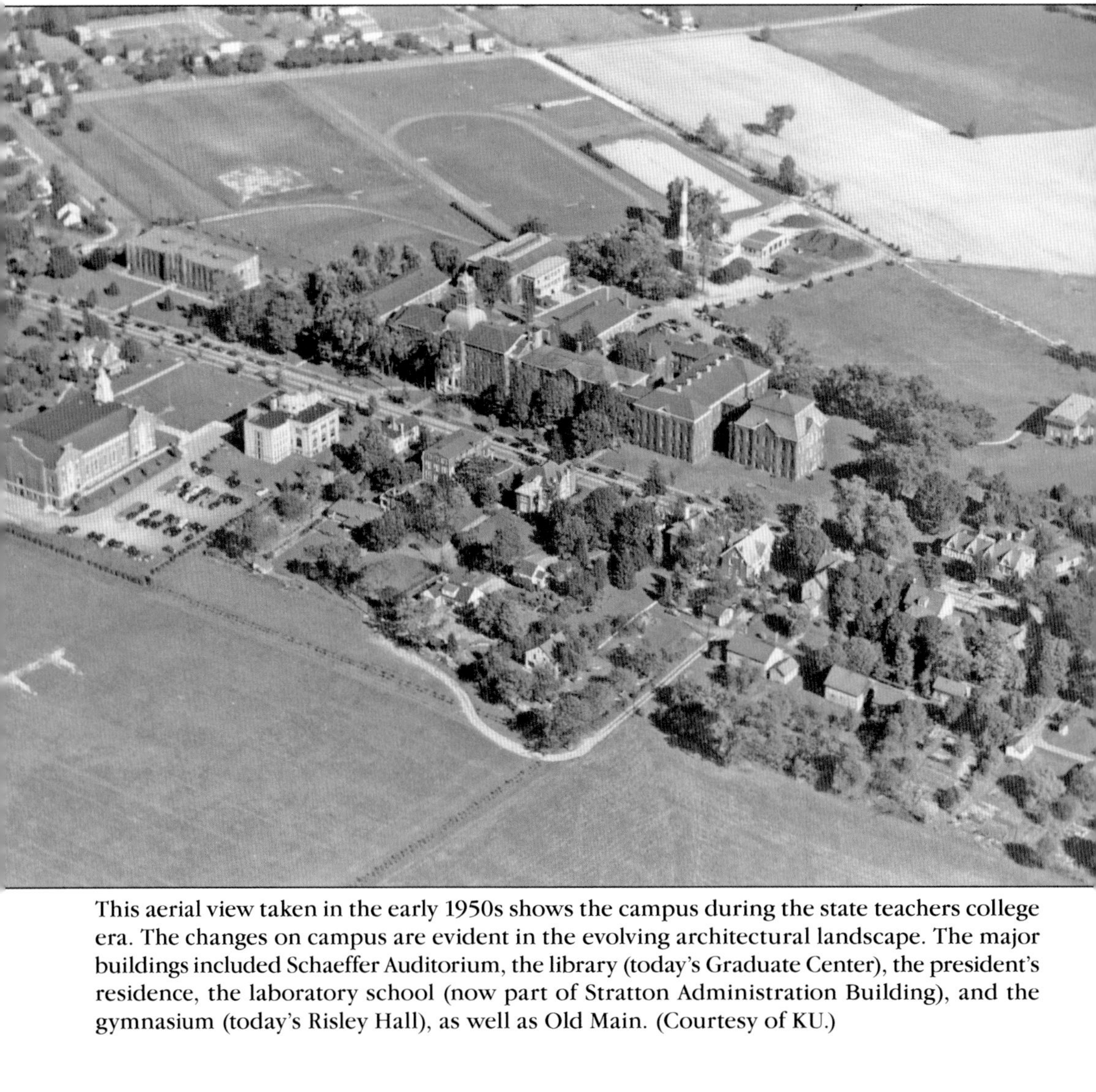

This aerial view taken in the early 1950s shows the campus during the state teachers college era. The changes on campus are evident in the evolving architectural landscape. The major buildings included Schaeffer Auditorium, the library (today's Graduate Center), the president's residence, the laboratory school (now part of Stratton Administration Building), and the gymnasium (today's Risley Hall), as well as Old Main. (Courtesy of KU.)

Three

KUTZTOWN STATE COLLEGE 1960–1983

On December 9, 1959, the state council of education finally approved the school's application to offer the master of education degree in the art and elementary fields, though the amendment to offer graduate work in secondary degrees was delayed. As president, Italo L. deFrancesco continued to pursue the goal of graduate work in the various secondary branches, and on November 10, 1964, his efforts were rewarded. The school had probationary approval for graduate teacher education programs in English, social studies, French, German, Spanish, Russian, biology, and mathematics.

On January 8, 1960, Kutztown State Teachers College became Kutztown State College (KSC) in conformity with common practice in many other states. President deFrancesco lost no time in preparing Kutztown State College for its role as a multipurpose institution by setting up a liberal arts program. The state council of education approved the granting of the bachelor of arts degree in liberal arts in the areas of the humanities, the social sciences, and the natural sciences on May 23, 1962, followed by the bachelor of fine arts degree on April 10, 1963. The first students in the new fine arts curriculum were admitted in January 1964. In the fall of 1964, the language department was completely revised, with 12 professors teaching language courses in French, Spanish, German, and Russian.

In 1966, the school celebrated its 100th anniversary. The centennial celebration included multiple events, along with the publishing of *Beacon on the Hill: A Centennial History of Kutztown State College*, a historical record of the school written by Lee Graver.

Among the many milestones that occurred during the time the school was a state college were the construction of a new library, the conversion of the old library building into the Graduate Center, the 50th anniversary of the art program, the installation of a telescope in the Grim Science Building, and the presentation of some great concerts at Keystone Hall in the 1970s.

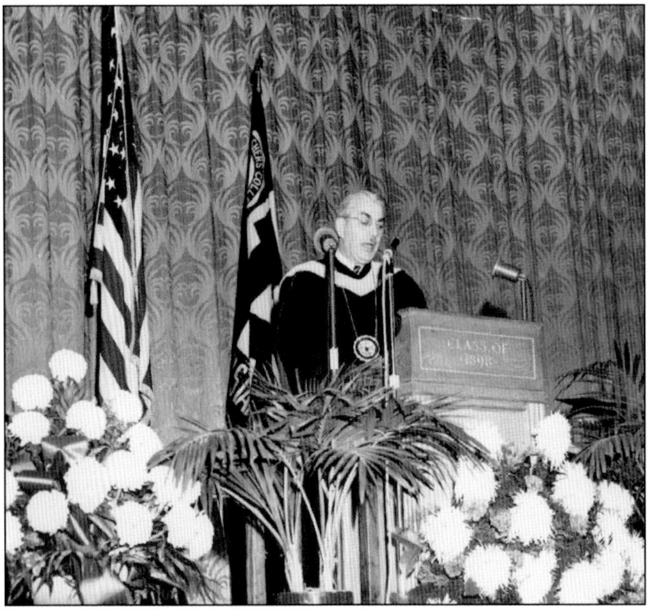

Italo L. deFrancesco (1901–1967) joined Kutztown State College's art department in 1936, and three years later, he became the director of art education, a position he held for 20 years before becoming the school's seventh president, from 1959 to 1967. "Dr. De," as he was affectionately called by his students, passed away while in office on May 27, 1967, due to a respiratory illness.

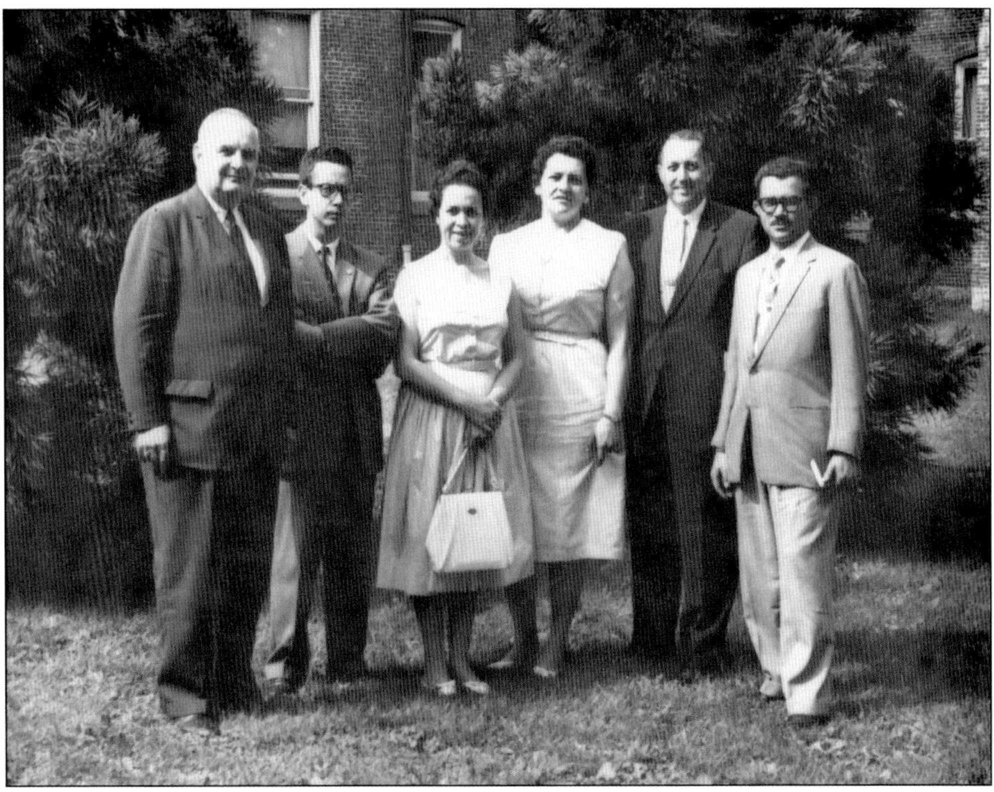

On September 14, 1961, a group of Latin American visitors came to the KSC campus to observe a school of the American Association of Colleges for Teacher Education. From left to right are Cyrus E. Beekey (dean of instruction at Kutztown), Oscar Flores (Guatemala), Eida Badille (Costa Rica), Margarita Guzman (Costa Rica), Ralph Geigle (superintendent of Reading Schools, Reading, Pennsylvania), and Andres Moreno (Nicaragua).

The 100th anniversary of the school was marked with multiple celebrations and events, including the play *One Hundred Yesterdays* written by Ruth E. Bonner, a 1921 graduate of the Keystone State Normal School. The play was performed in Schaeffer Auditorium on the centennial year's Alumni Day, which took place on May 28, 1966. Bonner returned to Kutztown, where she taught English and speech at Kutztown State Teachers College and Kutztown State College until she retired in 1965. In 1975, Bonner Hall was dedicated in her name.

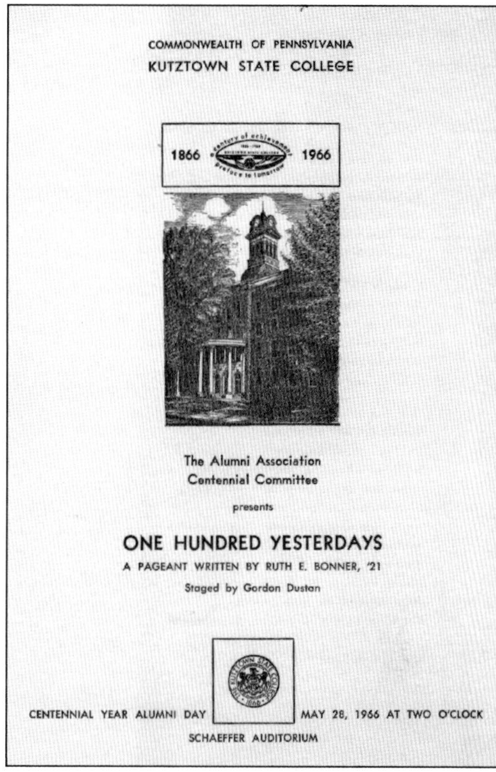

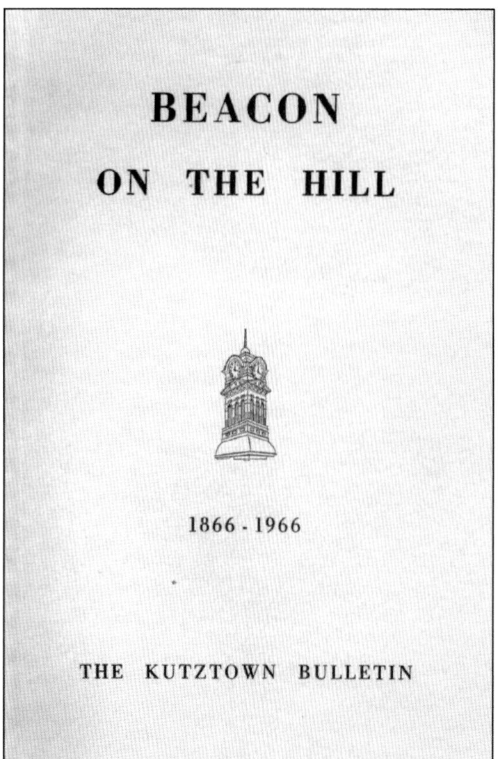

Beacon on the Hill was a centennial history book written by Lee Graver, professor and head of the Department of History and Political Science at Kutztown State College. Graver's book features stories and facts about the school in tremendous detail, dating from the founding of the school as a seminary to its centennial year in 1966.

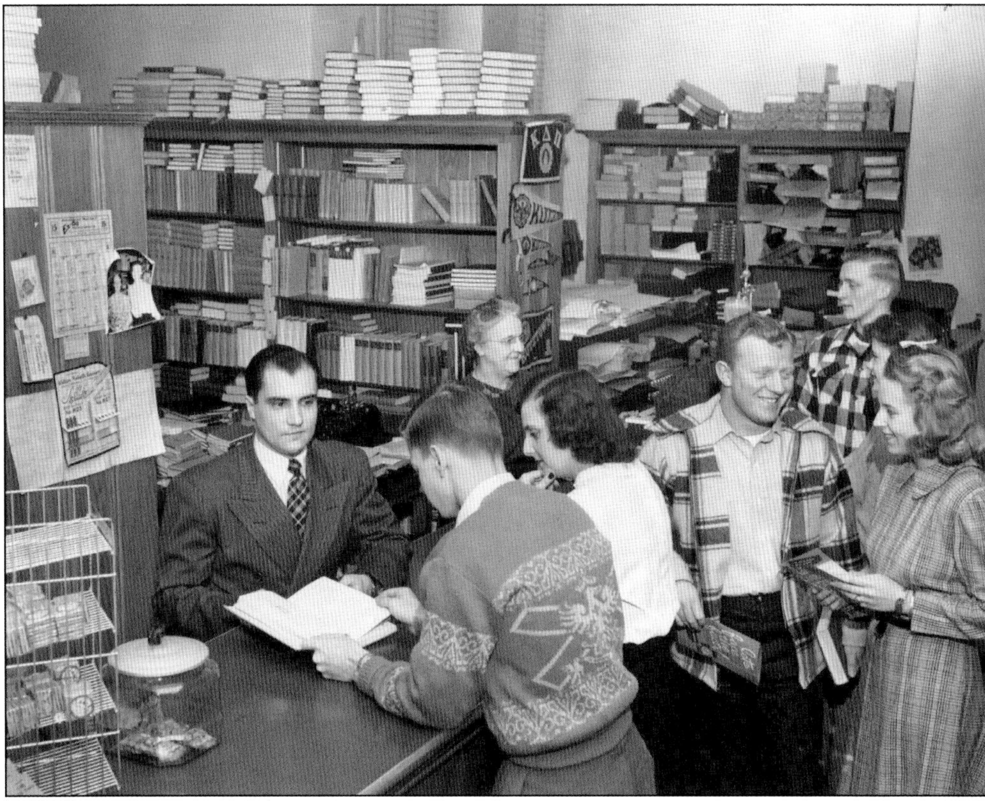

Students at Kutztown have always had the opportunity to purchase books, school supplies, and other merchandise from the school store. The reference library at the normal school was fortified with profits from the bookstore. The current-day student store is run by the Kutztown University Students Services Inc. (KUSSI), which was established in 1997 to generate funds for student activities through retail operations and special events.

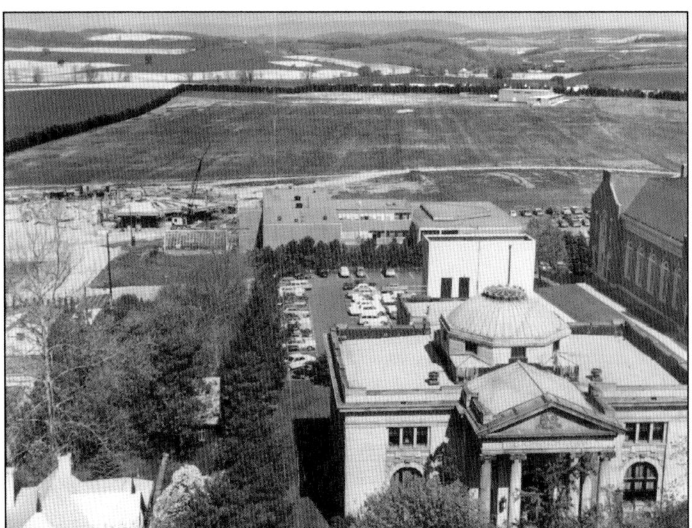

This c. 1966 photograph taken from the Old Main clock tower depicts the north campus. The Grim Science Building, completed in 1967, is seen under construction in the background to the left. Standing in the foreground is the school's original library. Directly behind it is the Boehm Science Center, which was completed in 1962. A 2015 view showing how the campus has evolved can be found on page 127.

Dr. Cyrus Ezra Beekey (1906–1974) started his career at the Kutztown State Teachers College in 1943 as a physics professor. Following President deFrancesco's death, Dr. Beekey was appointed as the eighth president of Kutztown State College and was inaugurated on November 18, 1967. During his term, he oversaw the construction of five buildings, along with an increase in enrollment and faculty. On August 1, 1969, Dr. Beekey retired from Kutztown State College because of a respiratory ailment.

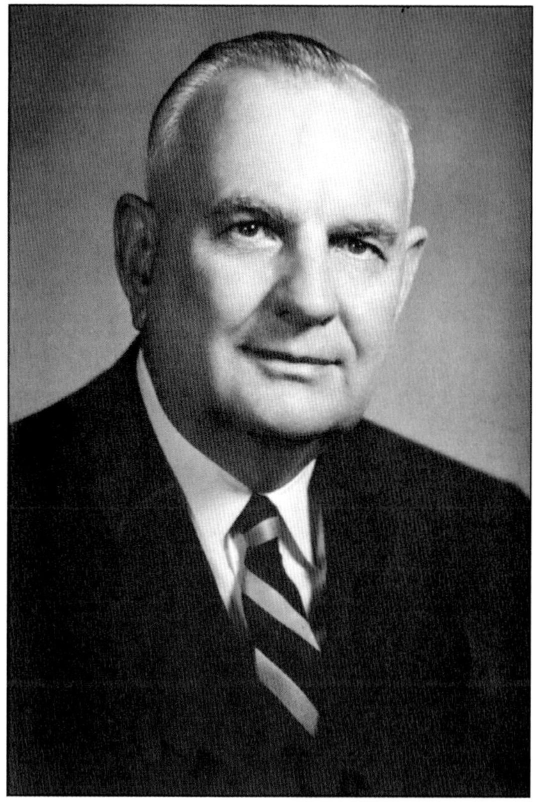

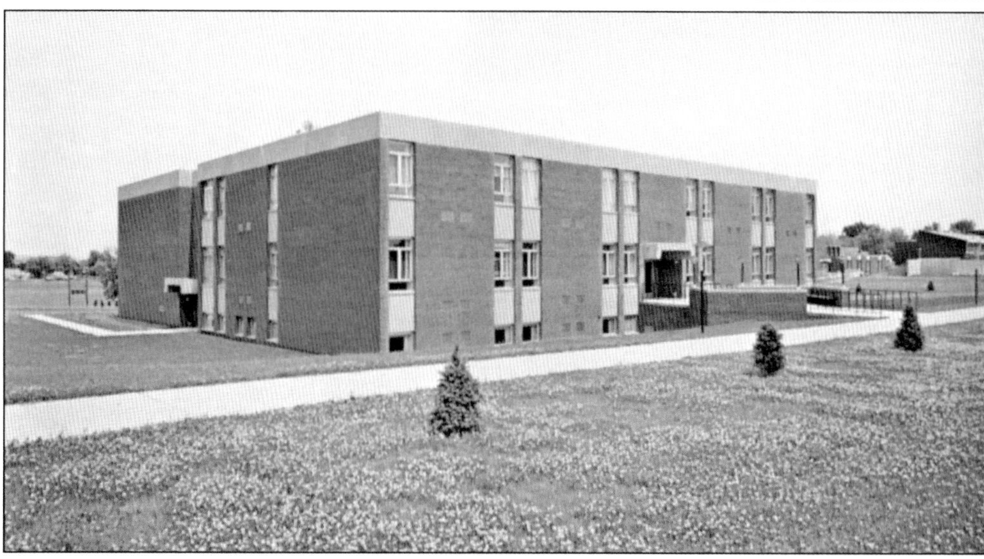

The cornerstone of the World Cultures Building was laid in 1968. Now named in honor of President deFrancesco, the building originally housed the social sciences, foreign languages, history, and political science departments. In 1993–1994, the building was renovated and expanded. Today, it houses the College of Business, the Department of Professional Studies, and the Department of Modern Language Studies. Most students refer to the building as "deFran."

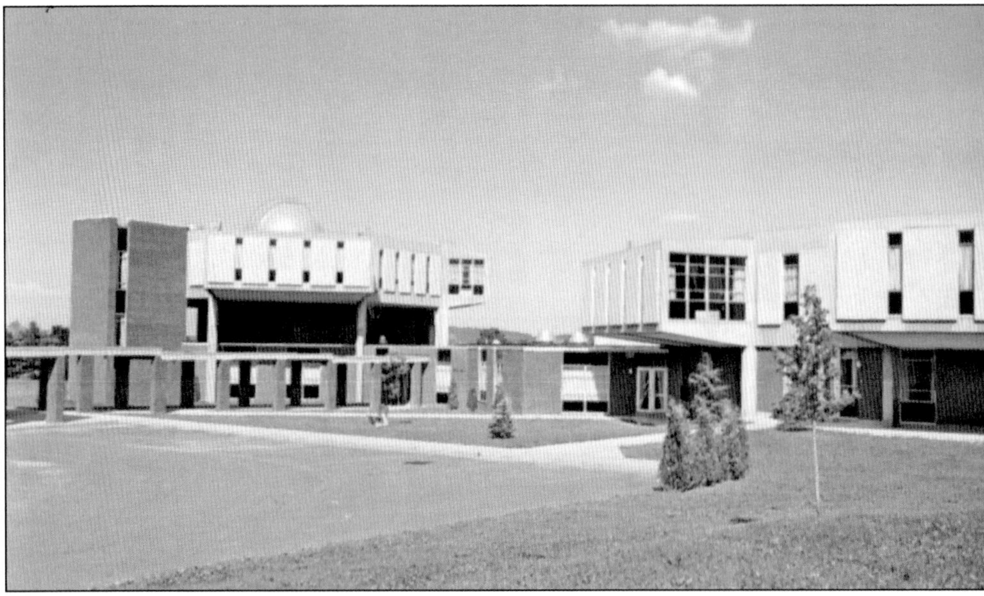

The Grim Science Building was named for 1893 KSNS graduate and science professor Dr. James Stewart Grim to honor his nearly 45 years of service to his students and his alma mater. Completed in 1967, the facility hosts the astronomy program in addition to an observatory and planetarium, originally named the Gruber-Knedler Planetarium and Observatory, where students learn about stars, constellations, and the universe.

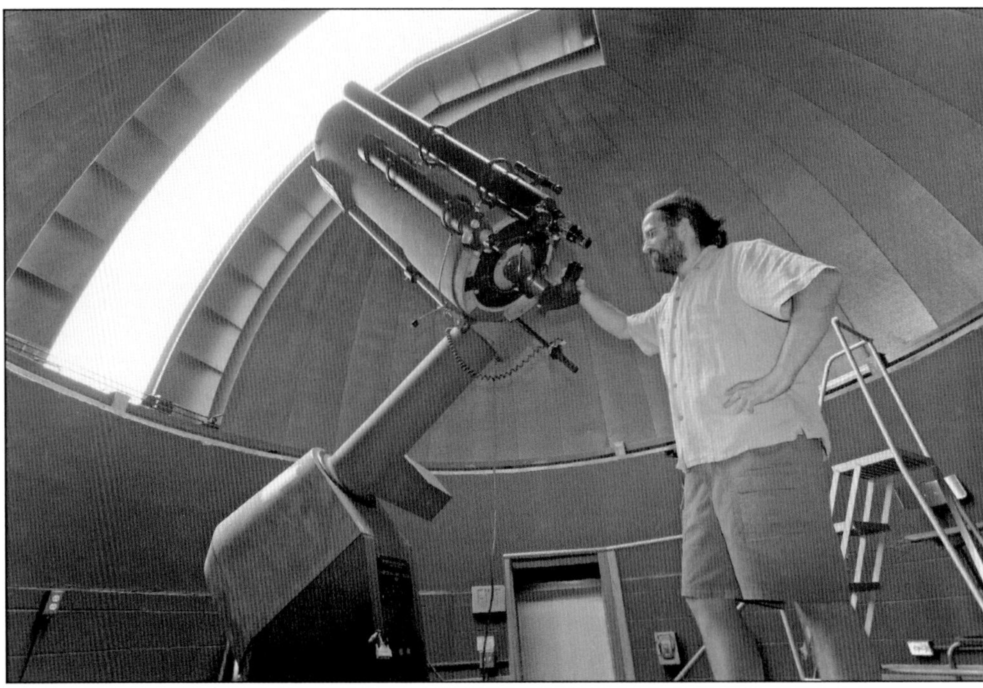

In 1968, a Tinsley Instruments telescope was installed in the observatory of the Grim Science Building. In 2012, the telescope was donated to the Lehigh Valley Amateur Astronomical Society after many years of being used for research. Featured in this photograph is astronomy professor Dr. Phillip Reed. (Photograph by Gary A. Becker, courtesy of Dr. Phillip Reed.)

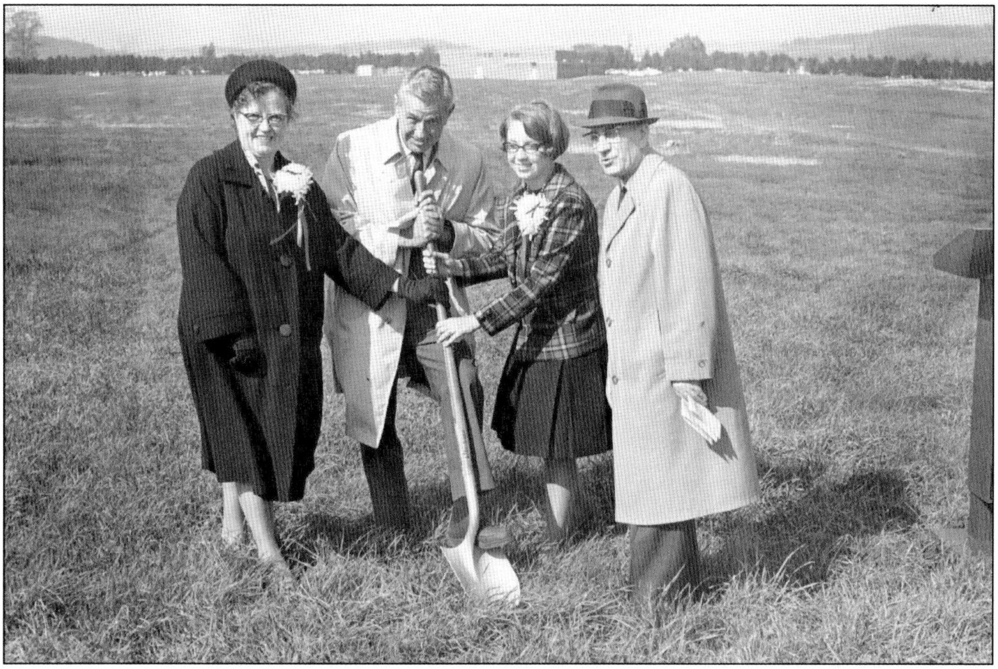

On October 26, 1966, ground was broken for the new library building. For 53 years, the school's original library was located directly across from Old Main, but growing enrollment and the need for more work and study areas required a larger library. Designed to hold 300,000 volumes, the new Rohrbach Library provided space for an updated research and learning center. The building was finished in 1968 at the cost of $1.3 million and was formally dedicated on May 24, 1969. In January 1997, construction was started to nearly double the size of the library. On September 19, 1998, a formal dedication was held for the newly expanded and renovated Rohrbach Library. Changes to the building included additional study spaces and computer wiring. The total cost for the project was over $8 million. Pictured above are, from left to right, head librarian Ruth K. Yost, director of library education Nicholas G. Stevens, college junior and president of Alpha Beta Alpha library fraternity Kathryn P. Kapoteh, and college president Dr. Italo L. deFrancesco. The photograph below depicts the current-day Rohrbach Library after the 1998 renovations. (Below, courtesy of KU.)

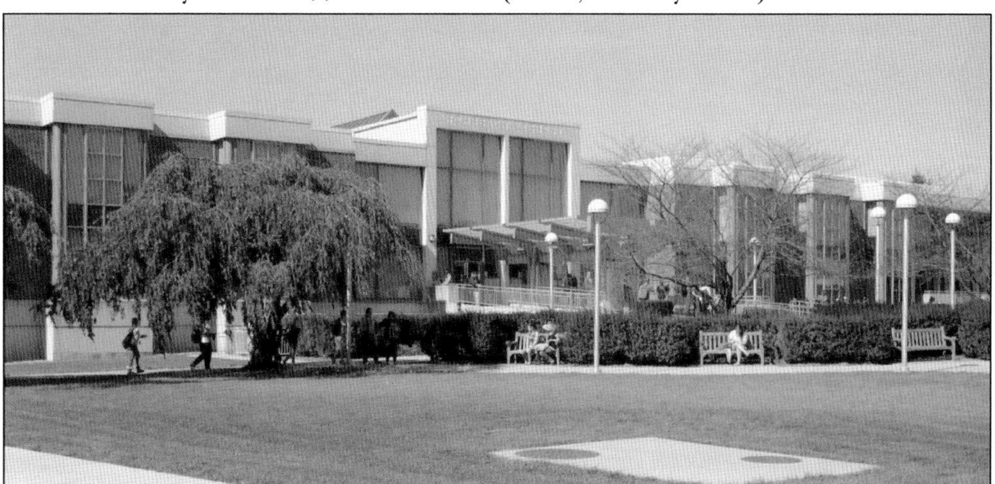

Commonwealth of Pennsylvania
KUTZTOWN STATE COLLEGE
Kutztown, Pennsylvania

Moving Day Schedule - Library Staff

WHO	WHERE	WHAT
Berg	Old Building (all day)	Periodicals
Bond	Old Building (½ day)	900's and Fiction
Borrell	New Building (all day)	Telephone
Fuller	Old Building (all day)	800's and 200's
Holloway	Old Building (all day)	Telephone
Liedberg	Old Building (½ day)	900's and Fiction
Mahle	Old Building (all day)	Mail and messages
Mateer	Old Building (all day)	300's a.m. 000'- Pa. & Ref. p.m.
Mengel	New Building (all day)	Russian
Oswald	New Building (all day)	upper floor
Parry	Old Building (all day)	Sending
Saul	Old Building (all day)	600, 100 & 400 - a.m. 700 - p.m.
Seaman	New Building (all day)	Messages
Sprankle	Old Building (all day)	370's a.m. & 500's p.m.
Toney	New Building (all day)	Periodicals
Woods	New Building (all day)	Periodicals a.m. Reference p.m.
Yost	New Building (all day)	Receiving

On November 14, 1968, students, emeriti professors, library staff, college personnel, community members, faculty, and their families took part in a "book walk" to transfer more than 100,000 volumes to the new library location. More than 2,000 people helped to move the materials a four-block distance between buildings. The book walk started at 8:00 a.m. and finished 75 minutes before the 4:00 p.m. deadline. Commuting students who came out to help were rewarded with a free buffet luncheon in the Georgian Dining Room. Most people volunteered to make 10 trips moving books from one library to the other, but some students managed to do 20 trips.

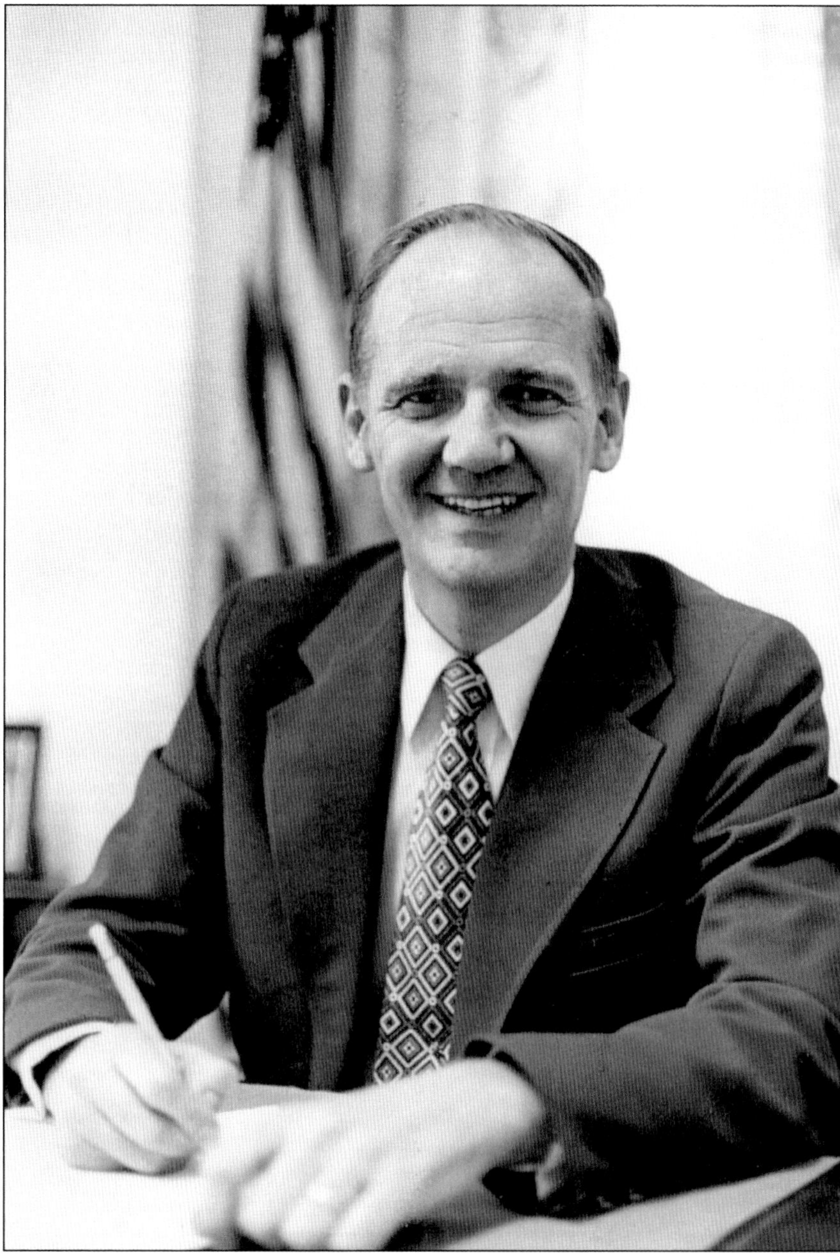

Dr. Lawrence M. Stratton served as Kutztown's ninth president from 1969 to 1987. During his term, the school changed from Kutztown State College to Kutztown University in 1983. Stratton helped to increase the undergraduate programs from 12 to 50 and the graduate programs from 6 to 13. Kutztown's campus grew not only through enrollment but also through academic programs and physical facilities. Stratton was known to have a sense of humor. On April Fools' Day 1974, he showed up to South Dining Hall to serve breakfast to the students. On October 29, 1987, Dr. Stratton died at the age of 59 after a near-yearlong illness while still serving as Kutztown's president. On May 7, 1988, the administration building was renamed in dedication of Stratton's commitment to Kutztown University. Prior to his death, Dr. Stratton was told of the university's plans to name the administration building for him.

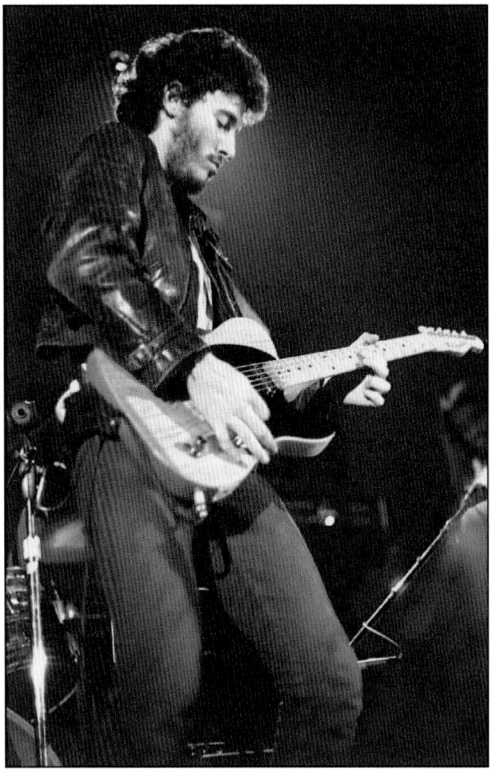

Bruce Springsteen played at Kutztown State College as the opening act for Stevie Wonder on March 29, 1973, supporting the release of *Greetings from Asbury Park*. On July 25–26 1975, Springsteen returned to Kutztown as a two-evening headliner. The set lists survive from these concerts, as well as bootleg recordings. Several songs from the soon-to-be-released *Born to Run* album were performed, including "Born to Run" and "Thunder Road." (Courtesy of Bill Uhrich.)

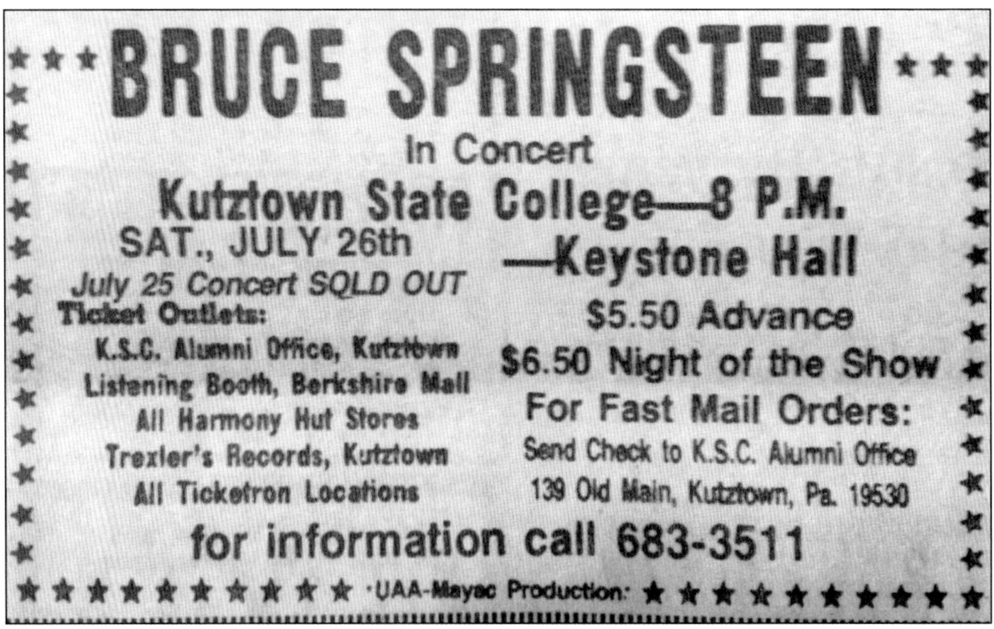

Springsteen and the band stayed at the Campus Inn during the 1975 concerts. Before the show on July 25, Springsteen's manager arrived with an acetate of *Born to Run*, and the musicians listened to the recording, but Springsteen started second-guessing himself and flung the acetate into the motel pool and wanted to rerecord. About a month later, that album was released, and Bruce Springsteen was a new sensation. (Courtesy of Bill Uhrich.)

The first half of the 1970s brought a wide range of musicians to the Kutztown campus, some of whom were not yet well known nationally. In 1971, Chicago and Jethro Tull arrived. Yes performed on March 7, 1972, while on their Fragile Tour. Procol Harum came in 1974, and the next year, Frank Zappa and Captain Beefheart appeared. Kutztown State College played a role in the rise of some of the era's great artists.

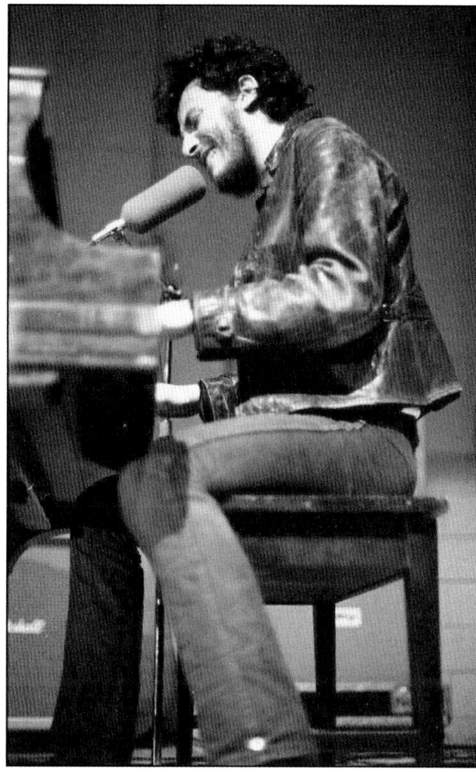

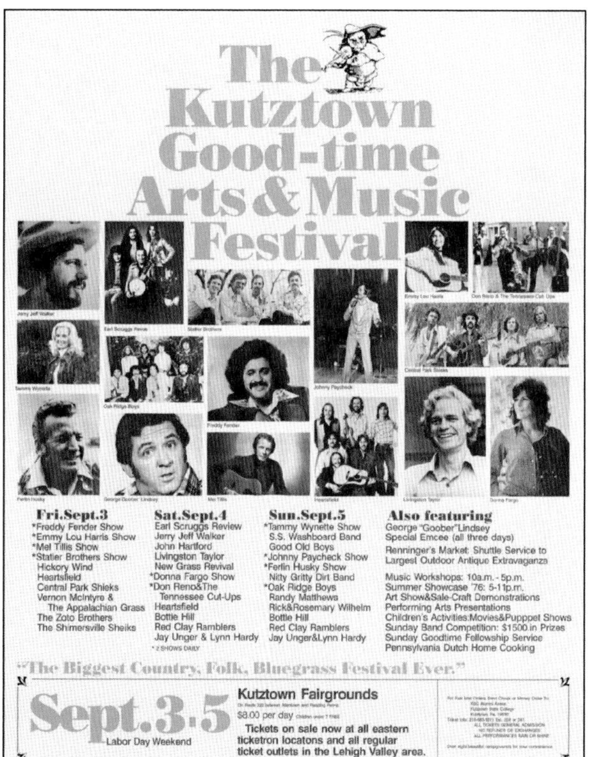

On Labor Day weekend 1976, the Kutztown Fairgrounds were home to the town's final celebration of the nation's bicentennial. Presented by the Kutztown Alumni Association, the Kutztown Good-time Arts & Music Festival featured at least 28 top country and bluegrass performers, including Freddy Fender, the Oak Ridge Boys, Emmylou Harris, and New Grass Revival. George "Goober" Lindsey from *The Andy Griffith Show* emceed. (Courtesy of Keith J. Weidner.)

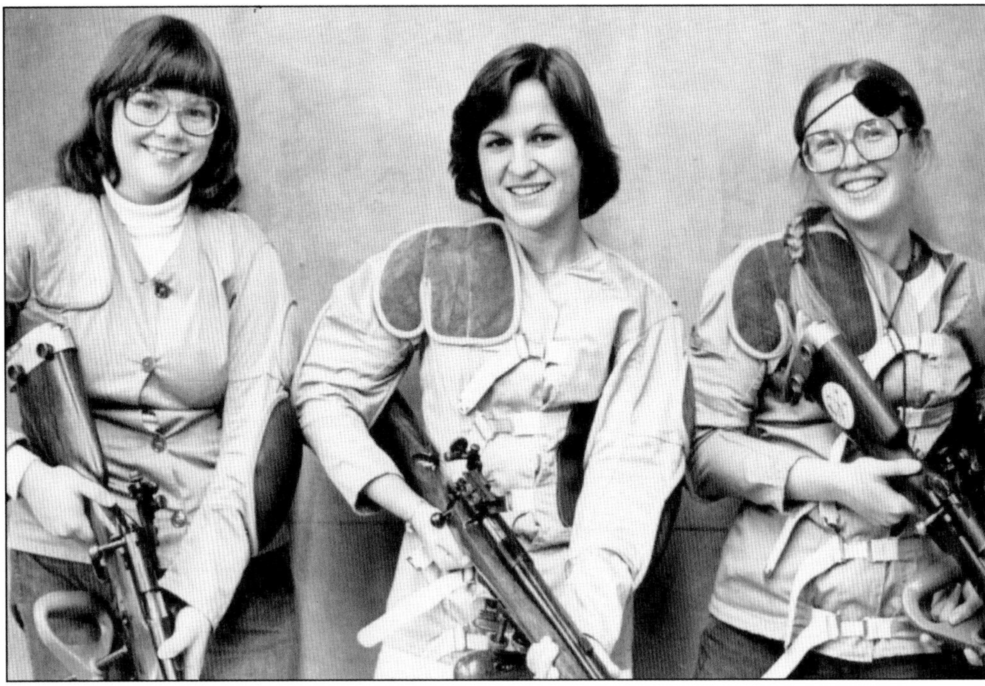

The rifle team competed throughout the 1970s and 1980s. Its rifle range was located in the basement of the Keystone Arena. The team was known to produce talented shooters, including Diane Walzer (left). During her sophomore year of 1975–1976, Walzer was one of the top four women shooters in the Eastern Pennsylvania Intercollegiate Rifle League.

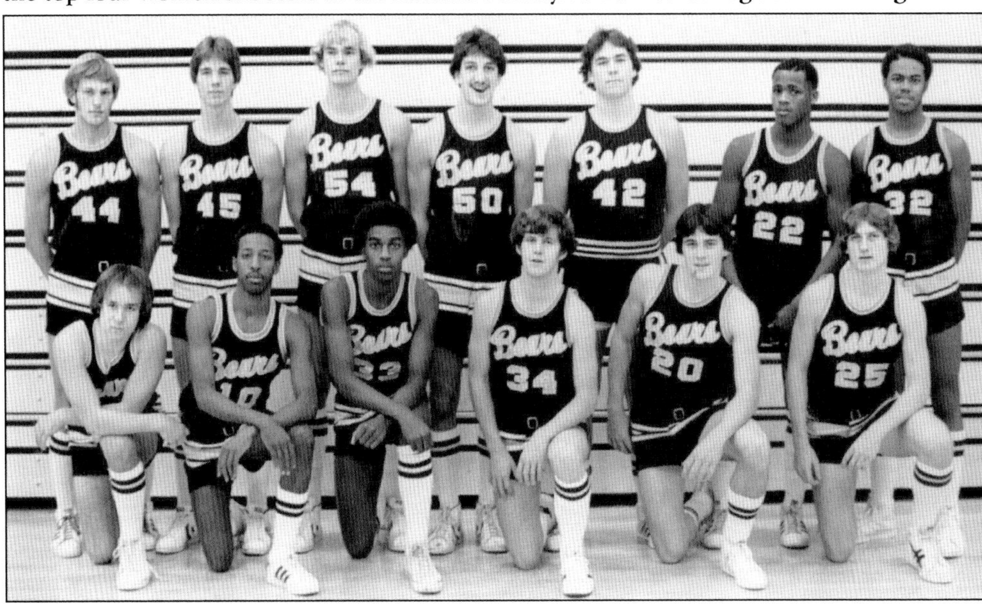

Men's basketball is thought to have come to the campus by 1902, before the completion of the new gymnasium (now Risley Hall). The program reached a high level of success in the late 1910s, winning two Pennsylvania State Normal School championships. The program's first title, and the first championship in any sport at the school, came in 1917. The 1978–1979 team pictured carried on the long-standing basketball tradition at Kutztown University.

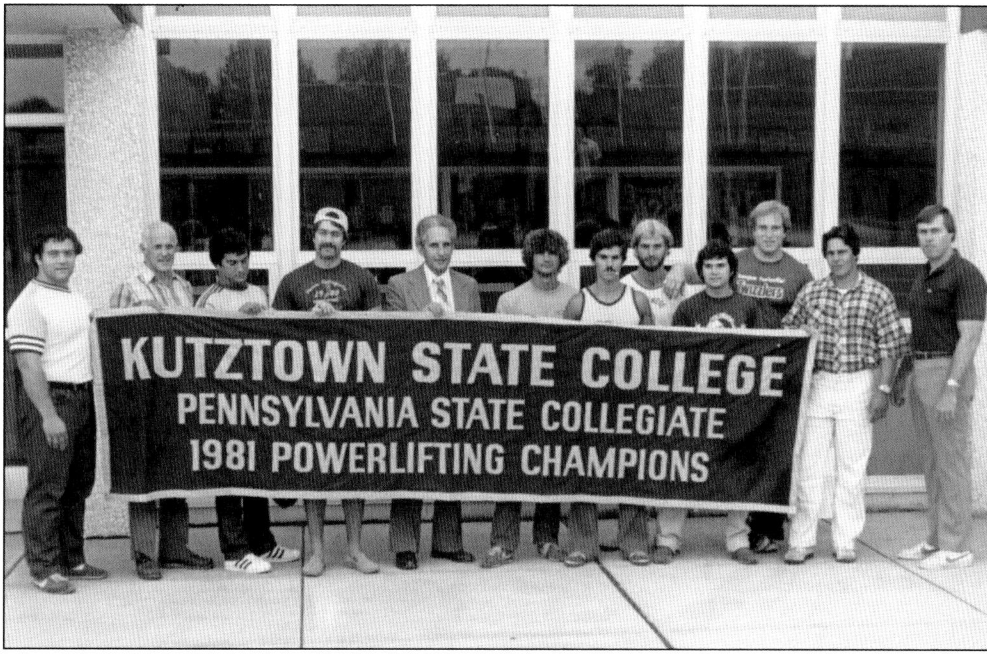

Started in a dorm basement in 1979, the Kutztown State College's powerlifters proved themselves as worthy athletes. Founded by Mark Sabatino (class of 1981), the team earned the Pennsylvania Powerlifting Champions title in 1979, 1980, and 1981. On March 19–21, 1981, Kutztown State College hosted the National Collegiate Powerlifting Championships. With a budget of only $200, the Kutztown powerlifters took home the title. (Courtesy of KU.)

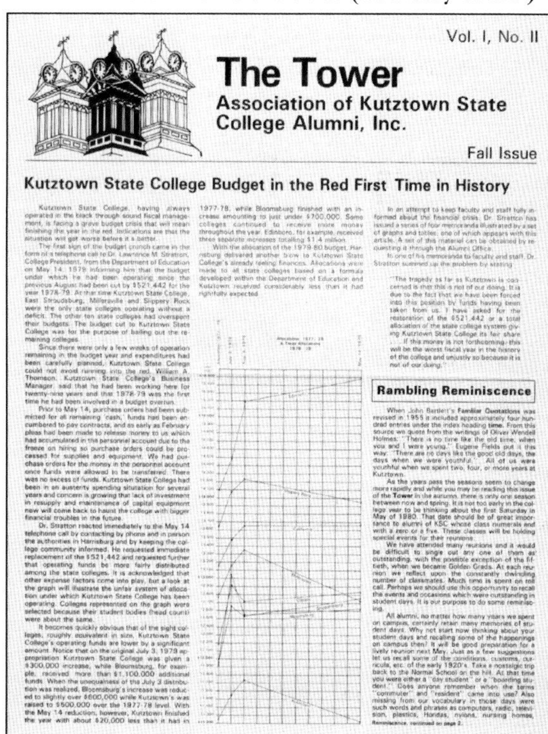

Vol. I, No. II

The Tower

Association of Kutztown State College Alumni, Inc.

Fall Issue

Kutztown State College Budget in the Red First Time in History

Kutztown State College, having always operated in the black through sound fiscal management, is facing a grave budget crisis that will mean finishing the year in the red. Indications are that the situation will get worse before it s better.

The first sign of the budget crunch came in the form of a telephone call to Dr. Lawrence M. Stratton, College President, from the Department of Education on May 14, 1979 informing him that the budget under which he had been operating since the previous August had been cut by $521,442 for the year 1978-79. At that time Kutztown State College, East Stroudsburg, Millersville and Slippery Rock were the only state colleges operating without a deficit. The other ten state colleges had overspent their budgets. The budget cut to Kutztown State College was for the purpose of bailing out the remaining colleges.

Since there were only a few weeks of operation remaining in the budget year and expenditures had been carefully planned, Kutztown State College could not avoid running into the red. William A. Thomson, Kutztown State College's Business Manager, said that he had been working here for twenty-nine years and that 1978-79 was the first time he had been involved in a budget overrun.

Prior to May 14, purchase orders had been submitted for all remaining 'cash,' funds had been encumbered to pay contracts, and as early as February pleas had been made to release money to us which had accumulated in the personnel account due to the freeze on hiring so purchase orders could be processed for supplies and equipment. We had purchase orders for the money in the personnel account once funds were allowed to be transferred. There was no excess of funds. Kutztown State College had been in an austerity spending situtation for several years and concern is growing that lack of investment in resupply and maintenance of capital equipment now will come back to haunt the college with bigger financial troubles in the future.

Dr. Stratton reacted immediately to the May 14 telephone call by contacting by phone and in person the authorities in Harrisburg and by keeping the college community informed. He requested immediate replacement of the $521,442 and requested further that operating funds be more fairly distributed among the state colleges. It is acknowledged that other expense factors come into play, but a look at the graph will illustrate the unfair system of allocation under which Kutztown State College has been operating. Colleges represented on the graph were selected because their student bodies (head count) were about the same.

It becomes quickly obvious that of the eight colleges, roughly equivalent in size, Kutztown State College's operating funds are lower by a significant amount. Notice that on the original July 3, 1978 appropriation Kutztown State College was given a $300,000 increase, while Bloomsburg, for example, received more than $1,100,000 additional funds. When the unequalness of the July 3 distribution was realized, Bloomsburg's increase was reduced to slightly over $600,000 while Kutztown's was raised to $500,000 over the 1977-78 level. With the May 14 reduction, however, Kutztown finished the year with about $20,000 less than it had in 1977-78, while Bloomsburg finished with an increase amounting to just under $700,000. Some colleges continued to receive more money throughout the year. Edinboro, for example, received three separate increases totaling $1.4 million.

With the allocation of the 1979-80 budget, Harrisburg delivered another blow to Kutztown State College's already feeling finances. Allocations were made to all state colleges based on a formula developed within the Department of Education and Kutztown received considerably less than it had rightfully expected.

In an attempt to keep faculty and staff fully informed about the financial crisis, Dr. Stratton has issued a series of four memoranda illustrated by a set of graphs and tables, one of which appears with this article. A set of this material can be obtained by requesting it through the Alumni Office.

In one of his memoranda to faculty and staff, Dr. Stratton summed up the problem by stating:

> "The tragedy as far as Kutztown is concerned is that this is not of our doing. It is due to the fact that we have been forced into this position by funds having been taken from us. I have asked for the restoration of the $521,442 or a total allocation of the state college system giving Kutztown State College its fair share . . . If this money is not forthcoming, this will be the worst fiscal year in the history of the college and unjustly so because it is not of our doing."

Rambling Reminiscence

When John Bartlett's **Familiar Quotations** was revised in 1955 it included approximately four hundred entries under the index heading **time**. From this source we quote from the writings of Oliver Wendell Holmes: "There is no time like the old time, when you and I were young." Eugene Fields put it this way: "There are no days like the good old days, the days when we were youthful." All of us were youthful when we spent two, four, or more years at Kutztown.

As the years pass the seasons seem to change more rapidly and while you may be reading this issue of the **Tower** in the autumn, there is only one season between now and spring. It is not too early in the college year to be thinking about the first Saturday in May of 1980. That date should be of great importance to alumni of KSC whose class numerals end with a zero or a five. These classes will be holding special events for their reunions.

We have attended many reunions and it would be difficult to single out any one of them as outstanding, with the possible exception of the fiftieth, when we became Golden Grads. At each reunion we reflect upon the constantly dwindling number of classmates. Much time is spent on roll call. Perhaps we should use this opportunity to recall the events and occasions which were outstanding in student days. It is our purpose to do some reminiscing.

All alumni, no matter how many years we spent on campus, certainly retain many memories of student days. Why not start now thinking about your student days and recalling some of the happenings on campus then? It will be good preparation for a lively reunion next May. Just as a few suggestions let us recall some of the conditions, customs, curricula, etc. of the early 1920's. Take a nostalgic trip back to the Normal School on the hill. At that time you were either a "day student" or a "boarding student." Does anyone remember when the terms "commuter" and "resident" came into use? Also missing from our vocabulary in those days were such words and phrases as computers, radio, television, plastics, Hondas, nylons, nursing homes,

Reminiscence, continued on page 2.

The *Tower*, created by the Kutztown State College Alumni Association, was first published as an alumni newsletter in 1979. Today, it is a full-color magazine published biannually. The *Tower* helps share news, special events, and memories of the school with alumni and others. Kutztown alumni are encouraged to submit their life events to the *Tower* for publication.

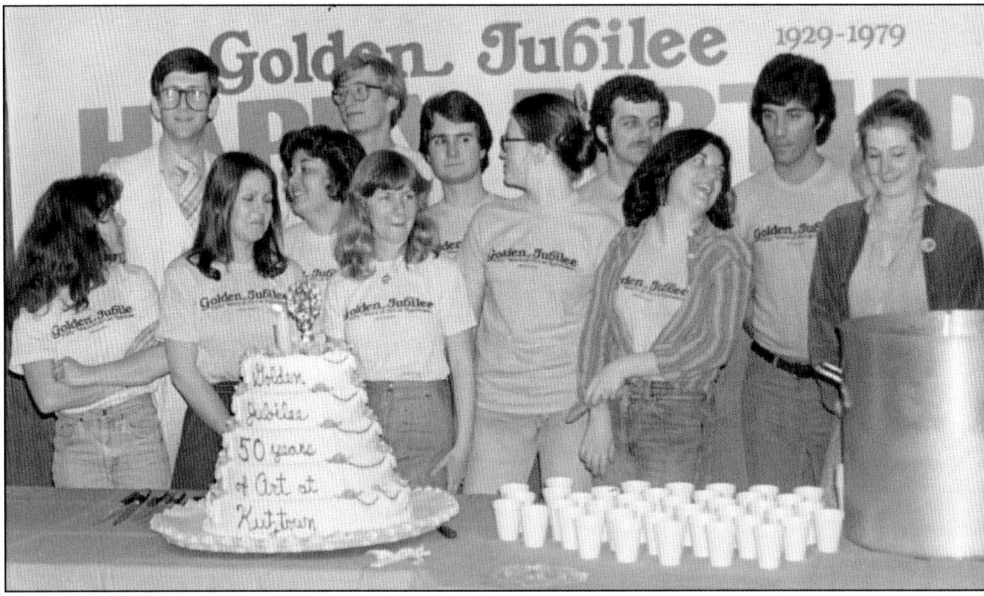

In 1979, Kutztown State College celebrated 50 years of art with its Golden Jubilee. The special occasion celebrated the expansion of degrees that included the bachelor of science in art education and a bachelor of fine arts. The committee, comprised of 11 students and three faculty members, invited the campus to the Jubilee party held on April 2, 1979. As pictured, Golden Jubilee T-shirts were printed for the occasion.

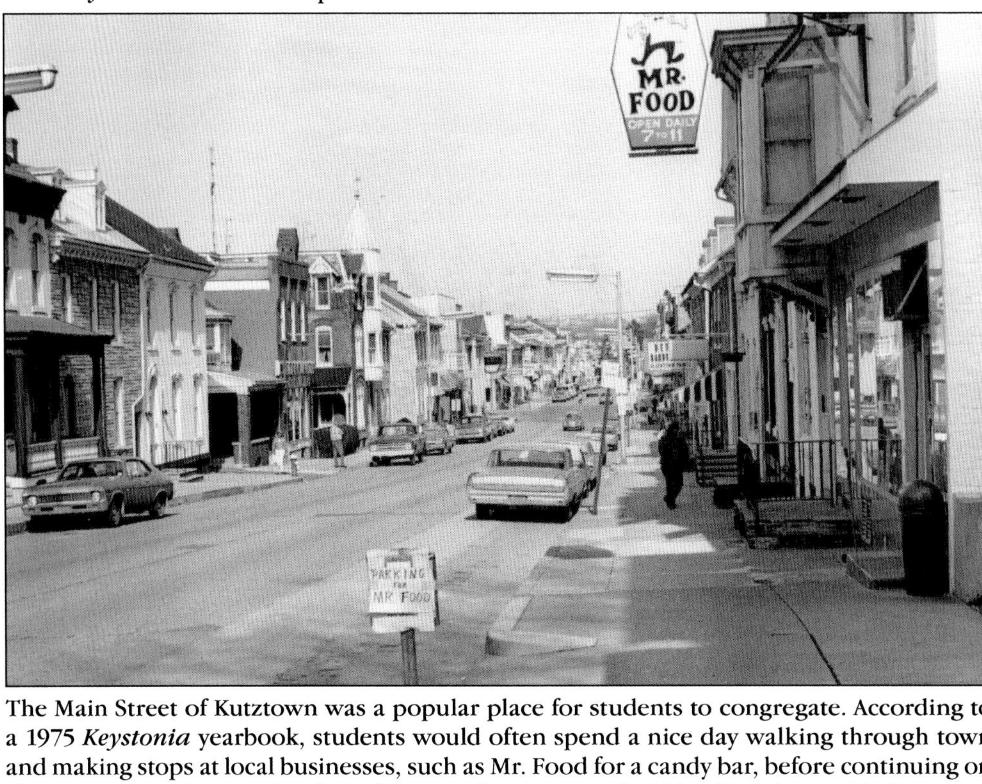

The Main Street of Kutztown was a popular place for students to congregate. According to a 1975 *Keystonia* yearbook, students would often spend a nice day walking through town and making stops at local businesses, such as Mr. Food for a candy bar, before continuing on their journey. Other yearbooks indicate students enjoyed visiting Renningers Market.

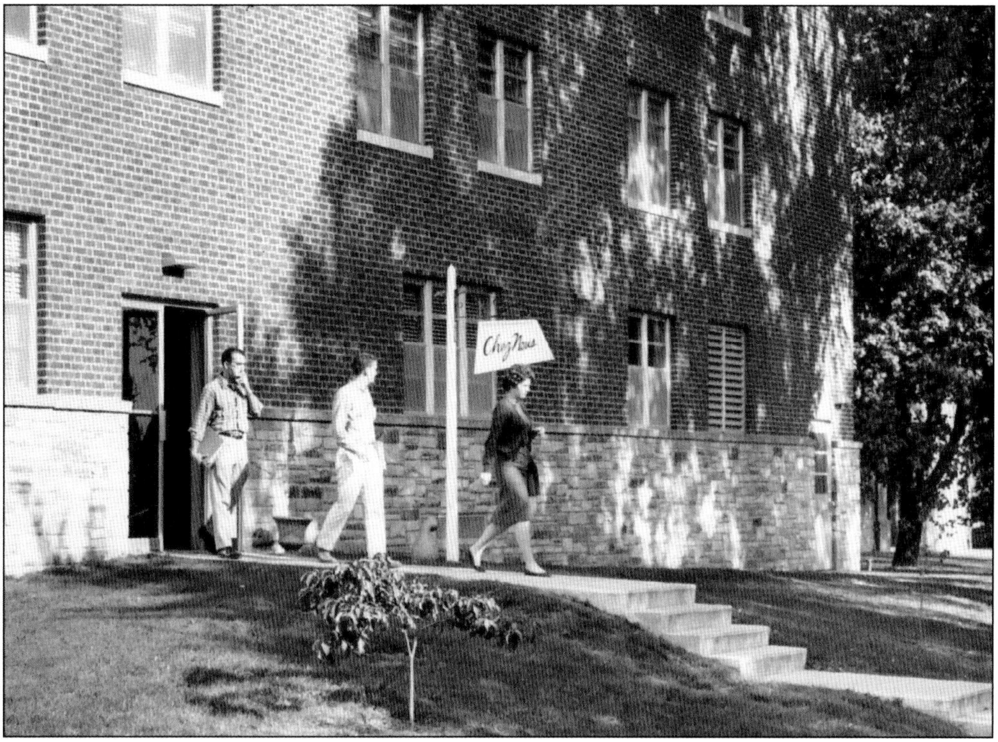

A favorite hangout from 1960 until 1990 was Chez Nous, a snack bar and lounge for students on the south side of campus. Originally located in Rothermel Hall, Chez Nous was moved under the Georgian Dining Room around 1983 and remained there until the late 1990s. Tous Chez, its north campus cousin, was frequented by students for snacks and as a place to hang out between classes.

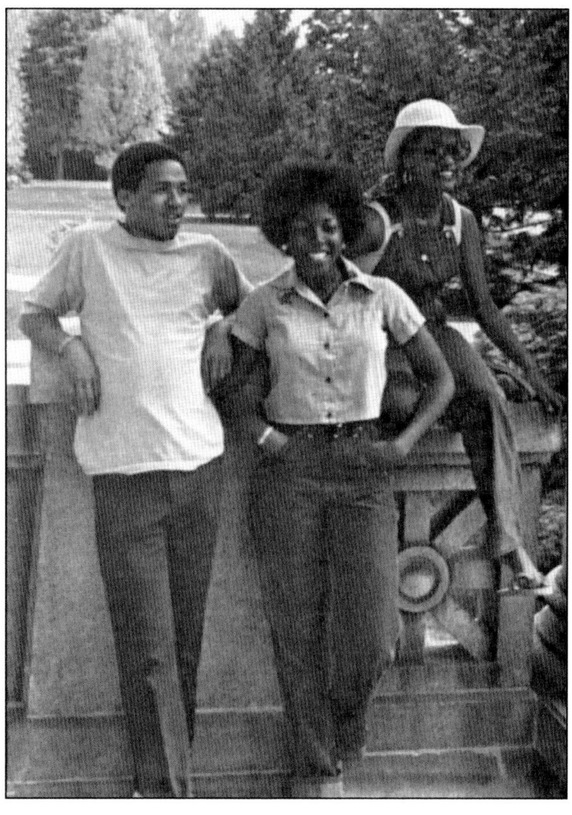

In the early days of Keystone State Normal School, students began their education at the school as early as eighth grade. Because of this, there were strict rules in place to ensure separation of the sexes. Unless given special permission to do so, students of the opposite sex were forbidden to mingle. With changing times, rules were relaxed, which allowed male and female students to eventually interact freely, as seen here.

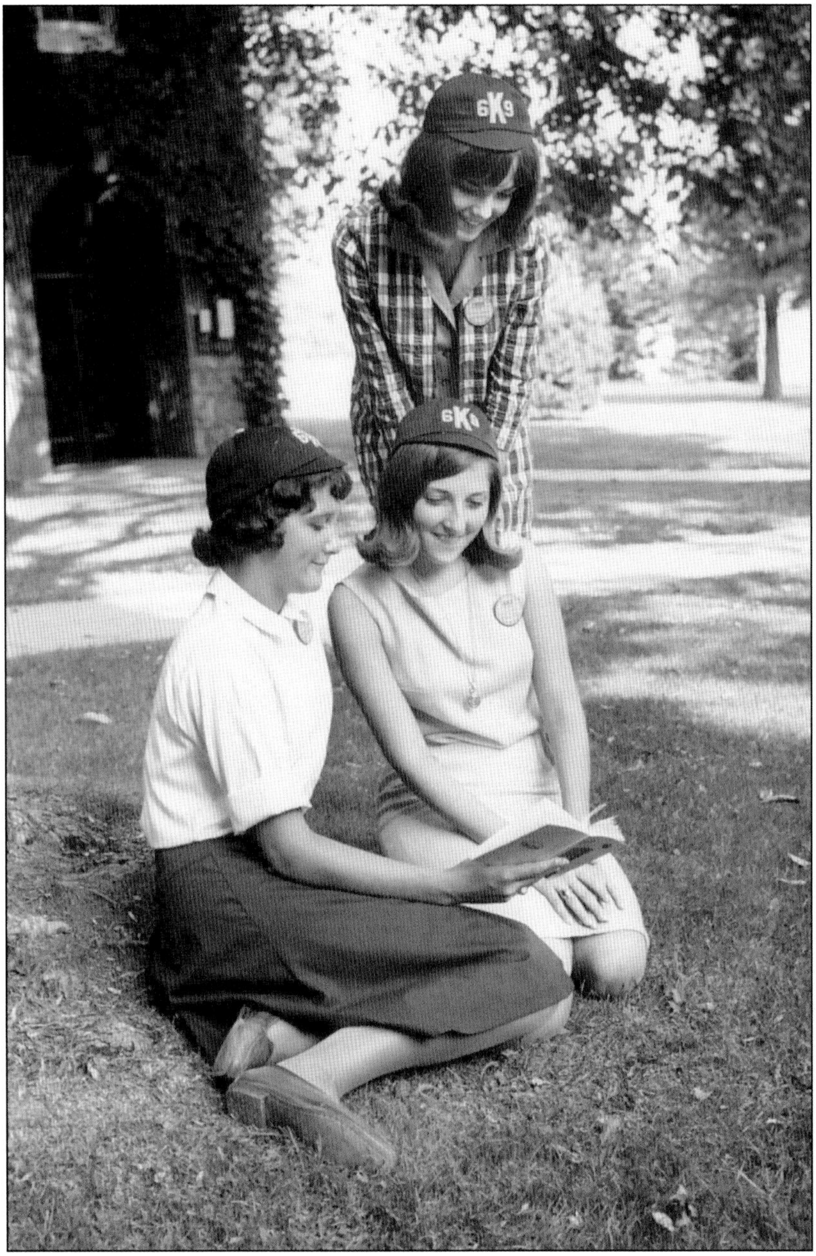

Featured in this image are freshmen students from the class of 1969. Each girl has on a "dink," sometimes called a freshman beanie, which denotes her graduation year. Freshmen were required to wear these, as well as the "frosh pins" each girl has on her shirt. These signifiers made freshmen stand out to the upperclassmen. Many graduates who were required to wear dinks have said they had to be prepared if an upperclassman asked questions or made them sing the alma mater. It is unknown when this tradition started, but the oldest known dink is from the class of 1905. In 1971, the last dinks were handed out to freshmen of the class of 1974. According to several alumni, when the school ran out of dinks, students were required to purchase material and make their own. Wayne's Drygoods, in Kutztown borough, is most likely where students went to purchase those supplies.

Four

KUTZTOWN UNIVERSITY 1983–PRESENT

On July 1, 1983, Kutztown State College became Kutztown University of Pennsylvania, part of Pennsylvania's State System of Higher Education. More commonly, the school is known as Kutztown University, or KU for short. Kutztown University offers a wide range of bachelor and master's degree programs across its four colleges: the College of Business, the College of Education, the College of Liberal Arts and Sciences, and the College of Visual and Performing Arts.

Students can individualize their experiences by adding the honors program or study abroad opportunities to their academic studies. In 2015, Kutztown University received approval to offer its first doctoral program, the doctor of social work, in conjunction with Millersville University under the College of Liberal Arts and Sciences. In 2016, the Pennsylvania State System of Higher Education Board of Governors approved Kutztown University to grant a doctorate in education in transformational teaching and learning.

Kutztown University offers a variety of academic majors and minors, along with a diverse mix of extracurricular activities, including academic organizations, clubs, and multicultural and athletic programs. Both men's and women's intercollegiate sports are offered, as well as several different fraternities and sororities.

In this era, Kutztown University emerged as a modern university that prepares its students to take on the challenges of the world around them. With dynamic faculty educated at some of the finest academic institutions, Kutztown University's professors bring world-class experience to their classrooms and are committed to helping their students succeed. Kutztown is large enough to be comprehensive yet small enough to be personal, ensuring that students have the educational opportunities they need to complete their degree requirements and graduate to pursue a successful career.

Reaching the sesquicentennial milestone allows Kutztown University to look back on its unrivaled past as a teacher training institute while looking forward to its unlimited future offering its students countless opportunities to succeed.

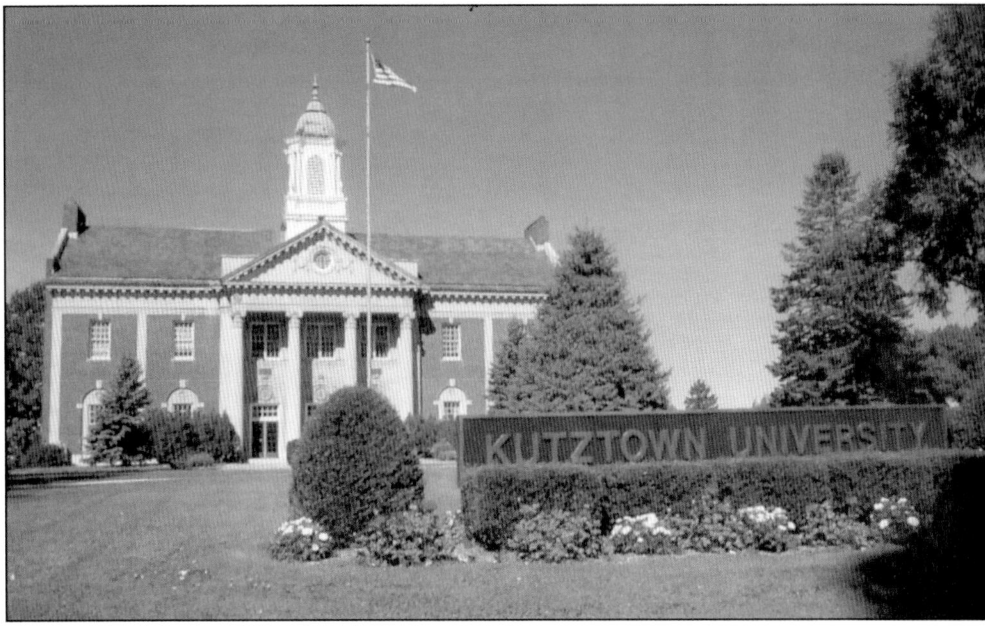

Kutztown University celebrates its 150th year as a state school on September 15, 2016. The university will cap its yearlong sesquicentennial celebration on the school's anniversary by placing a time capsule in its Alumni Plaza. The time capsule will be opened on September 15, 2066, Kutztown University's bicentennial year. (Photograph by Anthony L. Iezzi Photography Service, courtesy of Jason Graver.)

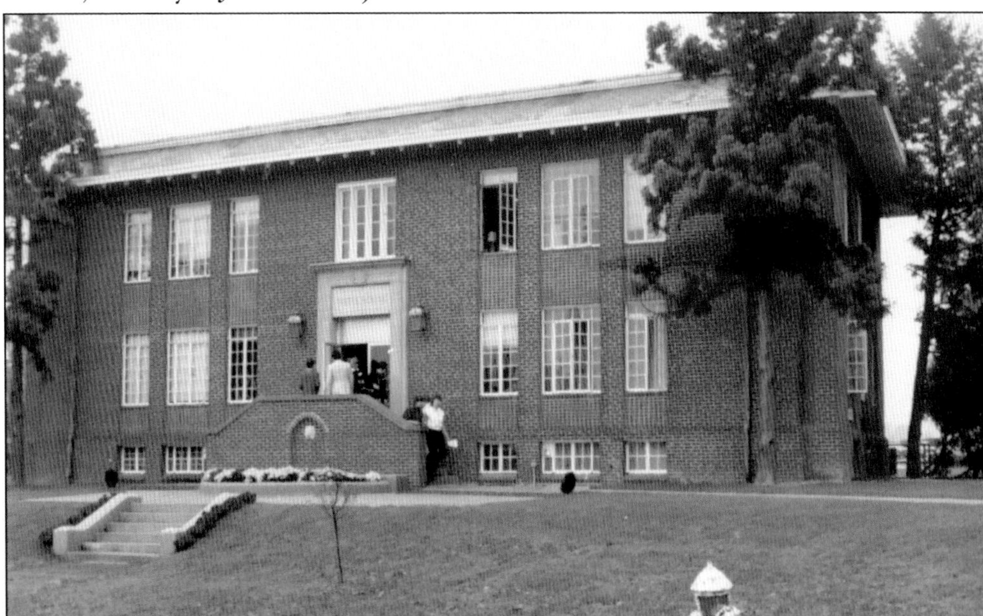

John B. White was a 1947 graduate of Kutztown State Teachers College. After graduation, White returned and served Kutztown for 22 years in various positions, including hall director, dean of men, director of athletics, and assistant to the president. In 1985, five years after White died unexpectedly, a residence hall for 36 international and computer science students was named for him. Currently, the John B. White House contains the Multicultural Center.

On May 6, 1989, Dr. David E. McFarland was inaugurated as the 10th president of Kutztown University. During his time as president, the Pennsylvania German Cultural Heritage Center was created, and the Kutztown University Foundation became responsible for the Kutztown Folk Festival. The university's honors program also grew in size from 35 students to 220. Upon retiring in 2002, McFarland moved to Tampa, Florida, where he works at Penson Associates. (Courtesy of KUR.)

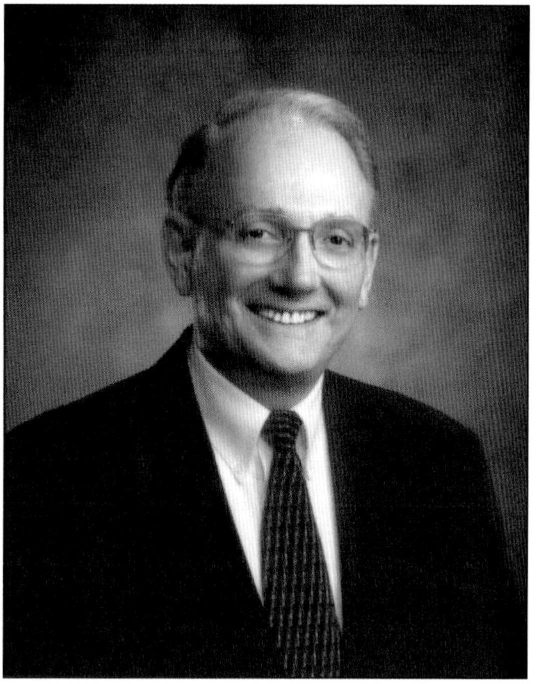

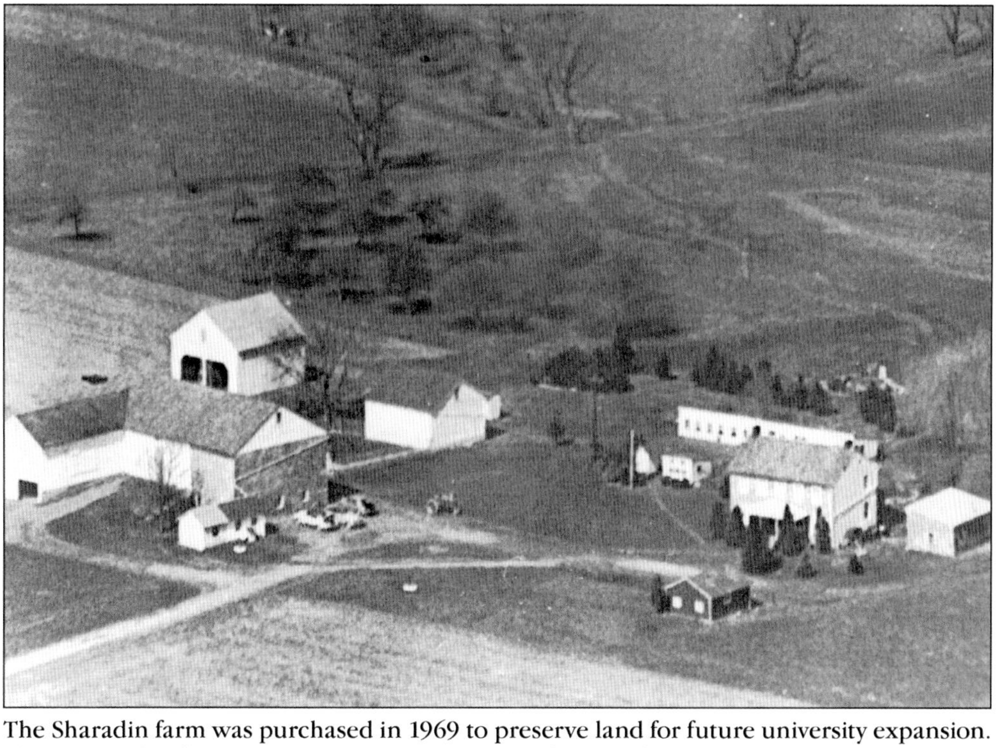

The Sharadin farm was purchased in 1969 to preserve land for future university expansion. The initial plan for the property was to place the football field and parking lots there. The stadium ended up on the south side of the campus, and the farmhouse and fields were rented. President McFarland realized that, without a purpose, the slowly deteriorating farm buildings were not likely to remain standing indefinitely. (Courtesy of PGCHC.)

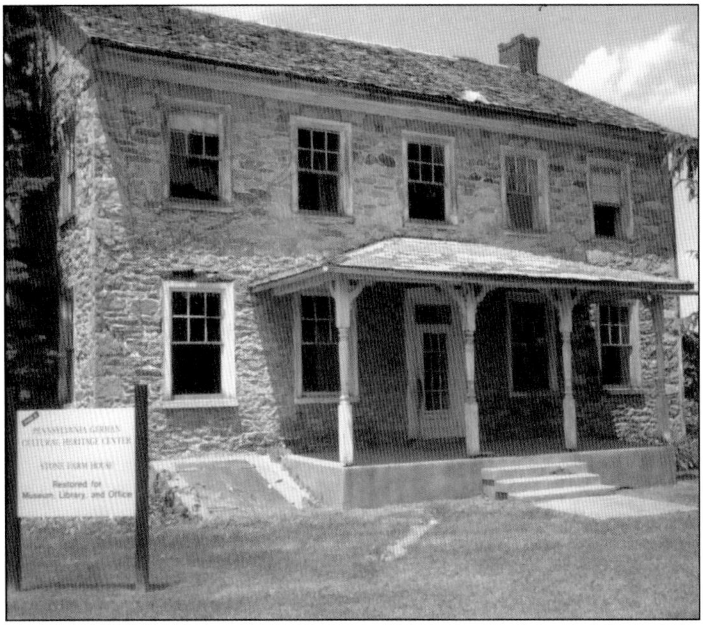

The transformation of the farm into a folklife center began in 1991. While the c. 1800 limestone farmhouse had seen better days, the home was rebuilt to maintain its structural integrity, but all surviving original features were preserved. The front porch, a later improvement, was taken off to restore an earlier appearance. Extending from the rear is a one-story stone kitchen wing that was added shortly after the front portion was constructed. (Courtesy of PGCHC.)

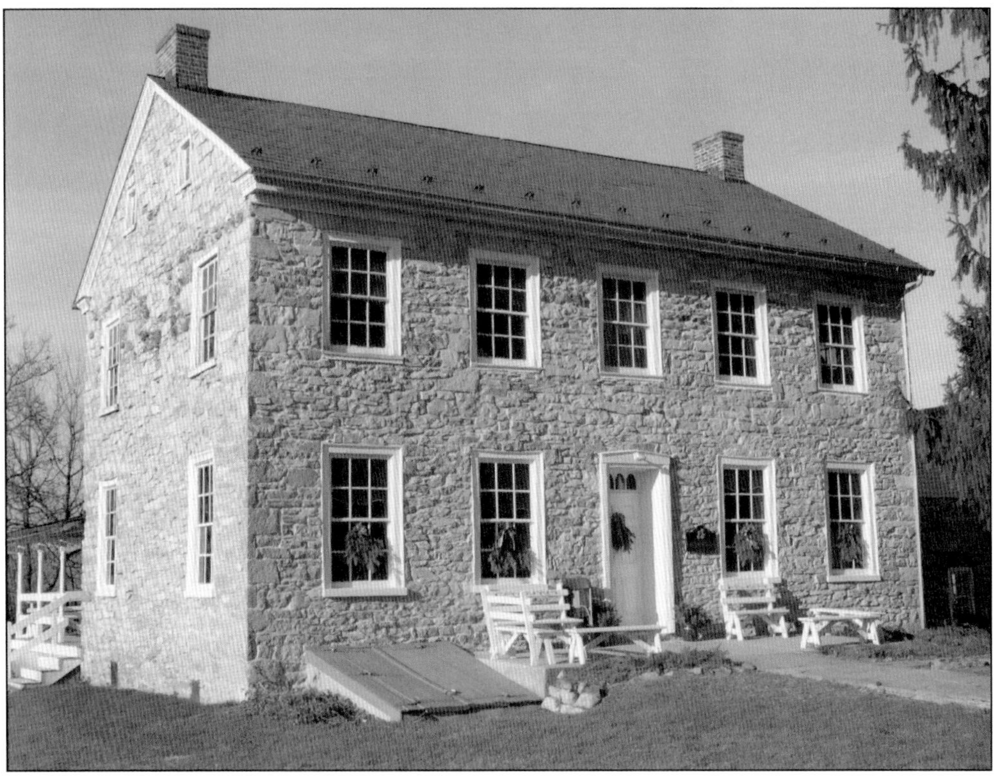

The Sharadin farmhouse is one of scores of similar homes built up and down the East Penn Valley at the turn of the 19th century. Second- and third-generation families constructed these homes to replace frontier log buildings with limestone structures meant to last centuries. The interior features typical regional furnishings with displays of various collections purchased and donated to highlight the material culture of the Pennsylvania Dutch. (Courtesy of PGCHC.)

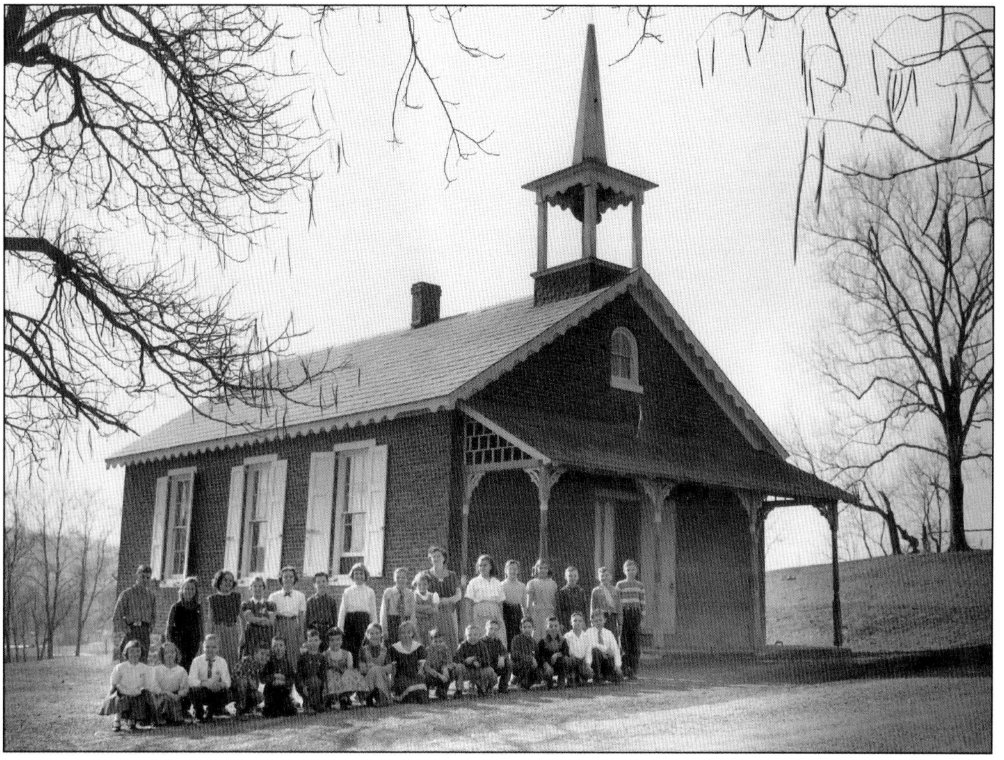

The one-room Stein schoolhouse was donated to the Pennsylvania German Cultural Heritage Center and relocated to campus. The bell tower and the roof were carefully removed, and the gable bricks were disassembled. After reinforcement, the building was jacked from its foundation, and steel I-beams were slid underneath to support the schoolhouse. Wheels under the I-beams allowed for the schoolhouse to be towed very slowly on the three-mile journey to campus. The schoolhouse traveled down Route 737 but did not fit under the Route 222 bypass, so the building was taken up on the highway, towed through farm fields, and slid onto a new foundation, where it was carefully restored. (Courtesy of PGCHC.)

The relocation of the schoolhouse occurred due to the generosity of Dr. Ruth Freyberger, a 1935 graduate of Kutztown State Teachers College. After careful restoration, the renamed Freyberger Schoolhouse received schoolhouse artifacts through the donation of the collections of the Pennsylvania Dutch Folk Culture Society, formerly located near the Deitsch Eck restaurant in Lenhartsville. Florence Baver led the merger effort, benefiting the thousands of visitors that attend events each year. (Courtesy of PGCHC.)

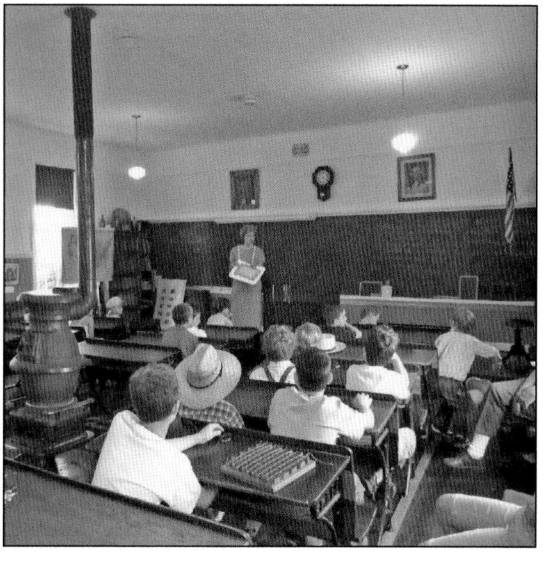

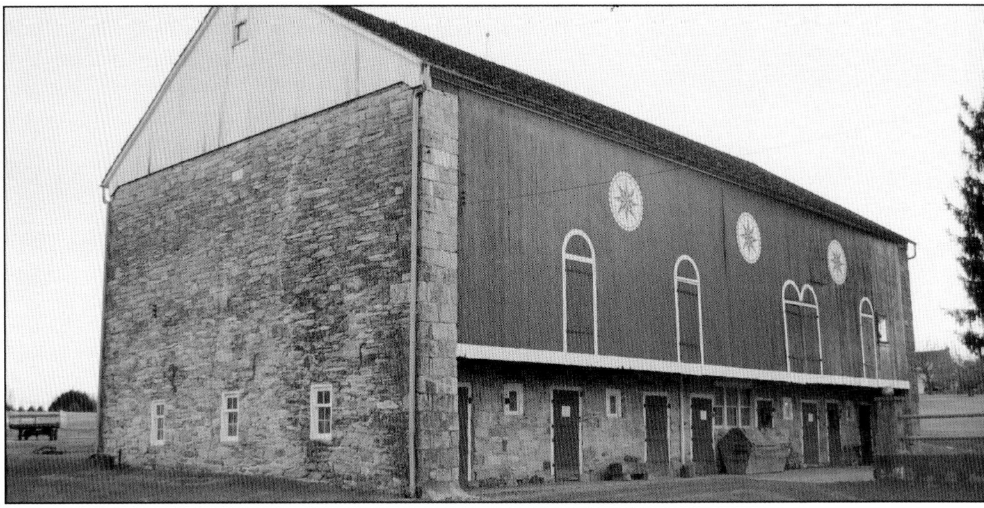

In its restored state, the classic 1855 Pennsylvania barn highlights the distinctive regional decorations of Berks County. The basement level remains largely intact from its use for a dairy herd in the 1940s. Eric Claypoole, the foremost regional barn painter, repainted the stars on the forebay. The vision to transform the farm into the Pennsylvania German Cultural Heritage Center was led by the Kutztown University Foundation and is now managed by Kutztown University. (Photograph by Ashley Nave.)

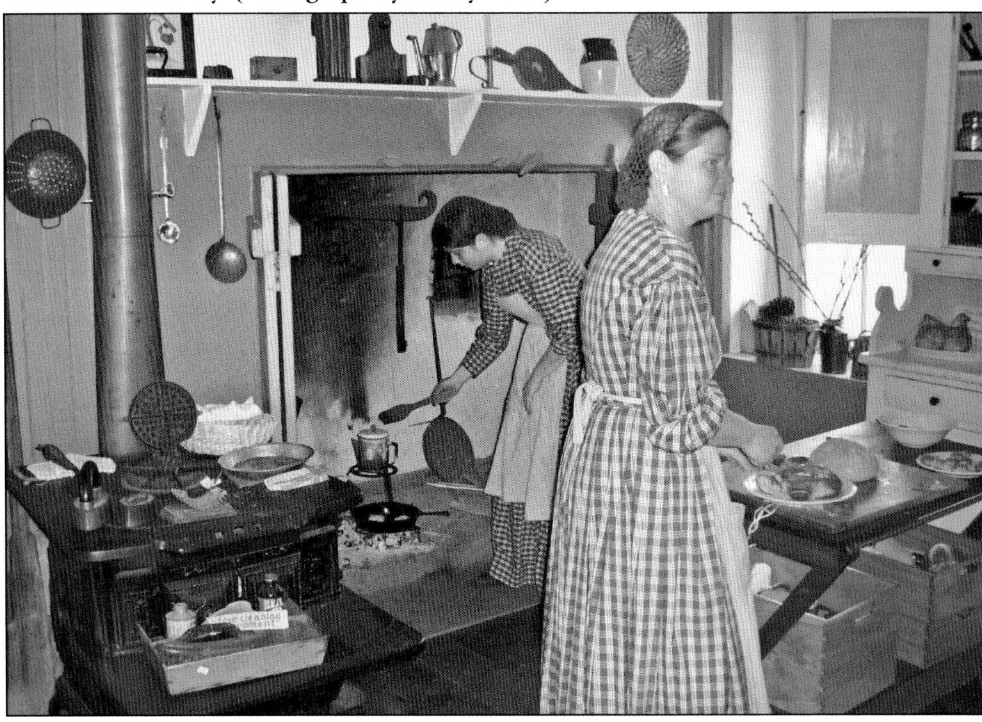

Today, the Sharadin farmhouse showcases regional folklife displays at annual heritage center events. Christmas and Easter celebrations demonstrate the unique traditions of the Pennsylvania Dutch to teach and inspire visitors. Volunteer Becky Manley (foreground) helps bring the Sharadin farmhouse to life with the smells of hearth-cooked foods during annual events. (Courtesy of PGCHC.)

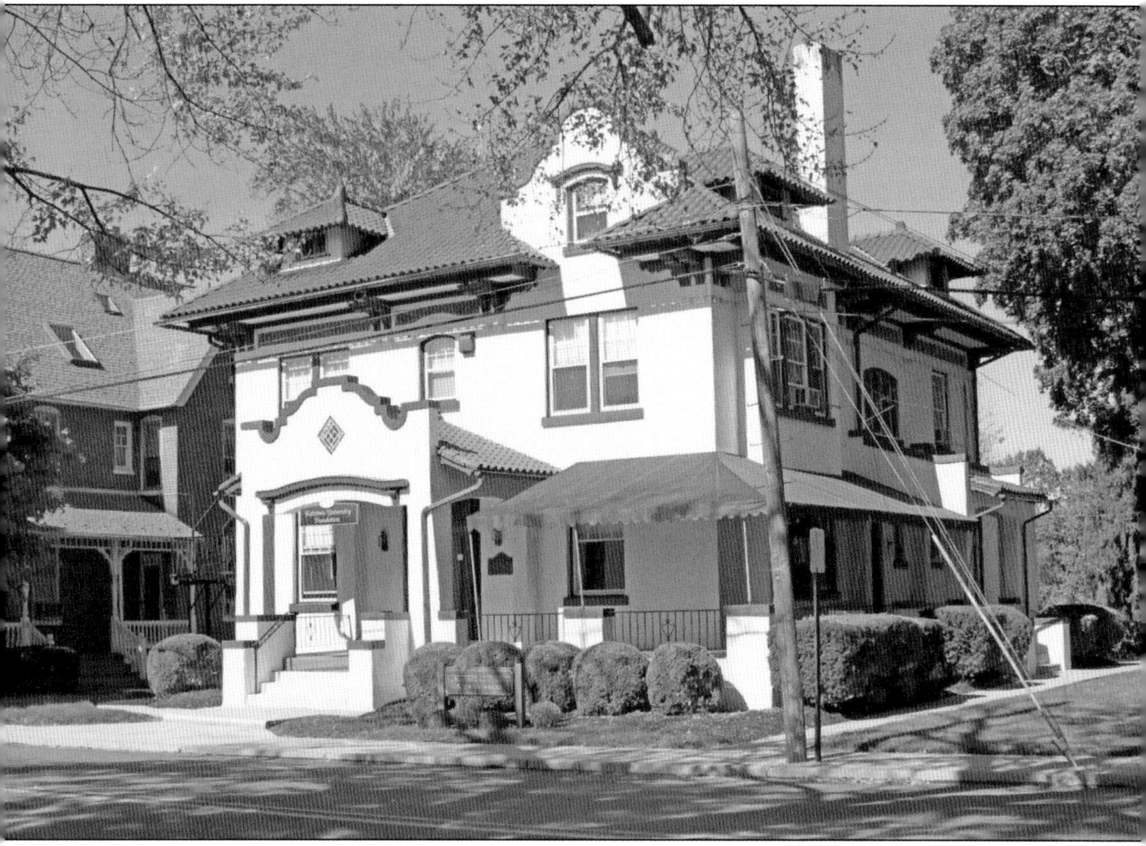

The Kutztown University Foundation was incorporated on July 1, 1983, from the George B. Hancher Fund, which was an endowment established to provide scholarships to KU students. The foundation has played a major role in the growth of the campus thanks to generous donations from alumni, faculty, staff, and university friends. Their contributions are evident in projects such as Alumni Plaza and Honors Hall, as well as the expansions of the Rohrbach Library, Sharadin Arts Building, and Schaeffer Auditorium. Funding through the foundation has been instrumental in the growth of the Pennsylvania German Cultural Heritage Center and the establishment of the Wiesenberger Alumni Center, pictured here. The alumni center was the former home of Henry Sharadin, the namesake of the Sharadin Arts Building. Donor gifts to the foundation have helped provide scholarships to KU students, assisting the future leaders of society while helping to enhance the university's mission. (Courtesy of KU.)

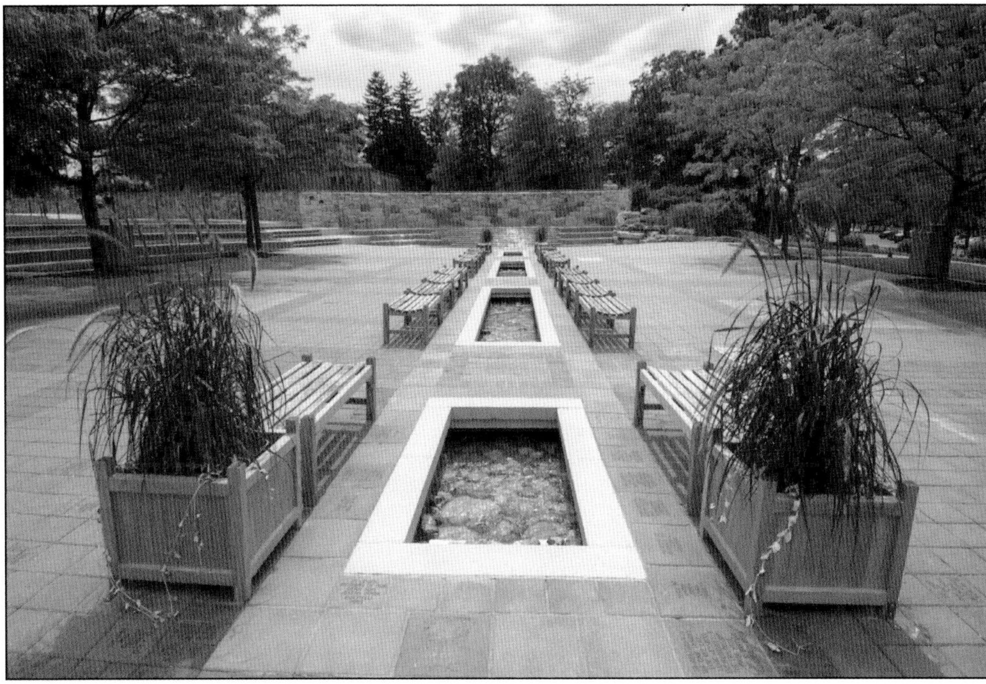

On April 24, 2003, ground was broken for Alumni Plaza. The plaza was officially dedicated during the 2003 homecoming festivities. Located in the middle of campus, this picturesque site features a waterfall, fountain, underground stream, amphitheater-type seating, and paths adorned with inscribed bricks of those who have contributed. The Alumni Plaza serves as a symbol of the past, present, and future. (Courtesy of KU.)

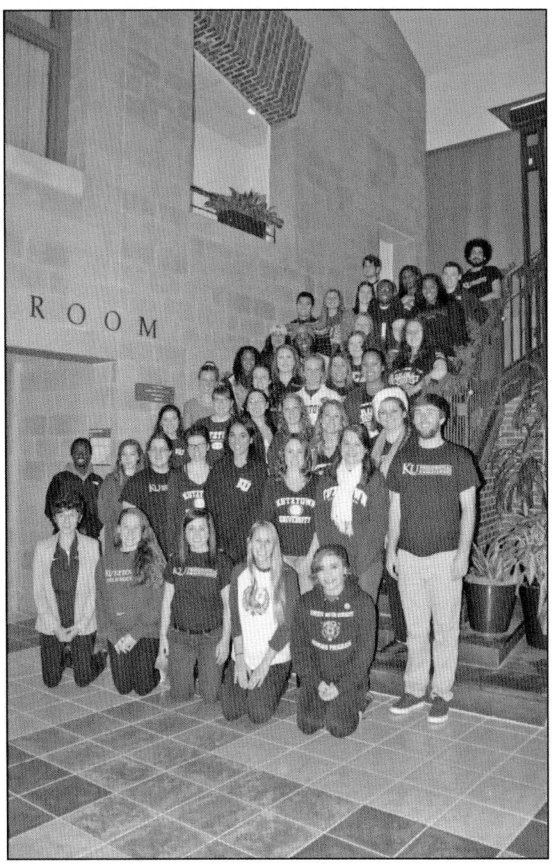

The Presidential Ambassadors, a student organization founded in 1997, works directly with the President's Office and the Kutztown University Foundation and Alumni Relations. Ambassadors connect current students with alumni, faculty and university friends, represent the university, start new traditions that enhance KU pride, and build philanthropy and stewardship with the Kutztown University community. (Photograph by Mary Neuenschwander, courtesy of Ashley Nave.)

Dr. F. Javier Cevallos served as president from 2002 to 2014. As the first Hispanic president of a Pennsylvania state university, he raised student body diversity from 6 percent to 19 percent during his term. Dr. Cevallos developed new academic programs and oversaw the renovation and expansion of the Sharadin Arts Building and the Schaeffer Auditorium. Dr. Cevallos left his position at Kutztown University to become president of Framingham State University. (Courtesy of KUR.)

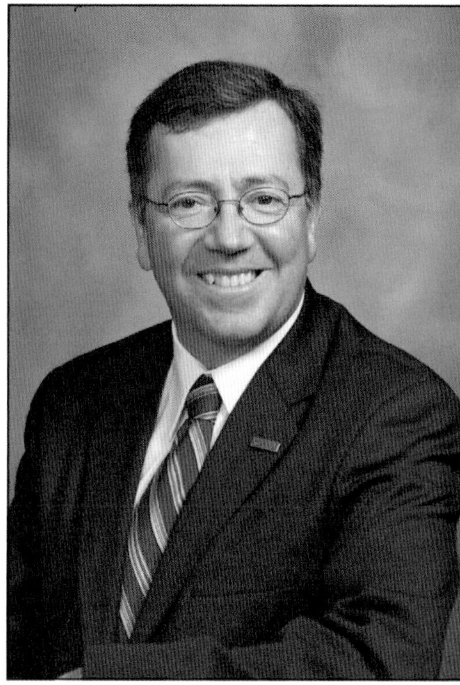

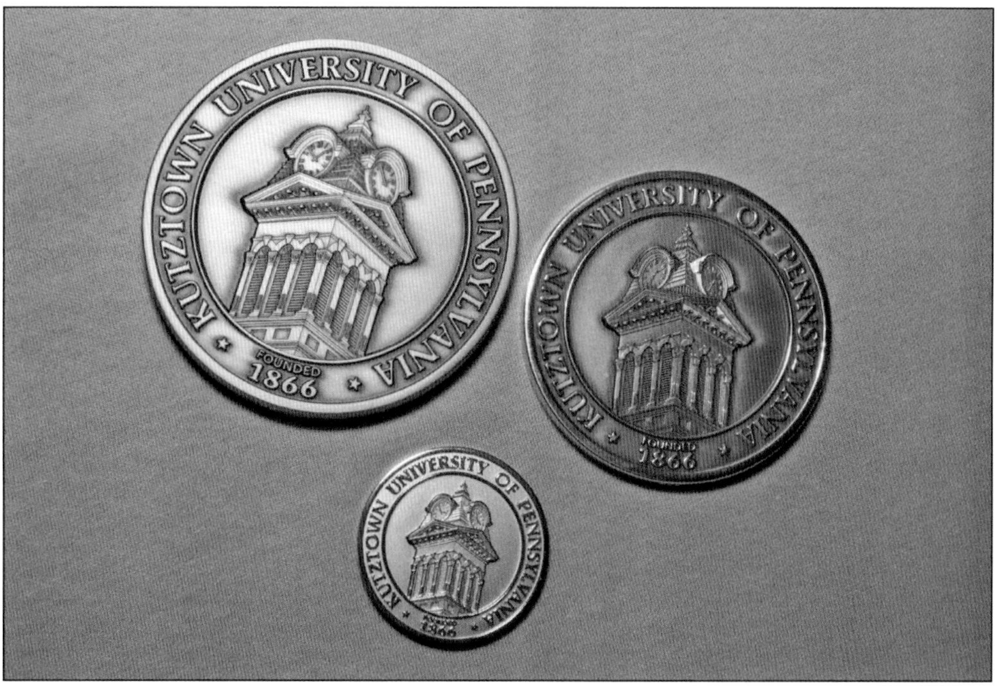

The Chambliss Academic Achievement Award was established through a donation provided by Dr. Carlson R. Chambliss, KU faculty member from 1970 to 2003. Faculty members nominate students who have made achievements in research, artwork, artistic performance, writing, athletics, or community service. The award is given annually to recognize the exceptional individual achievements of a select group of KU graduating seniors. Coin medallions of gold, silver, and copper are presented to the students. (Courtesy of KU.)

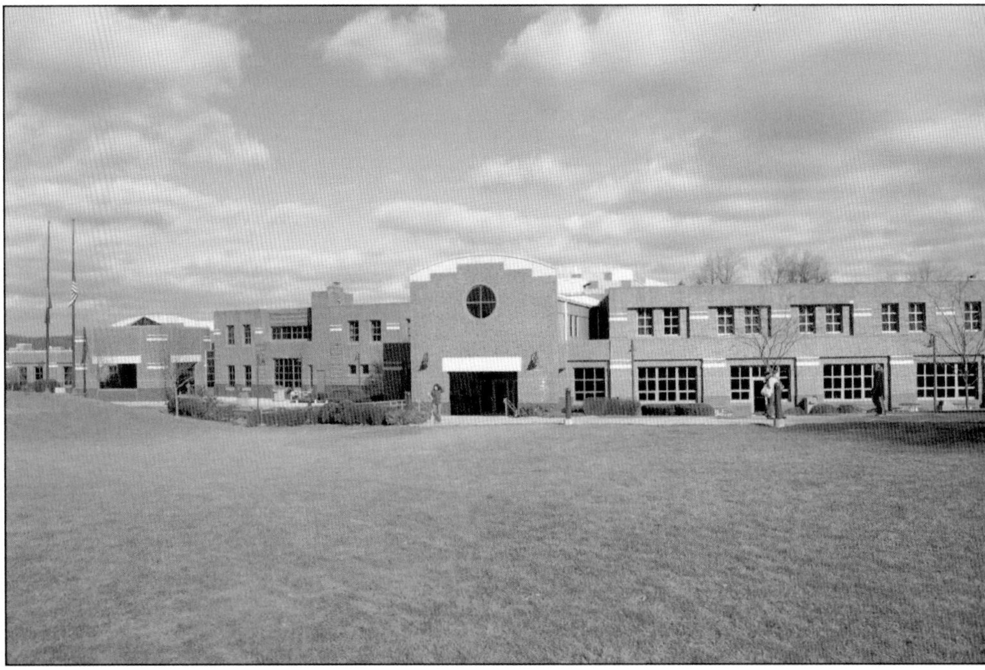

Named after former KU president Dr. David McFarland in 2002, the McFarland Student Union is home to many services for students, faculty, and staff. Student union amenities include the Cub Café, a Starbucks, three galleries, and the campus store. MSU staff pride themselves on running a versatile facility that offers space for a wide variety of university events and programming.

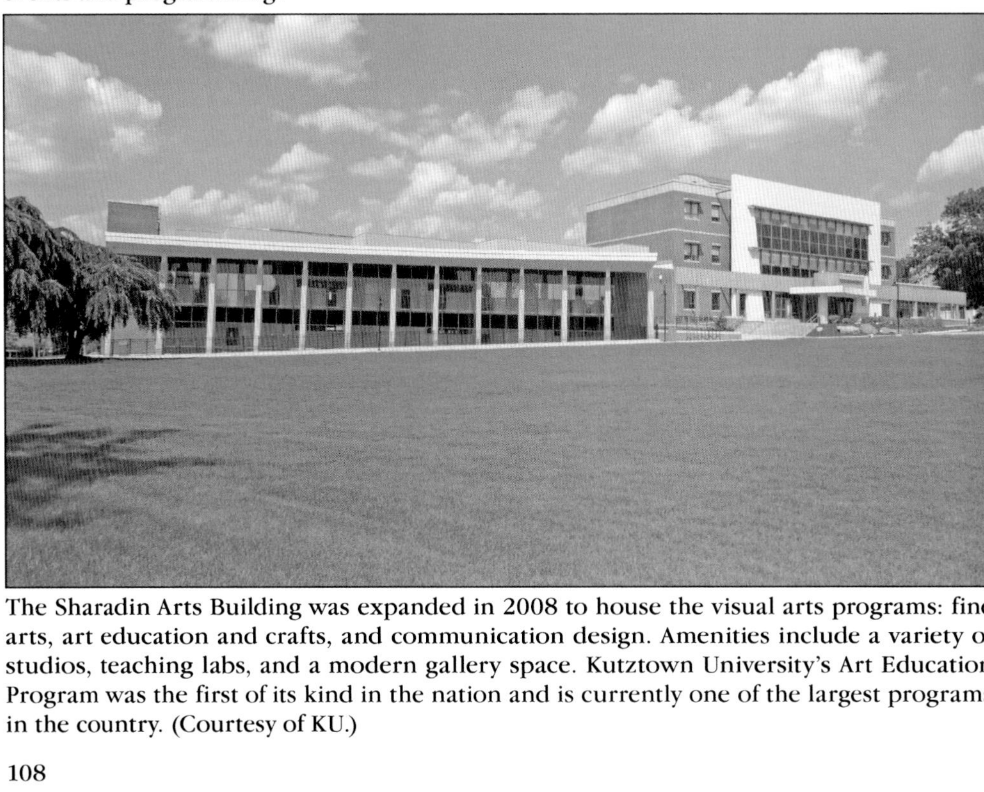

The Sharadin Arts Building was expanded in 2008 to house the visual arts programs: fine arts, art education and crafts, and communication design. Amenities include a variety of studios, teaching labs, and a modern gallery space. Kutztown University's Art Education Program was the first of its kind in the nation and is currently one of the largest programs in the country. (Courtesy of KU.)

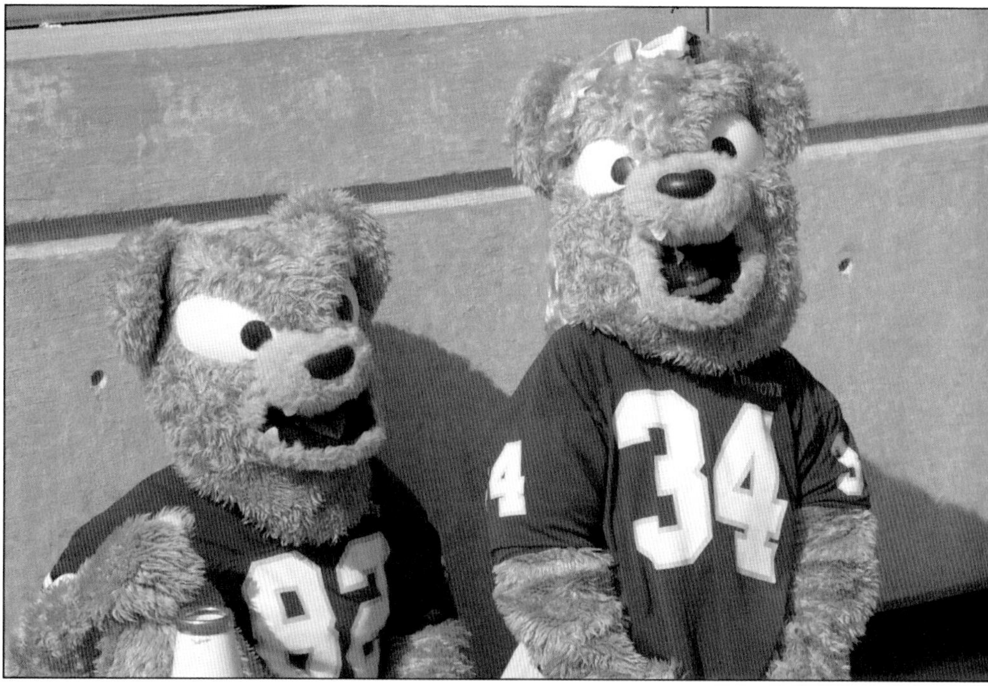

Mascots Goldie and Griz debuted in the mid-1990s. From the mid-1930s to 1960, the sports teams at Kutztown were nicknamed the "Golden Avalanche." It is said that "Golden" refers to the school colors of maroon and gold, while "Avalanche" refers to the fact that the football team was always being "snowed under." In 1961, the name Golden Bears replaced the old moniker. (Courtesy of KU.)

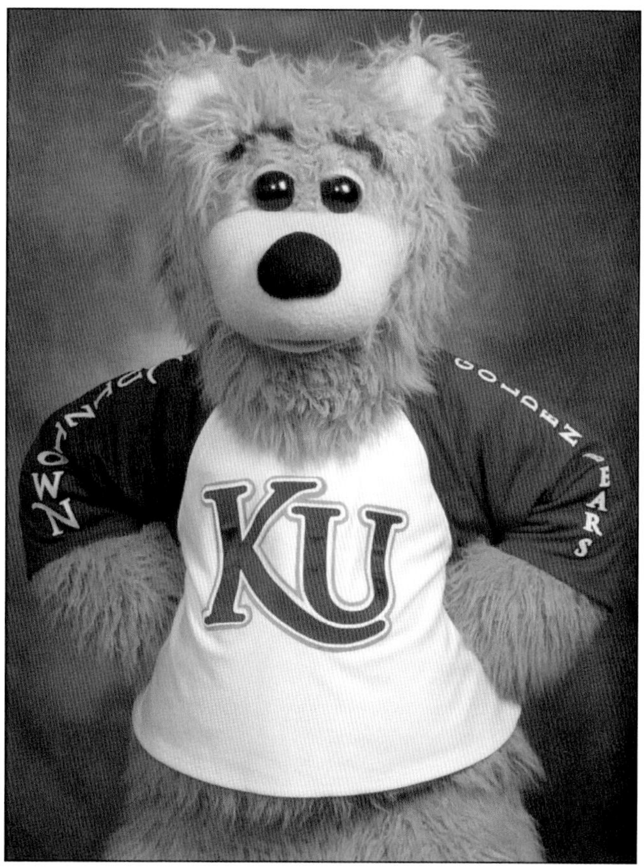

Following the "graduation" of former mascots Goldie and Griz, a new mascot was introduced to the school on October 1, 2005. Avalanche, the KU Golden Bear mascot, is named in honor of the "Golden Avalanche" nickname used by Kutztown sports teams from the 1930s to 1960. (Courtesy of KU.)

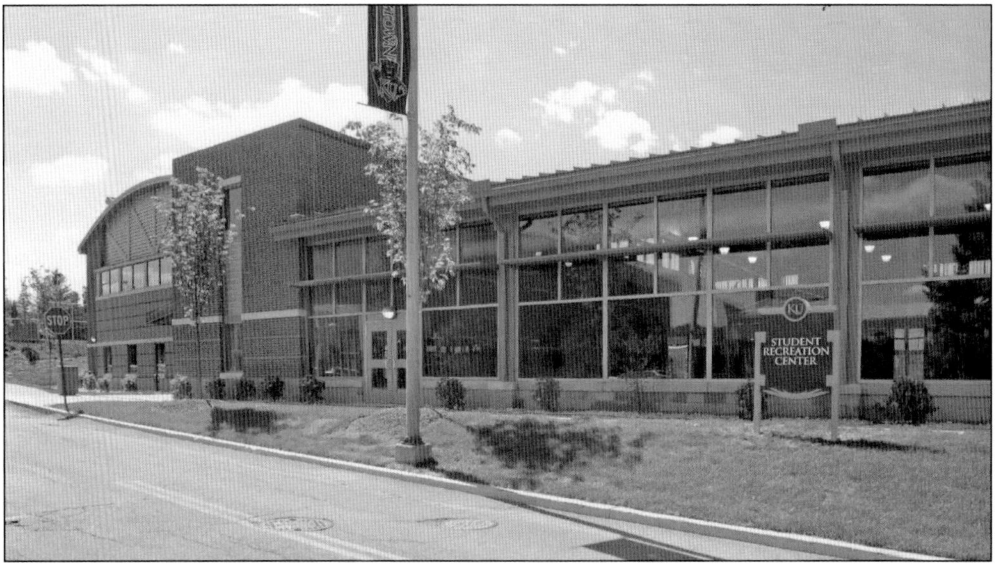

The Student Recreation Center opened in the fall of 2006 as an on-campus center for student recreation and fitness. Amenities include a nearly 9,000-square-foot fitness center and weight room, two group fitness studios, two racquetball courts, an indoor rock climbing wall, a synthetic surface gymnasium with curved walls for indoor sports, a synthetic surface half gymnasium, a suspended jogging track, a snack bar, and locker rooms with hot tubs. (Courtesy of KU.)

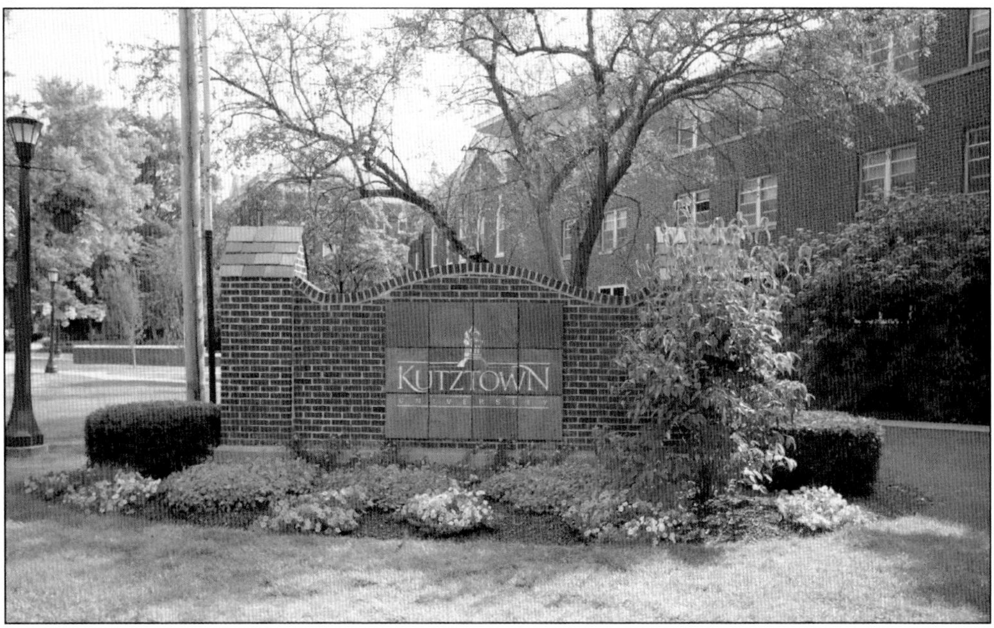

Many would say that Kutztown University focuses extra attention on campus landscaping. In 2009, the Professional Grounds Management Society agreed when it presented the university with its prestigious Green Star Honor Award for its more than 1,800 beautifully kept trees and countless flower gardens. Along with landscaping, the KU grounds crew is responsible for maintaining the athletic fields and decorating for the university's outdoor events. (Courtesy of KU.)

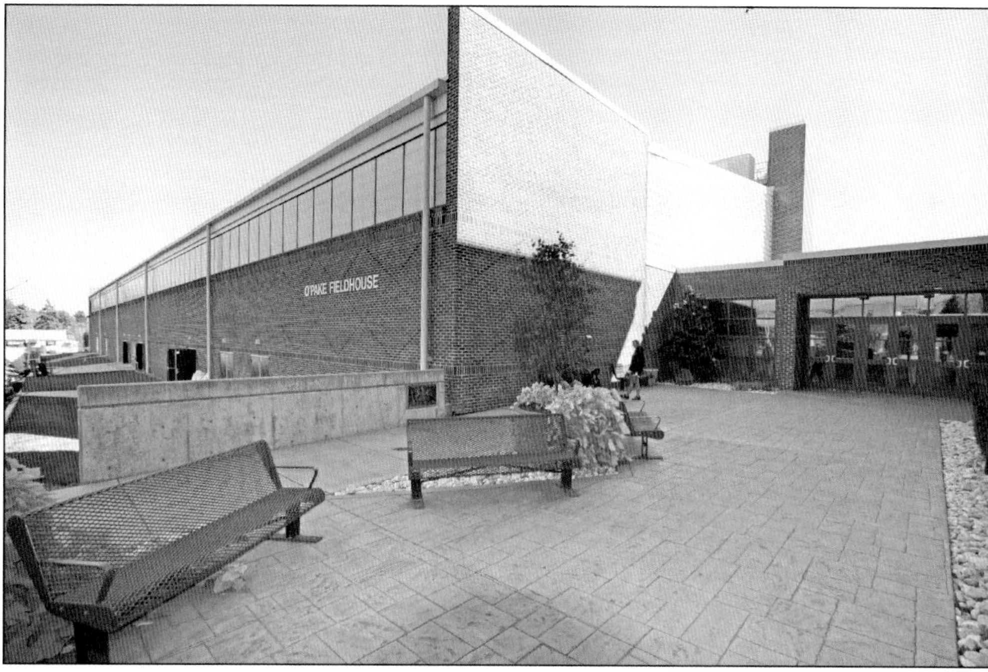

On September 30, 2011, Kutztown's field house was named for Michael A. O'Pake, a Democratic state senator who represented Kutztown and other Berks County areas from 1972 until his death in 2010. Senator O'Pake was born and raised in Reading and remained connected to the people of his district throughout his career as a lawmaker. The field house contains an indoor track and courts for basketball, tennis, and volleyball. (Courtesy of KU.)

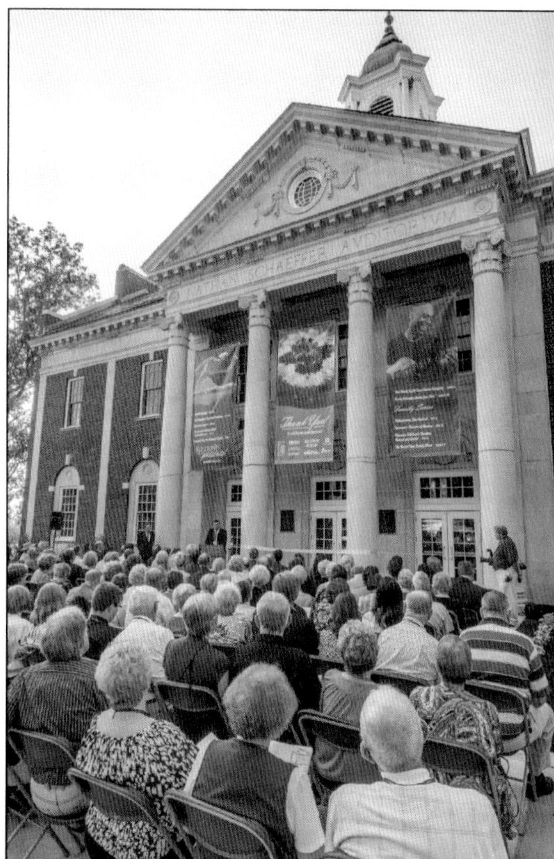

On September 10, 2013, a rededication ceremony was held to celebrate the expansion, renovation, and reopening of the Nathan C. Schaeffer Auditorium. Included in the 14,000-square-foot addition is a large rehearsal hall named in honor of Richard G. Wells, professor emeritus of music. The expansion and improvements made to the auditorium have proven helpful to the university's rapidly growing music program. (Courtesy of KU.)

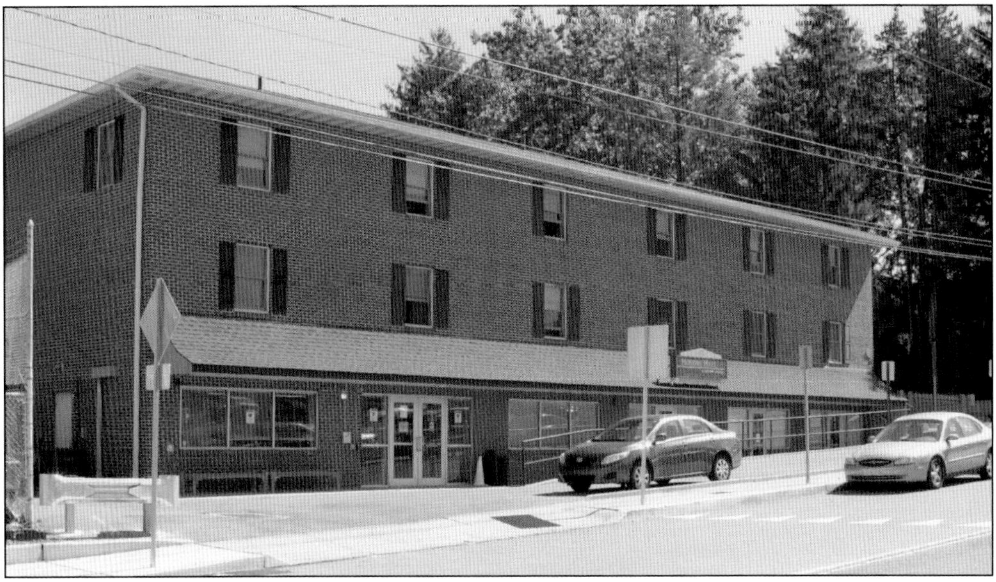

The honors program offers enriching academic and social opportunities for high-achieving students. Honors students select specially designed courses, courses by contract, independent studies, and internships to earn honors credit. In addition, a 30-hour service component supplements the honors coursework. This building includes honors student housing, where upperclassmen may choose to live in Honors Hall, which features fully equipped apartments with two double bedrooms, a kitchen, common area, and bathroom. (Courtesy of KU.)

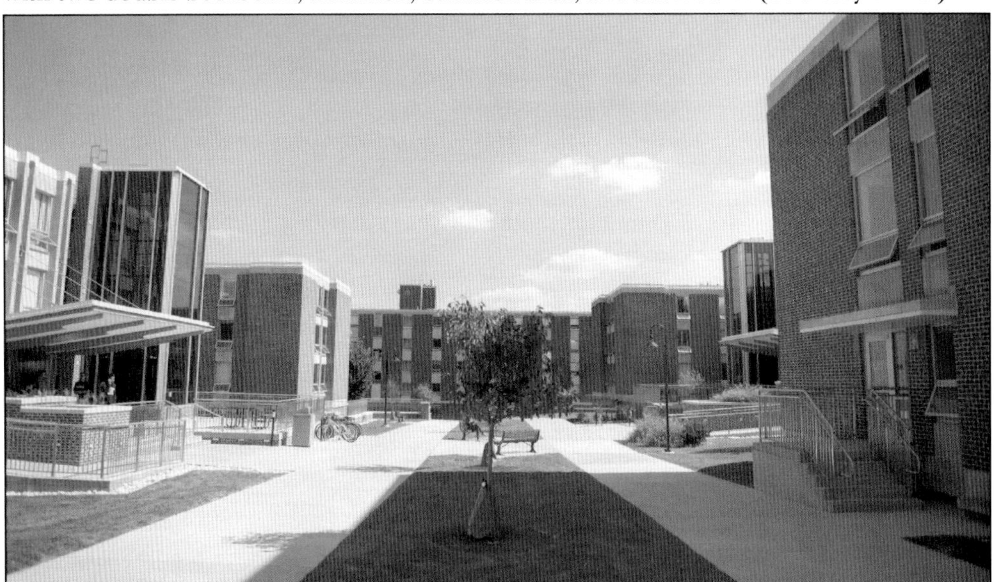

Berks, Lehigh, and Schuylkill residence halls were rededicated on September 18, 2015. These buildings were first constructed in 1964 as a women's dormitory complex and are named for the three counties that Kutztown University first represented as a state normal school. The tri-county halls went under renovations at a combined cost of $23,709,210. Each building houses specific majors and provides facilities and supplies that are beneficial to the residents. (Courtesy of KU.)

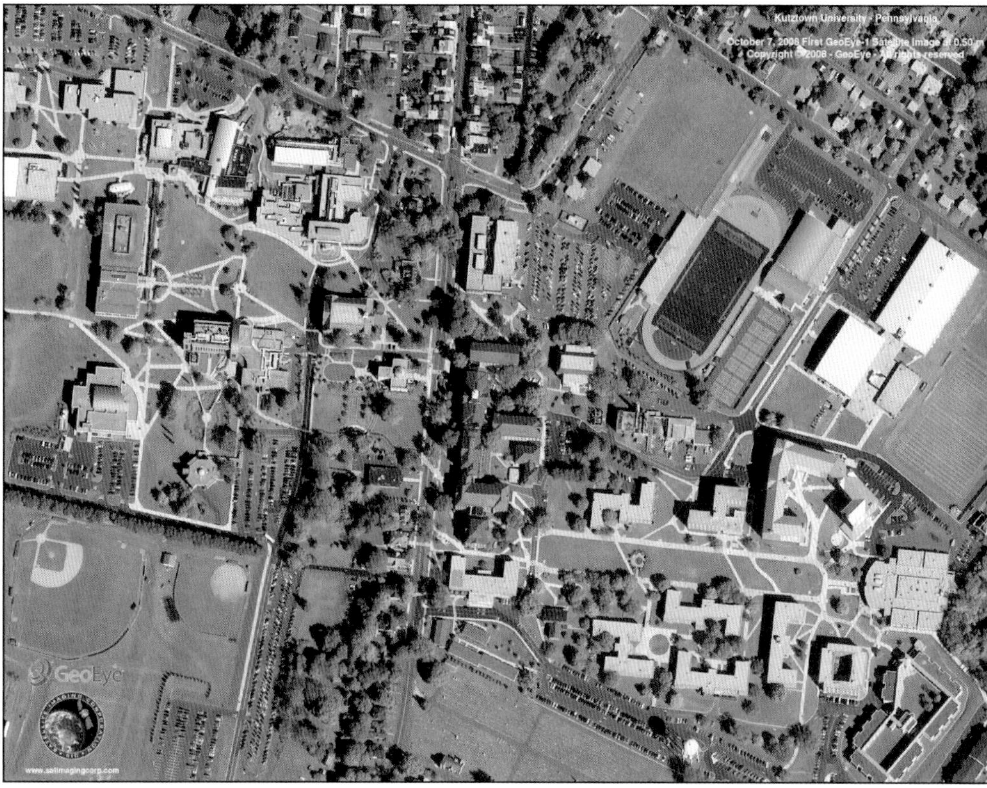

This aerial view of Kutztown University was the first natural color image collected by the GeoEye-1 satellite sensor. The satellite was launched from Vandenberg Air Force Base in California on September 6, 2008, and the image was collected on October 7, 2008. Kutztown University is featured in the Smithsonian National Air and Space Museum because of this photograph.

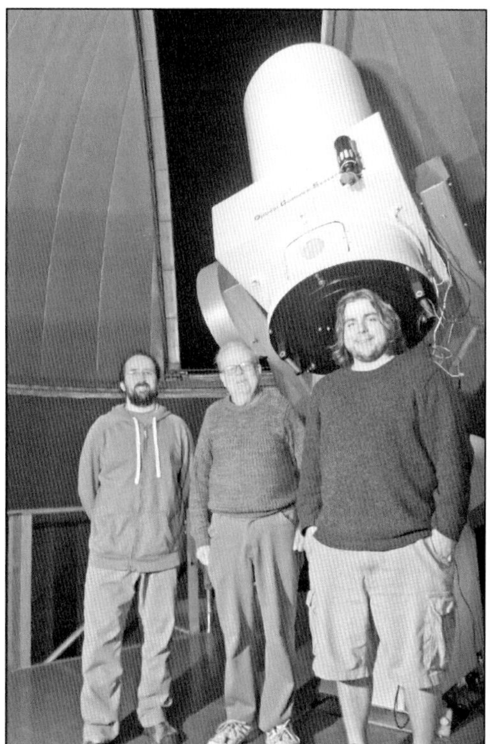

In 2012, a new telescope was installed in the observatory of the Grim Science Building. This investment has proven helpful in the discovery of at least three new extrasolar planets. From left to right are current professor Dr. Phillip Reed, retired professor Dr. Carlson Chambliss, and class of 2013 graduate Bernie Yuhas. (Courtesy of Dr. Phillip Reed.)

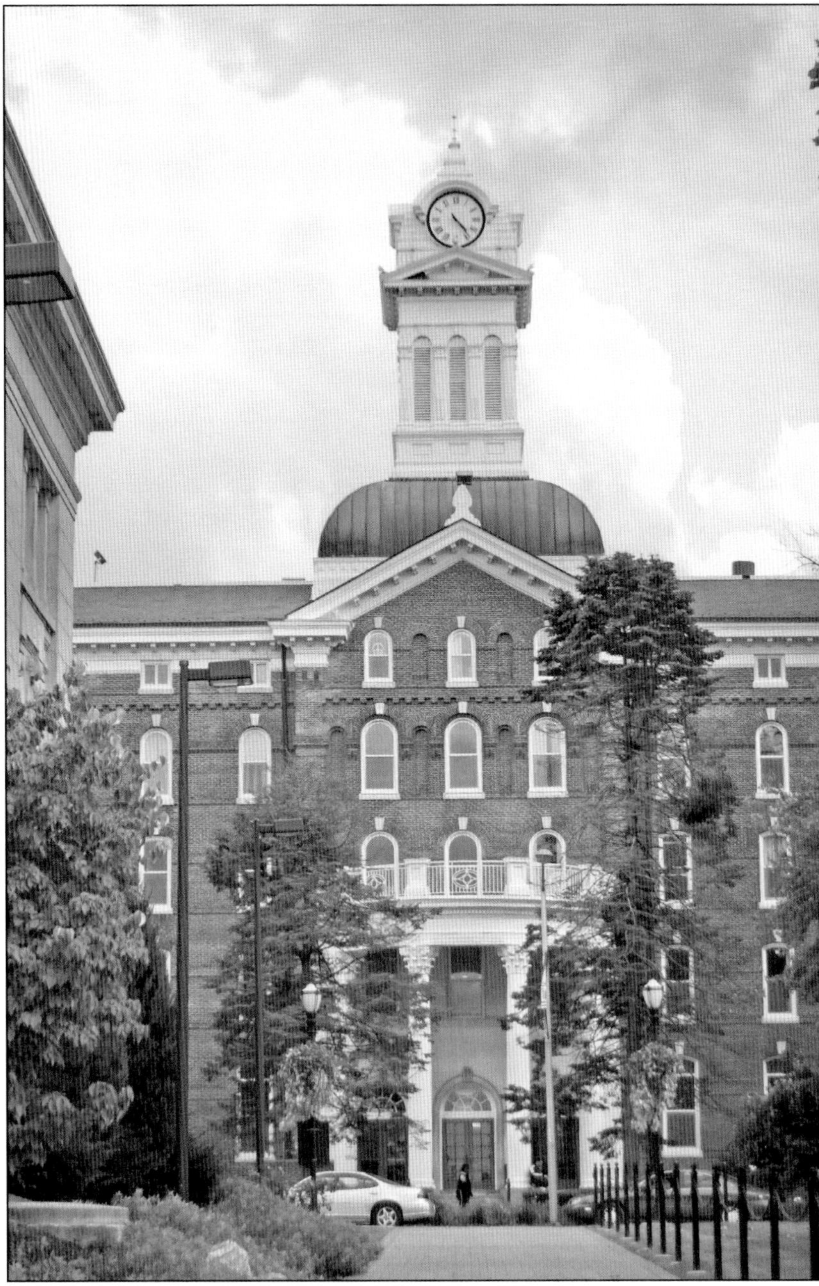

A ghost is rumored to haunt the fifth floor of the most significant campus building. The story of Mary, who supposedly committed suicide to cover up the fact that she was pregnant with a professor's child, has been told for decades. While this story has many versions, the only truth was her name. A KSNS student named Mary Snyder was set to graduate in 1895 at the age of 19. A day before her graduation, she fell ill with rheumatism and convulsions, which eventually led to her demise. Claims of her haunting include flickering lights, moving objects, and unplugged radios playing. Although Snyder passed away more than 120 years ago, the story about her will forever be told, as many believe she still walks the halls of Old Main's fifth floor. (Courtesy of KU.)

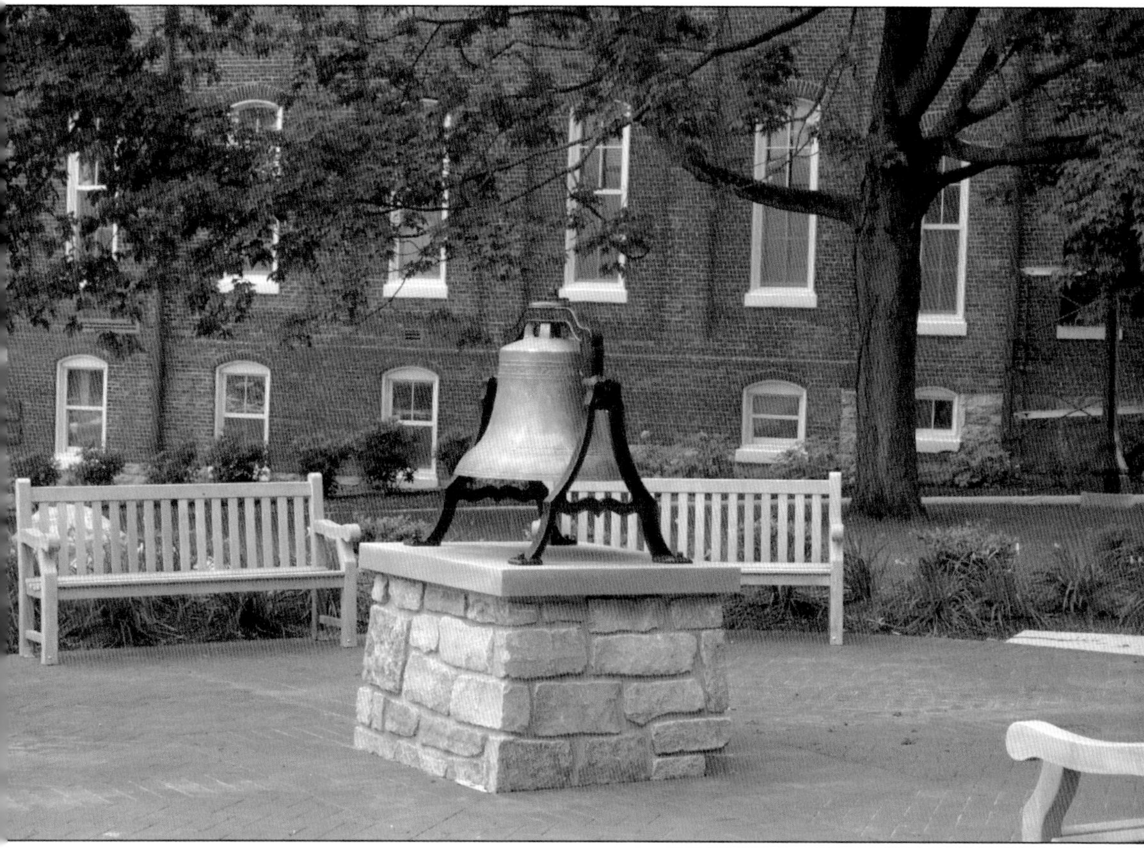

College Hill Memorial Grove was dedicated on May 9, 2013. Located between Old Main and Stratton, the memorial was dedicated to students, faculty, staff, and alumni who have died. The center of the grove features the bell that once hung in the clock tower. Every year, ceremonies are held in memory of those who have passed, including the anniversary of the 9/11 terrorist attacks in which four victims were KU alumni. (Courtesy of KU.)

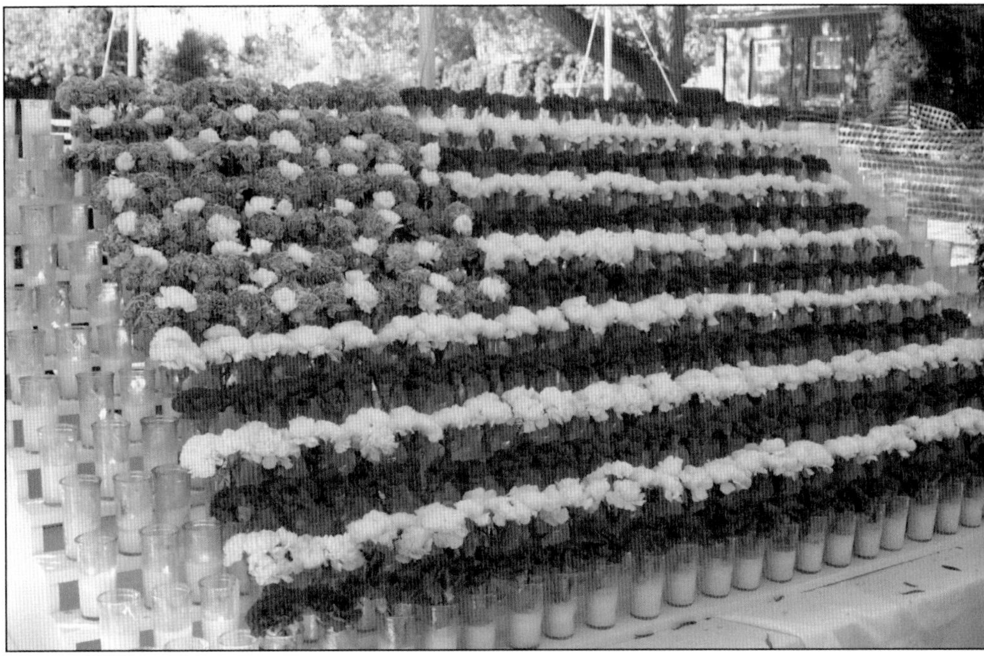

To honor the lives lost due to the terrorist attacks of September 11, 2001, a day of remembrance was held on the first anniversary of the tragedy. Students were encouraged to take a carnation from the flower flag and light a candle in remembrance. Among the more than 2,000 victims of September 11, four were KU alumni. They were Kevin Bowser (class of 1980), Paul Skrzypek (class of 1986), Gary Haag (class of 1987), and Robert Devitt (class of 1989). A tree was planted in front of Old Main with a plaque in memory of Gary Haag, an effort led by Steve Young, who organized and contributed to the memorial. (Both, courtesy of KUR.)

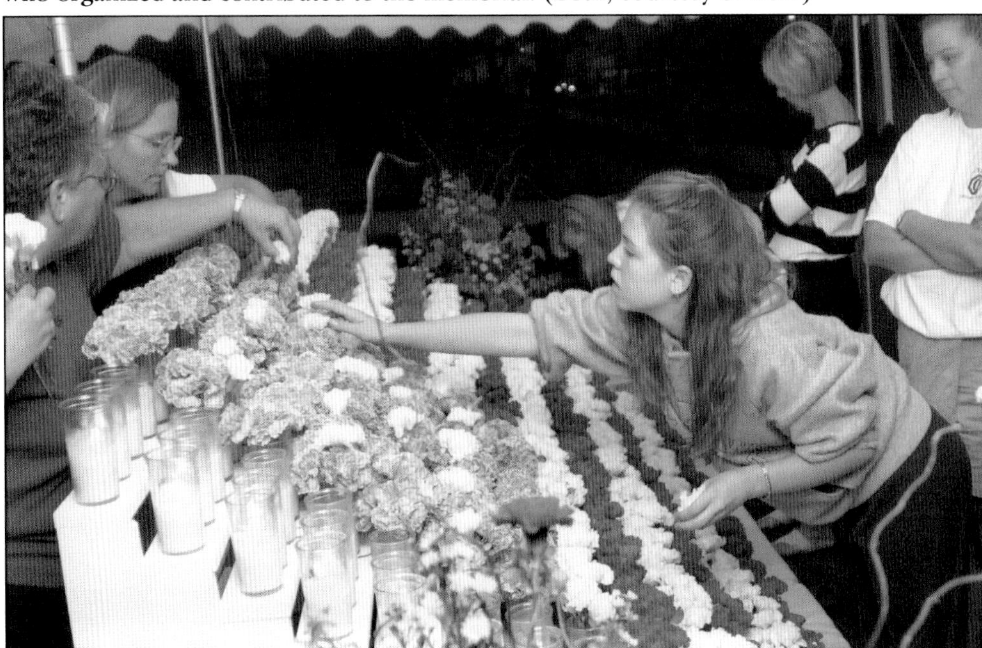

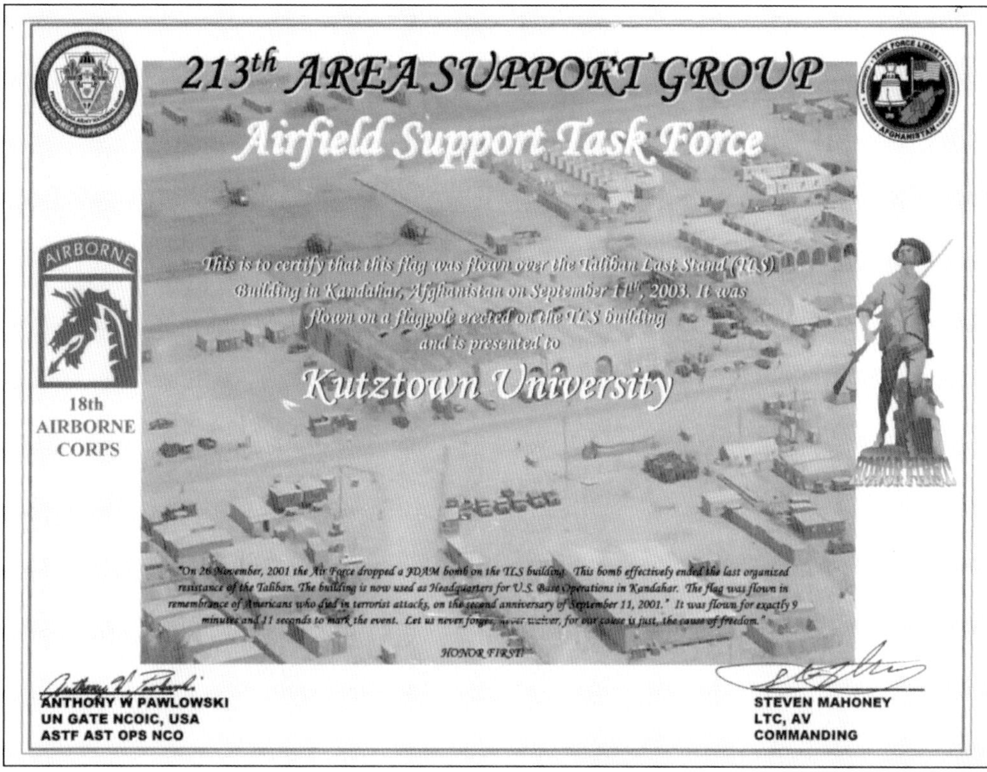

213th AREA SUPPORT GROUP

Airfield Support Task Force

This is to certify that this flag was flown over the Taliban Last Stand (TLS) Building in Kandahar, Afghanistan on September 11th, 2003. It was flown on a flagpole erected on the TLS building and is presented to

Kutztown University

"On 26 November, 2001 the Air Force dropped a JDAM bomb on the TLS building. This bomb effectively ended the last organized resistance of the Taliban. The building is now used as Headquarters for U.S. Base Operations in Kandahar. The flag was flown in remembrance of Americans who died in terrorist attacks, on the second anniversary of September 11, 2001." It was flown for exactly 9 minutes and 11 seconds to mark the event. Let us never forget, never waiver, for our cause is just, the cause of freedom."

HONOR FIRST!

18th AIRBORNE CORPS

ANTHONY W PAWLOWSKI
UN GATE NCOIC, USA
ASTF AST OPS NCO

STEVEN MAHONEY
LTC, AV
COMMANDING

This certificate and a framed flag were gifts from Sgt. Anthony W. Pawlowski, who was set to start his degree in commercial design when he was called upon to serve his nation. He later returned to Kutztown University and graduated in 2007. The flag was flown in Afghanistan for 9 minutes and 11 seconds on the second anniversary of the terrorist attacks of September 11, 2001.

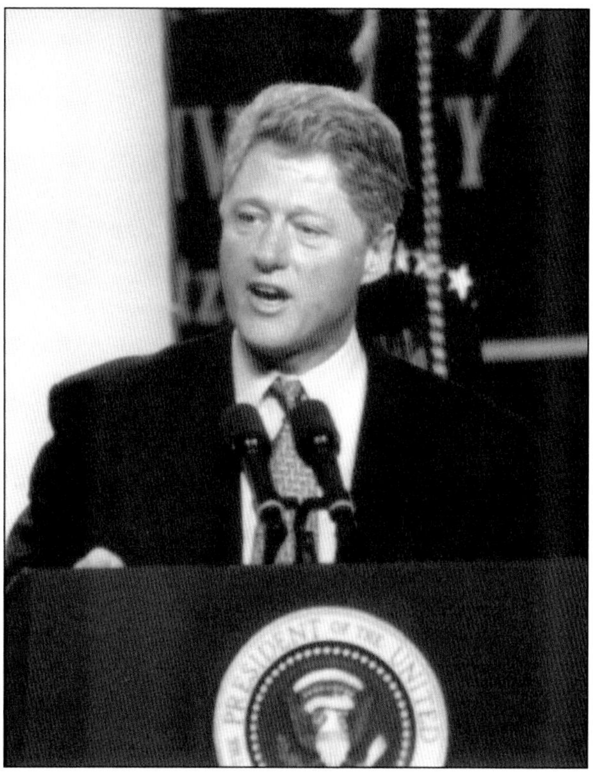

Kutztown University is no stranger to visiting dignitaries. On January 25, 1995, then president Bill Clinton spoke in the O'Pake Fieldhouse about his education initiative. This event not only drew from the student body, but local schools were invited to attend as well. Clinton served as the 42nd president of the United States. (Courtesy of KUR.)

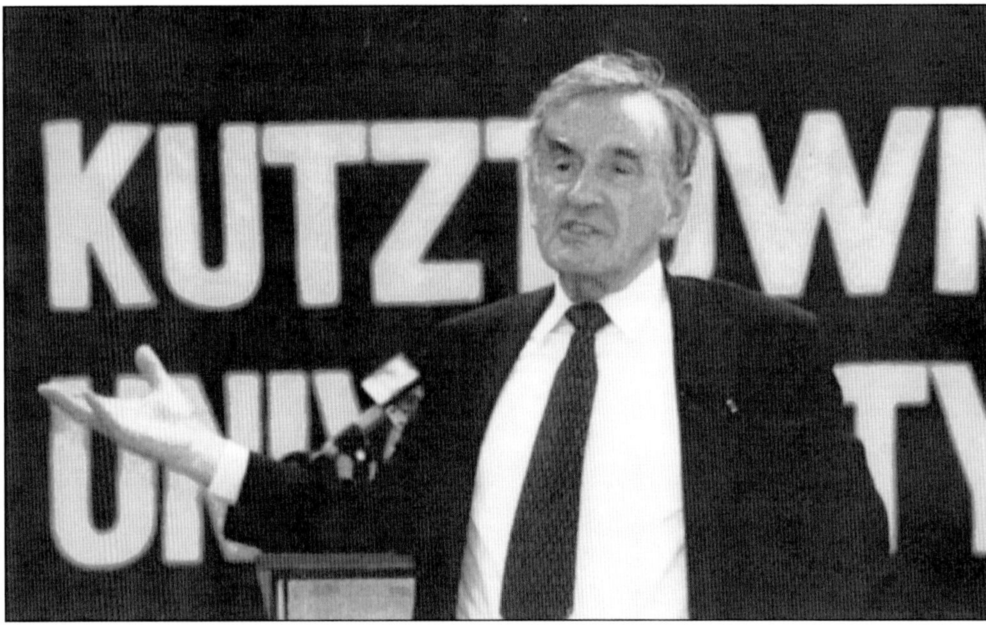

Author and holocaust survivor Elie Wiesel visited Kutztown University on May 1, 2001. His 1958 memoir *Night* was among the required reading for freshmen in the College of Liberal Arts and Sciences. *Night* describes Wiesel's experiences with his father in the Nazi concentration camps of Auschwitz and Buchenwald in 1944–1945. (Courtesy of KUR.)

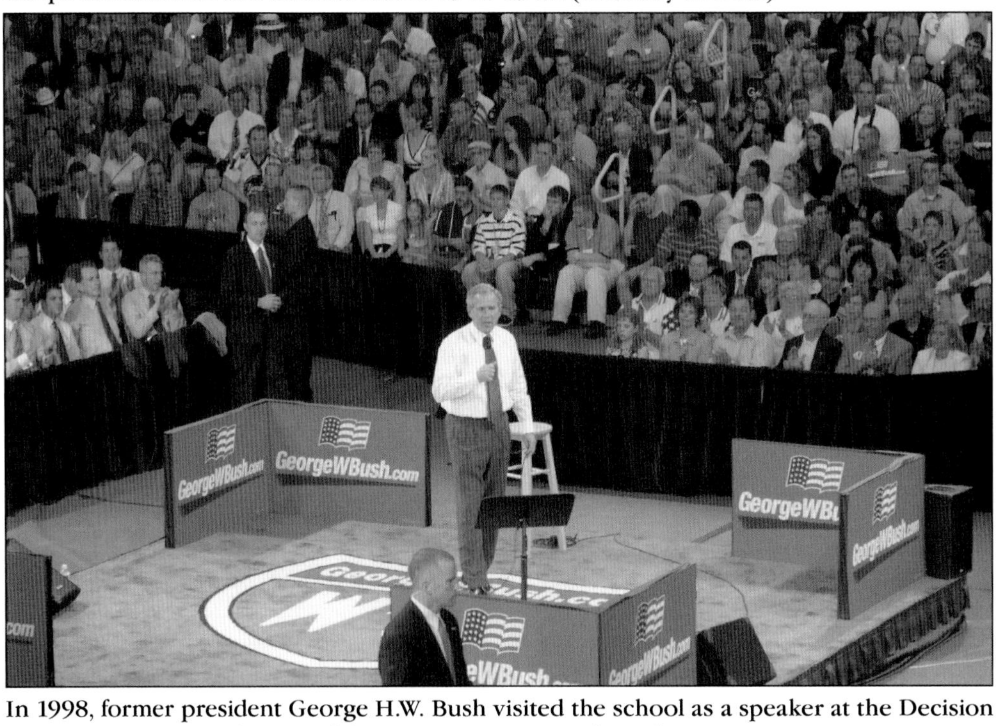

In 1998, former president George H.W. Bush visited the school as a speaker at the Decision Makers Forum. On July 9, 2004, his son George W. Bush made a campaign stop at Kutztown University and spoke in Keystone Arena, as pictured. Later, in 2008, Jeb Bush, George H.W.'s son and George W.'s brother, spoke at the Decision Makers Forum. (Courtesy of KUR.)

In March 2009, Barbara Walters served as a speaker of the 20th annual Decision Makers Forum held in Keystone Hall. Walters is an American broadcast journalist, author, and television personality. She is best known for her hosting roles on *The Today Show*, *The View*, *ABC Evening News*, and *20/20*. (Courtesy of KUR.)

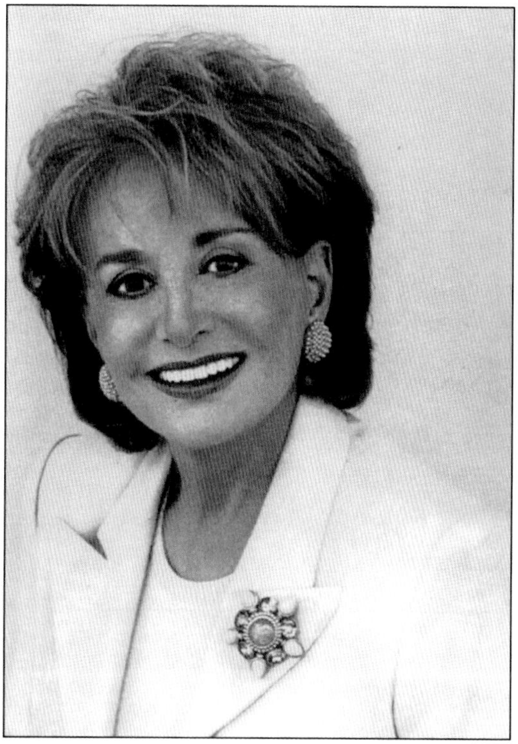

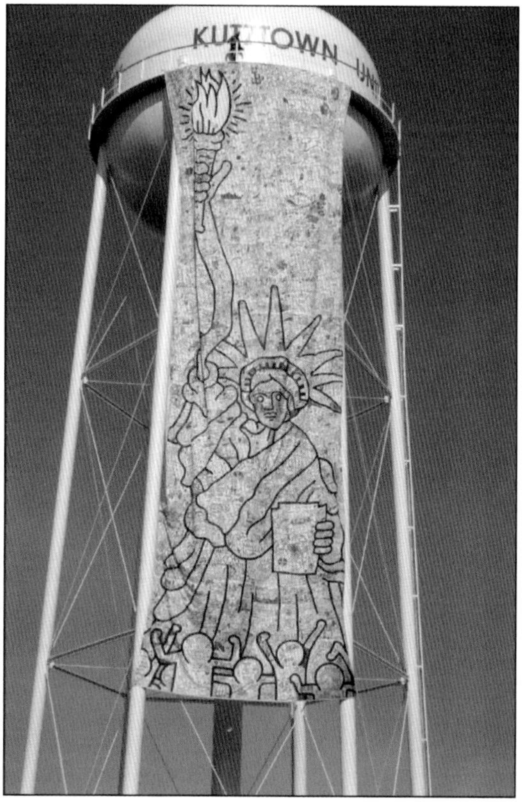

In the spring of 2006, a 90-foot banner by Kutztown native Keith Haring (1958–1990) hung from the campus water tower. Haring's public art in the subways of New York sought to break down the barriers between high and low art. In New York, he worked with Madonna and befriended Andy Warhol. Haring involved 1,000 children from the CityKids Foundation to create this mural of the Statue of Liberty. (Courtesy of KUR.)

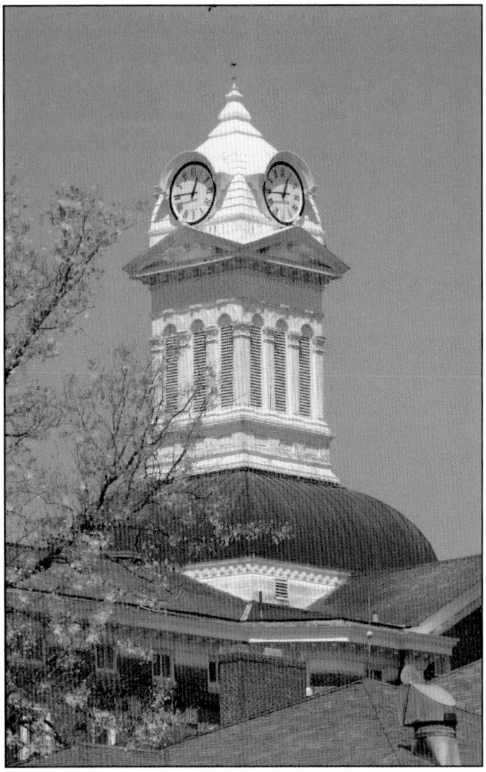

Rising above the trees is the clock tower of Old Main. Commonly known as the "Angry Chicken," this landmark received its clock faces in 1910. It is unknown when the tower started being called the Angry Chicken, but it is certain that the chicken will live for a long time. (Courtesy of KU.)

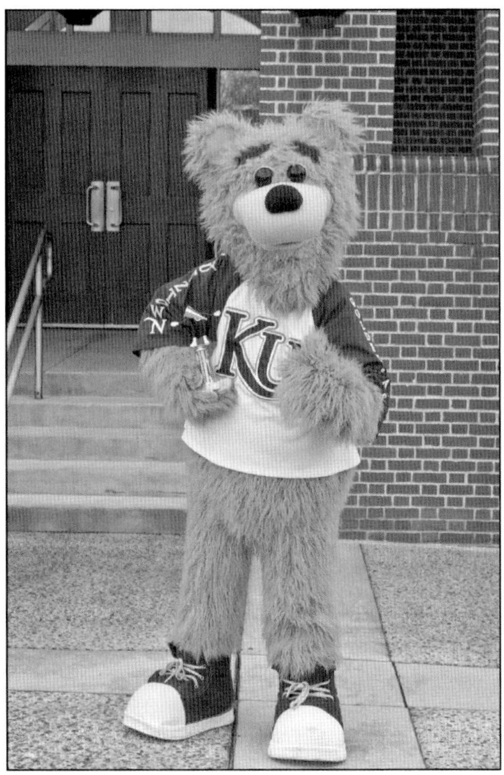

Avalanche was crowned the inaugural Mascot Madness Champion in 2015 after receiving more than 6,100 votes in a 15-hour period. With all 14 state schools battling in four rounds of social media voting, Avalanche reigned supreme. The last round, in order to determine the top mascot, ended in a 15-vote win over Slippery Rock's mascot, Rocky. In order to defend his title, Avalanche competed in the 2016 Mascot Madness. With another final round fought against Rocky, Avalanche won by less than 1 percent, making him a two-time mascot champion. (Courtesy of KU.)

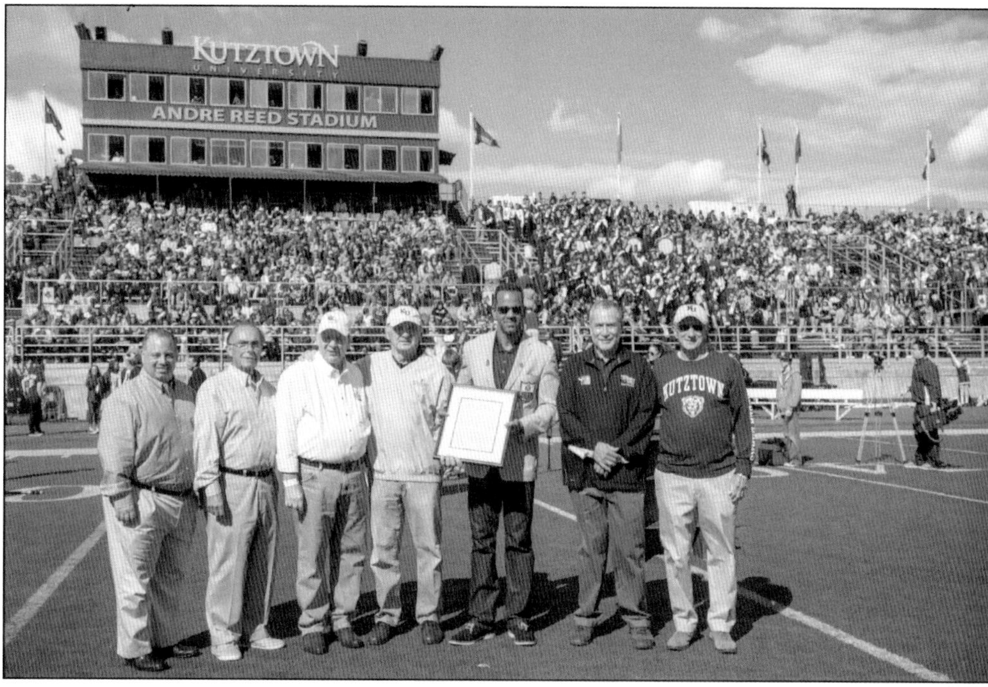

From 1981 to 1984, Andre Reed played football at Kutztown University, where he set nine school records and was named to the All-Pennsylvania State Athletic Conference team three times. Most of his 16-season professional career was spent with the Buffalo Bills as a wide receiver, and he played in four Super Bowls. The Pro Football Hall of Famer was honored with the naming of the Andre Reed Stadium on October 18, 2014. (Courtesy of KU.)

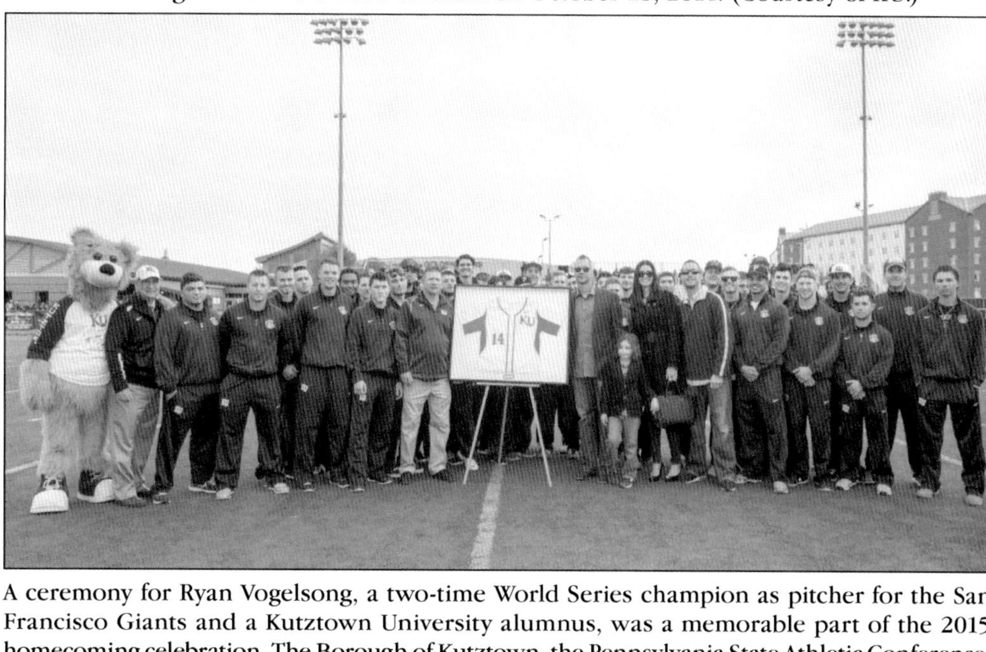

A ceremony for Ryan Vogelsong, a two-time World Series champion as pitcher for the San Francisco Giants and a Kutztown University alumnus, was a memorable part of the 2015 homecoming celebration. The Borough of Kutztown, the Pennsylvania State Athletic Conference, and the Kutztown University President's Office honored Vogelsong on October 19, 2015, when his No. 14 jersey was retired during halftime, as pictured. (Courtesy of KU.)

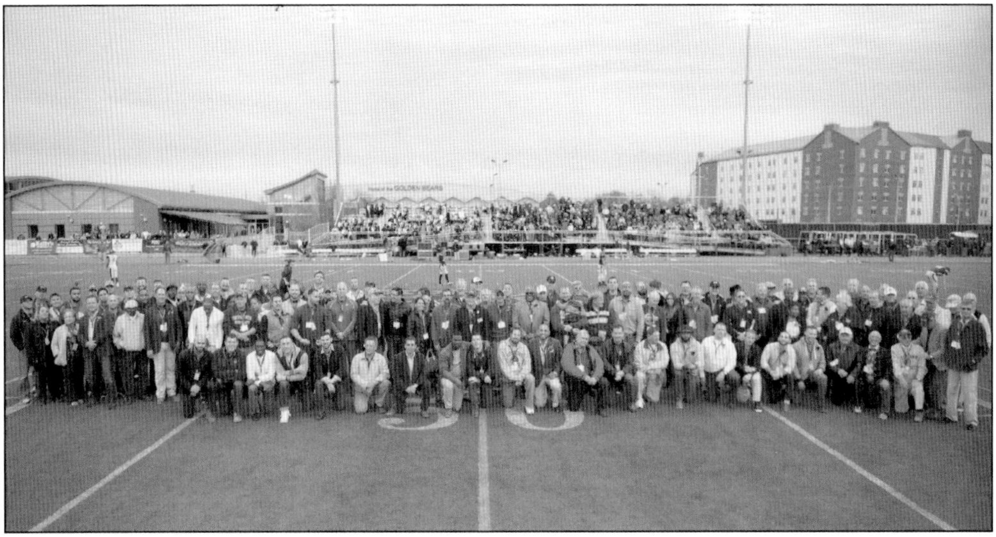

The year 2015 marked the 100th season of football at Kutztown. In celebration of this momentous occasion, 33 past players were selected for the All-Time Team. During a home game against Shippensburg University on November 7, 2015, members of the All-Time Team and KU football alumni were honored during halftime. Current players wore a "100" decal on their helmets throughout the season. (Courtesy of KU.)

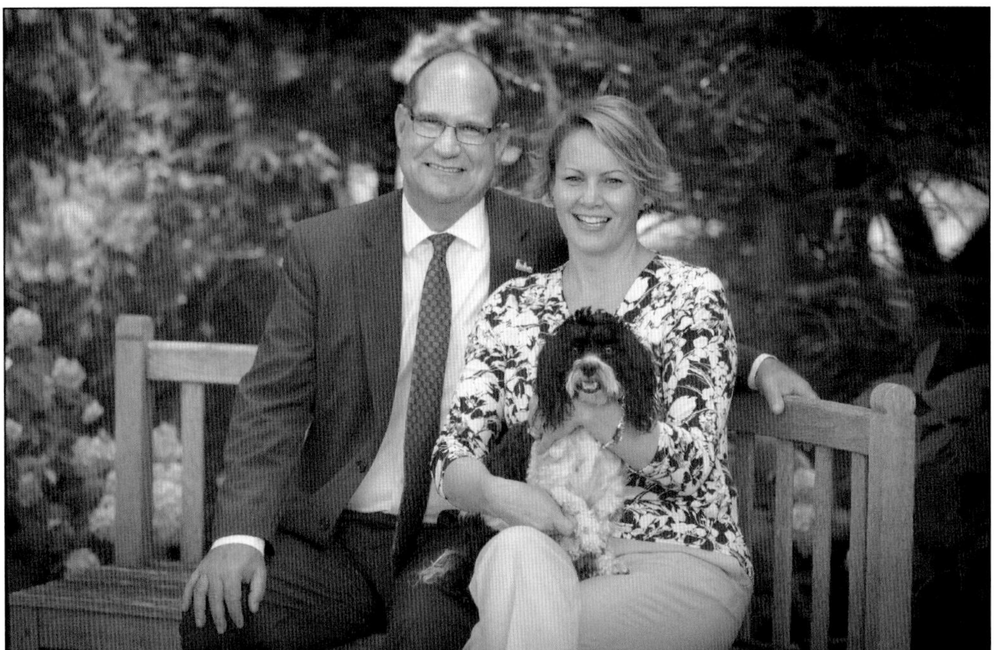

Dr. Kenneth S. Hawkinson joined the Kutztown University community on July 1, 2015. Dr. Hawkinson was provost at Western Illinois University before becoming Kutztown University's 12th president. In his first year as president, Dr. Hawkinson set more than 50 strategic goals to improve the quality and accessibility of higher education at Kutztown University. Dr. Hawkinson is pictured with his wife, Ann Marie Hayes-Hawkinson, and their dog, Wynnie. (Courtesy of KU.)

Kutztown University's newest president, Kenneth S. Hawkinson, and his wife, Ann Marie, established the weekly event "Walk with Wynnie," wherein they walk their dog, Wynnie, with students, faculty and staff, and townspeople for a meet-and-greet around campus. People were invited to bring their dogs along for the walk, followed by lemonade and cookies for the people and water and bisques for the dogs. Wynnie has been a hit on campus and has enjoyed playing the role of "First Dog" by greeting the many visitors to the president's residence and touring the campus each day. (Courtesy of KU.)

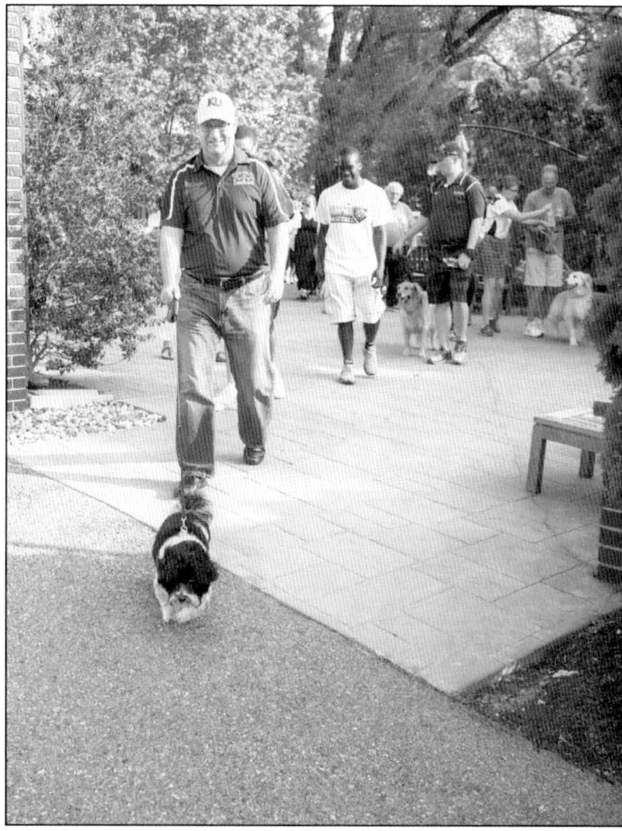

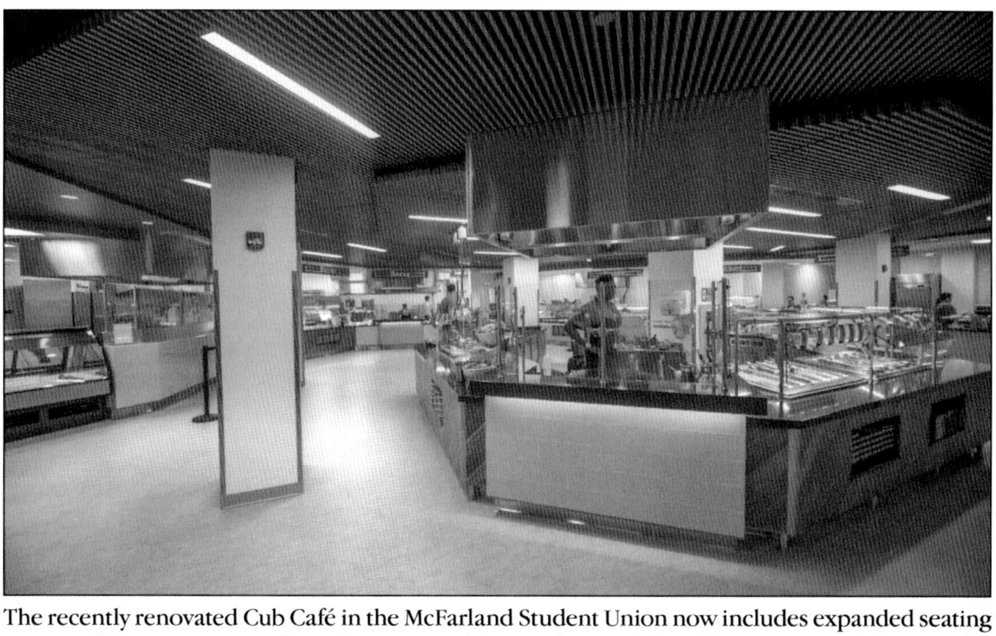

The recently renovated Cub Café in the McFarland Student Union now includes expanded seating areas and a new concept of serving open cuisine cooking, with grill, international, homestyle, deli, soup and salad, bakery, and beverage stations. This is a residential location for students, providing breakfast, lunch, and dinner sessions seven days a week. (Courtesy of KU.)

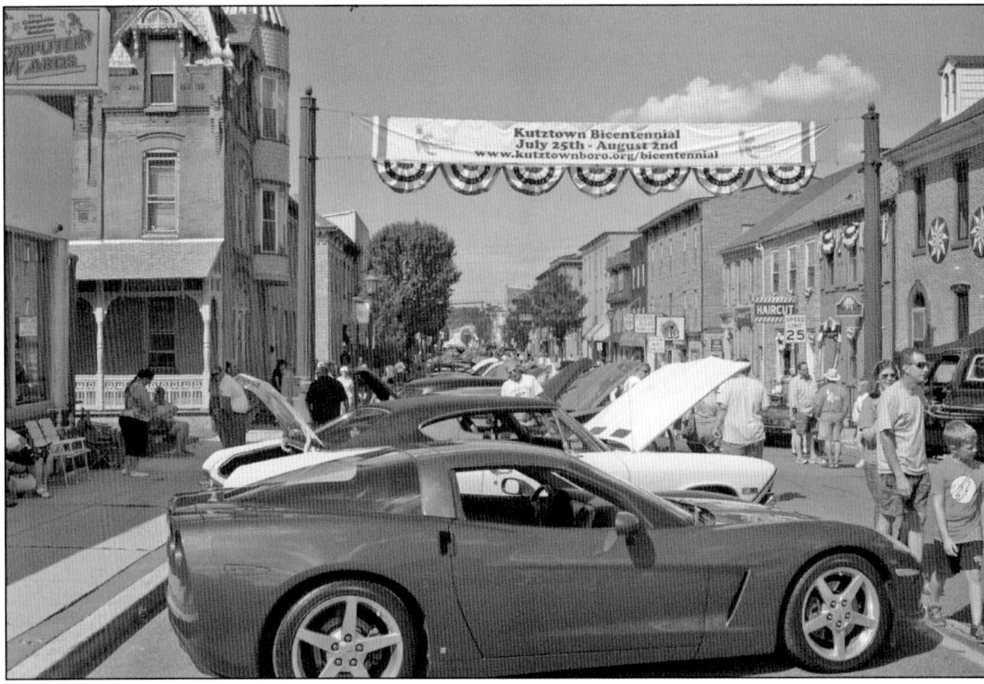

The year 2015 not only marked the beginning of a yearlong celebration of the university's 150th anniversary, but it was also the borough of Kutztown's 200th anniversary. Among the bicentennial events was a pageant in which two local KU students participated, as well as a parade that featured Dr. Hawkinson. Bicentennial week ran from July 25 through August 2. Pictured is the first event, the Kutztown Kruizz. (Courtesy of KHS.)

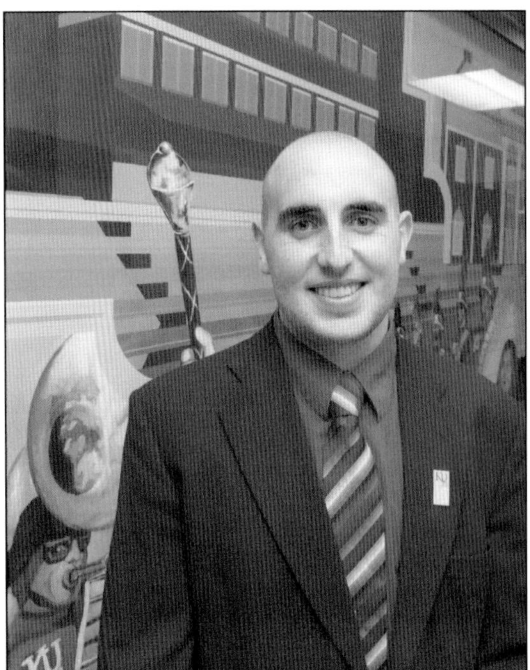

After more than 2,000 hours of planning and creation, the mural *Celebrating 150 Years of Music Through Public Art* was unveiled on August 20, 2015. It was designed and painted by Benjamin Hoffman, who graduated in 2015 with a bachelor of science in art education, a bachelor of fine arts with a concentration in painting, and dual minors in art history and music. The idea came when Hoffman heard of Schaeffer's 2013 renovations. He wanted to showcase the musical performers, as well as the connection between music and art. The sousaphone player in the lower left section is a self-portrait of Hoffman. In addition to art, Hoffman was a dedicated member of the KU marching unit. Not only did this mural play a role in the kickoff of the sesquicentennial celebration year, but it also served as Hoffman's honors capstone project. (Courtesy of KU.)

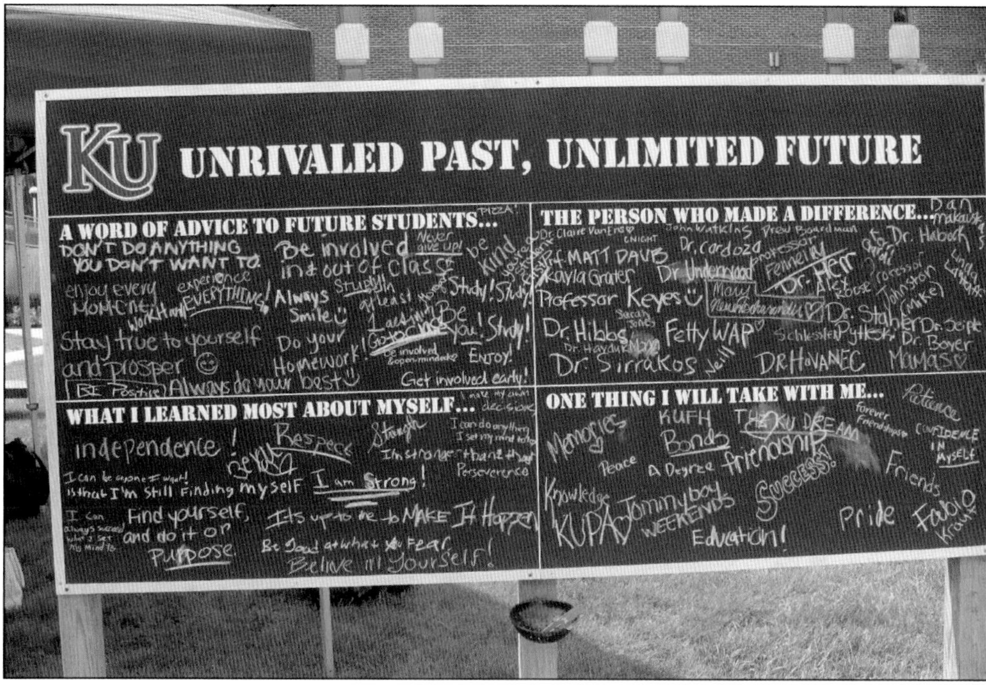

On September 1, 2015, the sesquicentennial chalkboard was unveiled in front of the McFarland Student Union, where everyone was encouraged to write advice and inspirational thoughts. The four parts of the board include "a word of advice to future students," "the person who made a difference," "what I learned most about myself," and "one thing I will take with me." These thoughts encapsulate the contemporary KU experience.

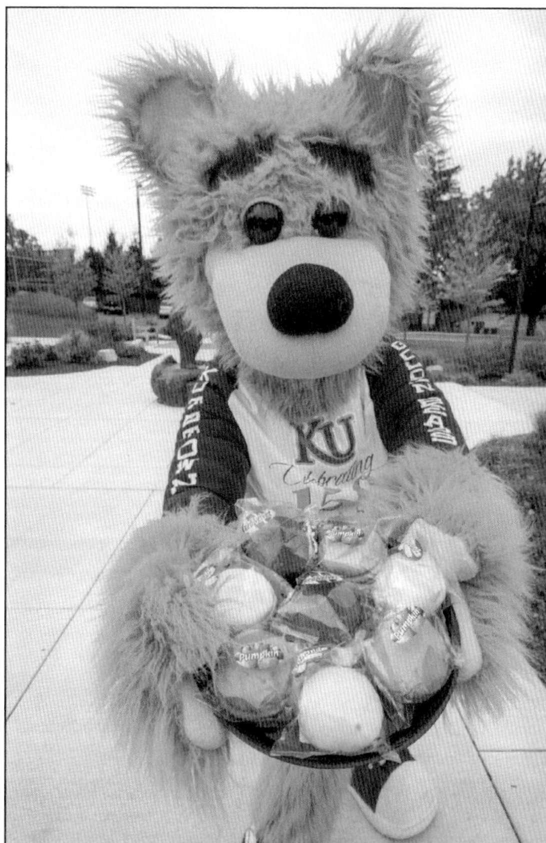

In honor of Kutztown University's 150th anniversary, the whoopee pie was named the official dessert of the sesquicentennial celebration. Since Avalanche's debut, it has been well known that whoopee pies are his favorite food. Matt Santos, director of university relations and chair of the Sesquicentennial Steering Committee, said that the whoopee pie was chosen as the dessert because it ties into the culture of the region and it is liked by many. (Courtesy of KU.)

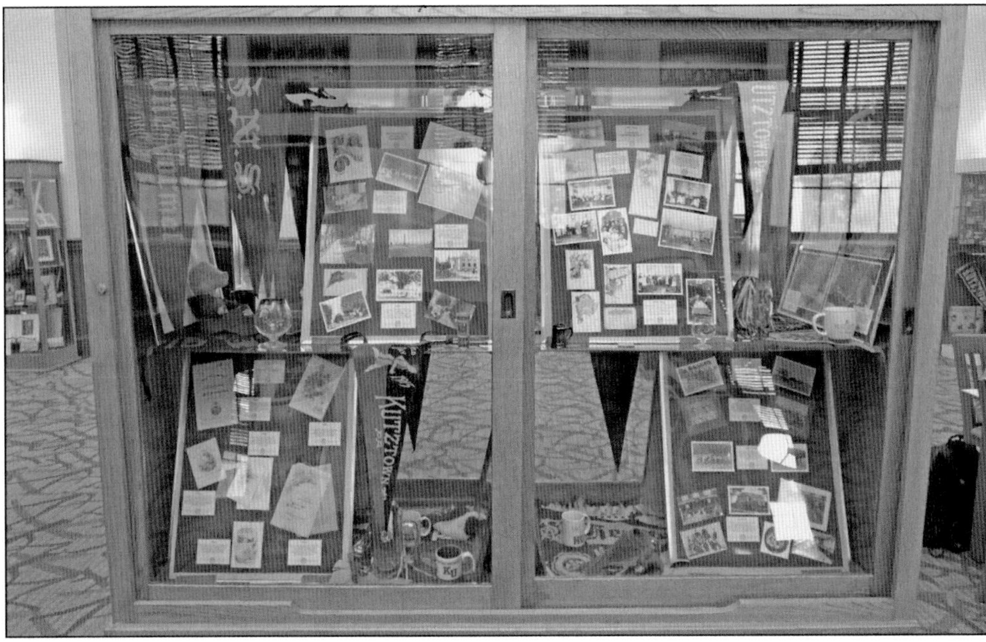

The celebration of Kutztown University's sesquicentennial started in the fall of 2015. The yearlong festivities included the unveiling of an inspirational chalkboard, a music mural, a 5K run, the whoopee pie as the official KU sesquicentennial dessert, and a history display in Old Main. The celebration concludes with Founder's Day, observed on September 15, 2016, which marks the 150th year of Kutztown University. (Courtesy of KU.)

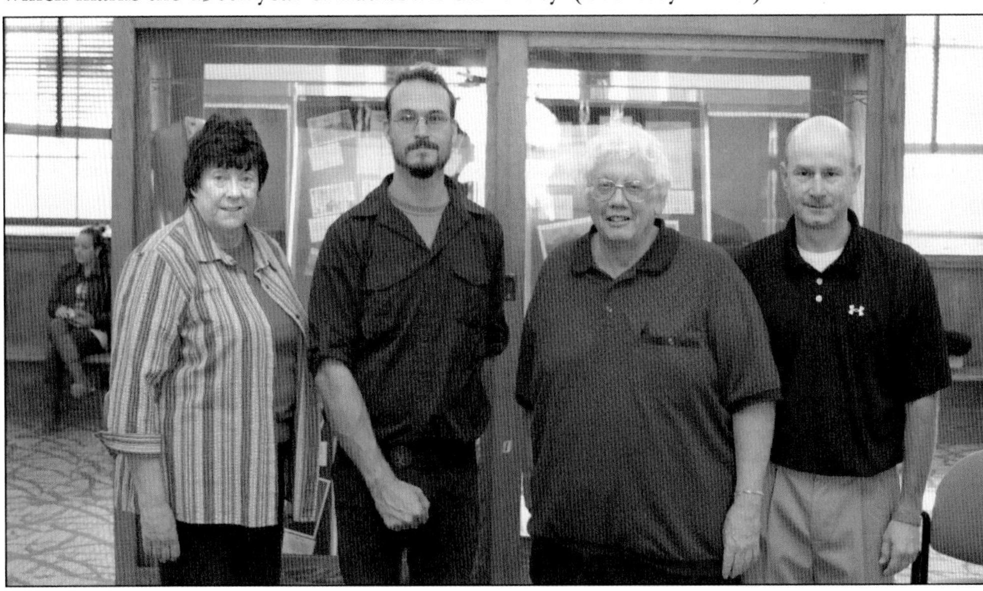

The sesquicentennial history display, located in the Old Main Concourse, includes 11 showcases containing historical photographs and other school artifacts dating back to Kutztown University's origins. Members of the Sesquicentennial History Subcommittee are, from left to right, Patricia Derr, Patrick Donmoyer (class of 2009), Bill Bateman, and Jason Graver (class of 1992). Other members include Sue Czerny (class of 1974) and Karin Graver (class of 1992). (Courtesy of KU.)

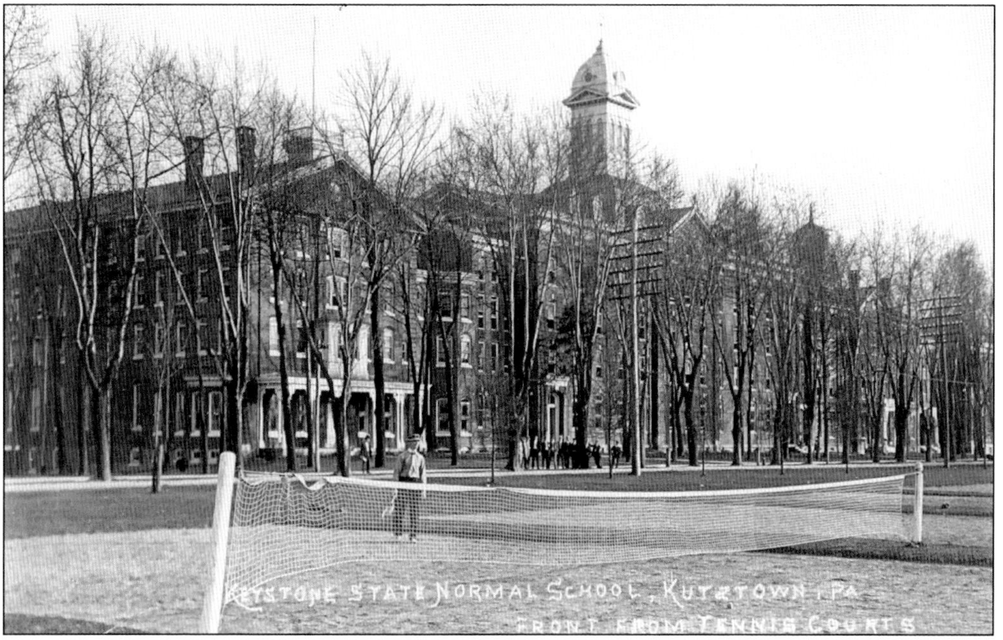

This tennis player beckons from the Keystone State Normal School. As time passes, the president would move from Old Main to an on-campus home, the tennis courts would give way to the lawn in front of Schaeffer Auditorium, and most of the trees in the allée would pass maturity and come down. The tower remains constant, maintaining that look of an angry chicken, a reminder to laugh and enjoy time spent on campus.

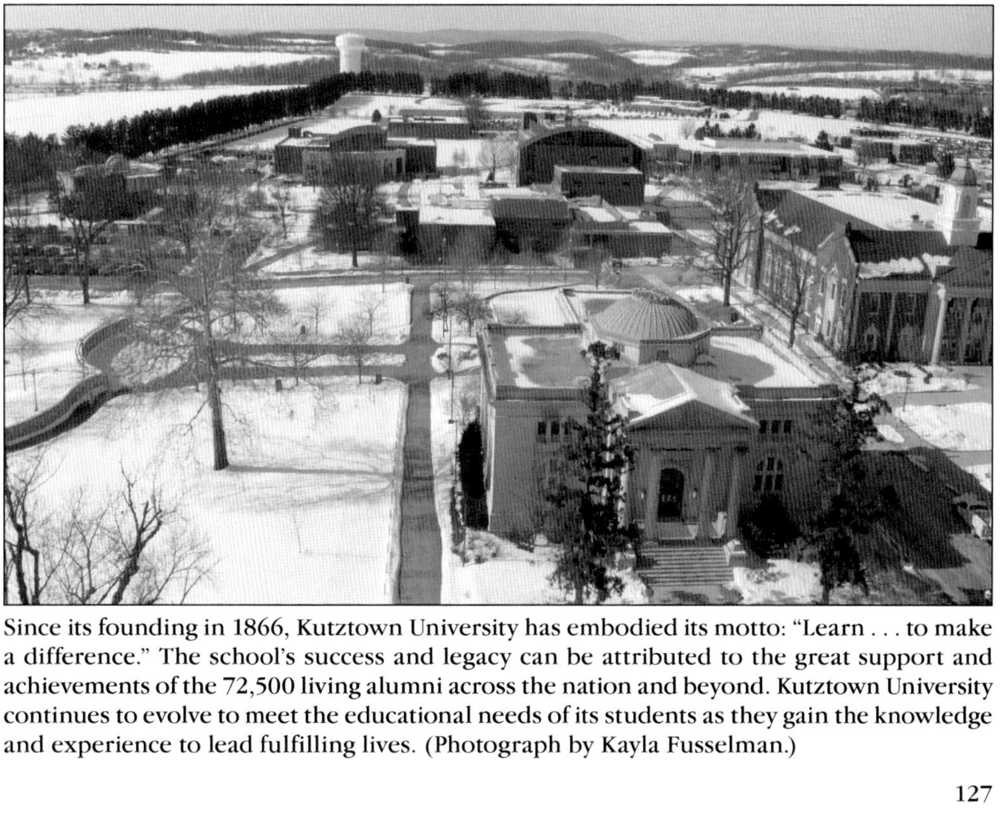

Since its founding in 1866, Kutztown University has embodied its motto: "Learn . . . to make a difference." The school's success and legacy can be attributed to the great support and achievements of the 72,500 living alumni across the nation and beyond. Kutztown University continues to evolve to meet the educational needs of its students as they gain the knowledge and experience to lead fulfilling lives. (Photograph by Kayla Fusselman.)